U.S. GOVERNMENT SERVICES CONTRACTING:
TOOLS, TECHNIQUES, AND BEST PRACTICES

GREGORY A. GARRETT

NAVIGANT

Wolters Kluwer
Law & Business

Editorial Director: Aaron M. Broaddus
Cover and Interior Design: Craig L. Arritola

Copyright Notice

Notice of Trademarks

Product No.: 0-4425-500

ISBN: 978-0-8080-2577-1

SUSTAINABLE FORESTRY INITIATIVE Certified Fiber Sourcing www.sfiprogram.org

CONTENTS

PREFACE

The U.S. government is spending more money than ever to acquire a wide range of professional services, from thousands of government prime contractors and subcontractors. Since an increasing number of the U.S. government contract requirements are for professional services, some of which involve unique research and development, the government frequently uses cost reimbursement, time-and-materials, labor-hour, and/or incentive type contracts or pricing arrangements to acquire professional services. Unfortunately, many members of the U.S. government's acquisition workforce are not adequately educated and trained in the unique aspects of services contracting. Further, many government prime contractors lack the quality business systems (accounting, estimating, purchasing, and earned value management systems) to effectively manage large complex services contract cost, schedule, and technical performance requirements. As a result, many U.S. government services contracts are delivered late, over budget, and fail to meet the needed performance requirements.

Thus, the best-selling author and leading government contracting consultant – Gregory A. Garrett, has created this practical and comprehensive "U.S. Government Services Contracting" book. This book provides a simple yet highly effective Buying and Selling Life-Cycle, composed of six key phases which the government and industry must jointly plan and execute to achieve success. This one-of-a-kind book on U.S. government services contracting contains numerous proven effective tools, techniques, and best practices. If you are involved in U.S. government services contracting, either in the U.S. government acquisition workforce, as a prime contractor, or a subcontractor, this book is a must read!

Shaw Cohe
Chief Executive Officer
AST, LLC

DEDICATION

I would like to dedicate this book to all of the men and women in the U.S. Federal Government, U.S. Military, and within industry who devote countless hours to ensure that the promises made in U.S. government services contracts are actually delivered!

To: Carolyn

I cannot imagine my life without you and our children. Thank you for your friendship, love, and support!

ACKNOWLEDGMENTS

I would like to thank the following people for their support and contributions to this book!

Dr. Rene Rendon, CPCM, CFCM, PMP

Steven Stryker

Uday Apte

Geraldo Ferrer

Ira Lewis

Julie McKillip

Jessica Spencer

ABOUT THE AUTHOR

Gregory A. Garrett

Gregory A. Garrett, CPCM, C.P.M., PMP is the Managing Director and practice leader of the Navigant Consulting, Inc. Government Contractor Services practice, headquartered in Vienna, Virginia. He is an internationally recognized expert in government contracting, cost estimating, contract pricing, risk management, and project management. Plus, he is a best-selling author, highly acclaimed speaker, and during the past 25+ years, he has managed more than $30 Billion of large complex contracts and projects in both the U.S. government and industry. He has taught and consulted with more than 25,000 professionals in 40+ countries. He has served as a lecturer at The George Washington University Law School and the School of Business and Public Management. He is the recipient of numerous national and international business awards for his writing, teaching, consulting, and leadership.

Mr. Garrett provides client support in assessing business risk and providing recommendations for performance improvement of contractor purchasing systems, cost estimating systems, cost accounting systems, bid/proposal management practices, contract pricing systems, contract administration systems, earned value management systems, supply-chain management processes, and program management methodologies. He also serves as an expert witness in support of client claims/litigations.

Mr. Garrett has served as a highly successful industry executive for more than 17 years. Prior to joining Navigant Consulting, he served as Chief Operating Officer (COO) for Acquisition Solutions, Inc. where he lead over 200 consultants providing professional services for more than 30 U.S. federal government agencies. He served 9 years with Lucent Technologies, Inc. as Chief Compliance Officer (CCO) and Vice President of Program Management for all U.S. federal government programs. Previously, he served as Partner and Executive Director Global Business at ESI International.

Formerly, he served as a highly decorated military officer for the United States Air Force, including assignments as: program manager Space Systems Division, warranted contracting officer Aeronautical Systems Division professor of contracting management Air Force Institute of Technology, and acquisition action officer, HQ USAF the Pentagon.

A prolific writer, Mr. Garrett has authored 20 books and more than 100 published articles on bid/proposal management, government contracting, project management, cost estimating, contract pricing, contract negotiations, risk management, supply-chain management, and leadership.

INTRODUCTION

The focus of this book is to serve as a practical and informative reference guide, for all of the business professionals in U.S. federal government agencies, government prime contractors, and subcontractors who are involved in U.S. government services contracting. This book is truly a comprehensive guide to planning and implementing the buying and selling of professional services to and for the U.S. government. Our hope is that you will find this text to be a valuable resource to explain and enlighten people about what it takes to effectively manage U.S. government services contracts.

This book provides a wide range of discussion on all aspects of the U.S. government services contracting buying and selling life-cycle, including: requirements determination, solicitation planning and preparation, opportunity and risk assessment, proposal development and evaluation, negotiations and contract formation, to contract administration and closeout. Plus, the book provides a wealth of proven effective tools, techniques, and best practices which are available and adaptable to help improve services contracts and related project performance results.

CHAPTER

U.S. GOVERNMENT SERVICES CONTRACTING

By Gregory A. Garrett

INTRODUCTION

The U.S. federal government now spends more money each year purchasing a wide range of professional services than it spends buying airplanes, tanks, ships, and computers. In fact, of the more than $600 billion spent by U.S. federal government agencies in fiscal year 2010, with the exception of the $787 billion American Recovery and Reinvestment Act of 2009 follow-on spending, over 61% of the money was spent acquiring professional services from industry to support the needs of our nation.

For many years, six U.S. federal government agencies (see Table 1-1) have typically spent 90% of the discretionary budget dollars acquiring a wide range of professional services, systems, products, and integrated solutions. The remaining 10% of the discretionary federal budget is spent by more than 50 other U.S. federal government departments and agencies for acquiring services, systems, products, and solutions.

Table 1-1 U.S. Federal Government Percent of Total Dollars Spent by Executive Department and Agency (Average FY 2007-2010) Top Six List		
Rank	**Executive Department / Agency**	**Percent of Dollars**
1	Department of Defense (DoD)	73%
2	Department of Energy (DOE)	6%
3	Department of Homeland Security (DHS)	3%
4	Department of Health & Human Services (HHS)	3%
5	Department of Veterans Affairs (VA)	3%
6	National Aeronautics & Space Administration (NASA)	3%
	Total	90%

Source: Federal Procurement Data System-Next Generation

This chapter provides an overview of the sphere of U.S. government services contracting. Specifically, the following key questions will be addressed:

- What professional services are most commonly acquired by the U.S. government?
- What are the size and nature of U.S. government contract actions?

- What are the challenges of managing the U.S. government and industry multi-sector services workforce and the role of insourcing?
- What is the U.S. government's progress in implementing the Services Acquisition Reform Act (SARA) of 2003?
- What is the U.S. Department of Defense plan to improve services acquisition?

WHAT PROFESSIONAL SERVICES ARE MOST COMMONLY ACQUIRED BY THE U.S. GOVERNMENT?

The U.S. federal government departments and agencies typically acquire a highly diverse range of services from industry, including education, training, studies, installation, construction, maintenance, research, testing, relocation, engineering, and other professional and administrative support services. Table 1-2 includes a list of the most frequently acquired services by the U.S. federal government departments and agencies.

Table 1-2 U.S. Federal Government Departments and Agencies' Most Frequently Acquired Services (FY 2007-2010)	
• Telecommunications	• Professional Support Services
• Maintenance & Repair	(Accountants, Lawyers, Engineers, etc.)
• Construction	• Medical Services
• Research & Development	• Social Services
• Architect/Engineering	• Operation of Government-Owned Facilities
• Installation of Equipment	• Technical Support Services
• Education & Training	• Natural Resources Management
• Transportation	• Utilities and Housekeeping
• Lease/Rent Facilities	• Travel and Relocation
	• Testing and Inspection

Source: Federal Procurement Data System-Next Generation

WHAT ARE THE SIZE AND NATURE OF U.S. GOVERNMENT CONTRACT ACTIONS?

Figure 1-1 illustrates how the vast majority (83%) of U.S. federal government contract actions between FY 2007-2010 are valued, on average, at less than $25,000. While on average about 10% of U.S. federal government contract actions are valued between $25,000 and $100,000, about 6% on average are valued between $100,000 and $1,000,000. Thus, only about 1% of all U.S. federal government contract actions are typically valued at more than $1,000,000.

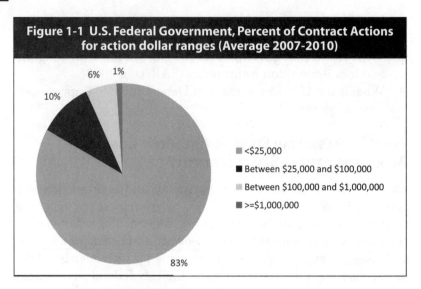

Figure 1-1 U.S. Federal Government, Percent of Contract Actions for action dollar ranges (Average 2007-2010)

Source: Federal Procurement Data System-Next Generation

However, Figure 1-2 illustrates the inverse relationship between the average dollar value of the federal government contract actions between FY 2007-2010 and the overall sum of dollars spent for contract action dollar ranges. Simply stated, while only 1% of the contract actions on average for FY 2007-2010, were more than $1,000,000, they typically accounted for 79% of the total dollars spent. Conversely, while 83% of the average U.S. federal government contract actions between FY 2007 and FY 2010 were valued at less than $25,000, they represent on average only about 2% of the total dollars spent.

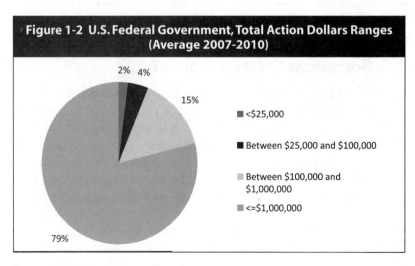

Figure 1-2 U.S. Federal Government, Total Action Dollars Ranges (Average 2007-2010)

Source: Federal Procurement Data System

ONE

What Are the Challenges of Managing the U.S. Government and Industry Multi-Sector Workforce and the role of Insourcing?

As a result of a dramatic increase in contract spending by the U.S. federal government over the past decade, with little increase in the hiring of U.S. federal acquisition workforce until 2008 (see Figure 1-3), the U.S. government has spent a great deal of money hiring government contractors to fill vacancies and to perform a wide range of acquisition management support services, including:

- Systems acquisition planning,
- Systems engineering and safety,
- Contract management planning,
- Contract administration,
- Project management,
- Cost estimating/analysis,
- Logistics management,
- Contract cost accounting/auditing,
- Contract closeout, and
- Others

At the start of the Obama administration, a new public law required hiring government employees to replace contractors whenever possible; the new policy is called insourcing. The government has focused on what it considers to be inherently governmental functions and/or critical positions.

Figure 1-3 U.S. Federal Government Contract Spending and Acquisition Workforce Since FY2002

*Does not include $787 billion ARRA Funding
Source: Federal Procurement Data System and the Federal Acquisition Institute

During the period FY 2002 through FY 2010 the growth in spending for professional services has increased each year in both total dollars and percentage– from 51% in FY 2002 to over 63% in FY 2010–according to the Federal Procurement Data System.

Acquisition and Contracting Improvement Plans and Pilots (2009) According to the Office of Management and Budget (OMB)

Federal agencies utilize both government employees and private-sector contractors to deliver important services to citizens. Management practices must recognize the proper role of each sector's professional services labor force and draw on their respective skills so that the government operates optimally.

Twenty-four federal agencies have launched pilot projects to begin this process. The pilots give each agency the opportunity to create the tools and internal collaboration necessary to plan and develop the workforce as a whole. Each agency will focus on at least one internal organization where concerns exist about a potential overreliance on contractors and will take steps to address any identified weaknesses. The pilots provide agencies with an opportunity to develop processes and practices– from mapping the organization in its current state to its future ("to be") state in order to identify appropriate remedies to improve the organization's performance.

Pilots were selected based on several criteria, including the potential erosion of in-house capability, insufficient contractor oversight, or the potential for improved performance or cost savings through in-house performance. Roughly one third of the pilots involve acquisition offices or functions. Another one third focuses on information technology support. The remaining pilots address a wide range of programs and functions. Agencies were to report to OMB by May 1, 2010, on a pilot project's results. Assessments could lead to a number of actions, such as insourcing or adding resources to contract management. A summary of results will be made public.

The initial review of the pilots shows that agencies are using cross-functional teams with human capital, acquisition, and program officials to determine the best mix of professional service skills and workforce size for the organization. The cross-functional teams provide agencies with technical support and capture lessons and best practices, driving better government performance.

The pilot initiatives give each agency the opportunity to reshape its workforce and strike a balance between staffing positions with permanent federal employees in order to build and sustain its in-house capabilities and, where appropriate, to utilize the professional services expertise and capacities of contractors available in the marketplace.

The pilot projects can be broken down by the following individual focus areas:

Acquisition Management Services

Seven agencies, Commerce, Defense, Education, Interior, Labor, GSA, and NASA, are studying acquisition management services.. While contractors can be beneficial in some supporting activities, they must not perform inherently governmental functions, such as awarding contracts, nor should contractors be utilized as a substitute for the strong internal capacity required for an agency to provide sufficient management and oversight of its contractors. Studying these roles will complement other efforts to strengthen the capabilities and capacity of the acquisition workforce.

Information Technology (IT) Management Services

Nine agencies, Agriculture, Energy, Homeland Security, Housing and Urban Development, Treasury, Veterans Affairs, NASA, SBA, and USAID, are analyzing IT management services performed by their Office of the Chief Information Officer. Most of these agencies have reported that they rely heavily on contractors and question whether the agency has the ability to maintain control of its mission and operations. Frequent turnover of contractors at some of the agencies has caused further concern that institutional and technical knowledge will be lost. At least two agencies, HUD and Treasury, are coordinating their pilot activities with related IT modernization efforts.

Veteran's Employment and Training Services

The Department of Labor (DOL) uses contractors to provide significant support for its Veteran's assistance programs, including the Homeless Veterans Reintegration Program and the Jobs for

Veterans State Grant program. Contractors perform operational analysis, provide information technology services, and offer general administrative and budget support. DOL will assess whether the mission and requirements of these programs are effectively served by the current mix of in-house and contractor support.

Environmental Remediation Services

The Environmental Protection Agency (EPA) will study the Technology Innovation and Field Services Division (TIFSD) in the Office of Solid Waste and Emergency Response. TIFSD provides critical support to the Superfund program, including field assistance in responding to incidents and spills, analytical work, and training on field investigations and remediation technologies. Under the pilot, EPA will determine whether the agency's extensive reliance on contractor support to accomplish the missions is impairing its ability to maintain control of operations.

Financial Management Services

The Department of Justice's (DOJ) Consolidated Quality Assurance Audit Team is responsible for ensuring a clean financial audit opinion for the Department. Under the pilot, DOJ will review the team's work processes and labor mix to improve efficiencies, ensure future knowledge transfer from its contract employees to in-house staff for long-term continuity, and assure that inherently governmental functions have not been outsourced.

Technical and Clerical Services

The Office of Personnel Management (OPM) will review its use of contracted staff that provides clerical and technical support to a wide range of important programs, including its investigations, retirement, legal, financial management, and public affairs functions. These support services were outsourced in 2004. As OPM reviews the mix of skills and amount of labor required in light of its mission and performance goals, it will inform it assessment based on its experiences with contract support since 2004 and with federal employee support prior to that time.

Consulting Services

The National Science Foundation has identified its Business and Solutions Services area within the Division of Information systems for evaluation to determine the best mix of federal and contract workers.

Insourcing Issues

(As Reported by Government Executive.com)

Pentagon Abandons Insourcing Effort (August 10, 2010)

In 2009, the U.S. Department of Defense announced it would reduce the number of service support contractors by about 33,000 by 2015. The Pentagon had planned to replace those services contractors during the next five years with 39,000 new full-time government employees, 20,000 of whom would be acquisition professionals.

As the Pentagon reduced contractors, it did not see the savings it had hoped from insourcing.

Based on data available after the first year, Secretary Gates said that he was "not satisfied with the progress made to reduce our overreliance on contractors." As part of a department wide effort to save $100 billion from overhead costs and return the funding to the warfighter, Secretary Gates instructed officials to reduce by 10 percent their spending on service support contractors during each of the next three years. The cuts will not affect contractors operating in Iraq or Afghanistan.

DoD had planned to insource contracted services in areas such as logistical support of aviation systems, safety engineering, cost accounting, anti-terrorism training, and religious support. To date, the department has hired about 5,000 new employees, nearly two thirds through insourcing, according to Defense officials.

"With regard to insourcing, other than changes planned for fiscal 2010, no more full-time positions in these organizations will be created after this fiscal year to replace contractors," Gates said.

The insourcing initiative essentially became irrelevant when Gates froze the number of employees within the Office of Secretary of Defense, military agencies, and combatant commands at their fiscal 2010 levels for the next three years.

Industry groups, which had criticized the department's insourcing agenda as capricious and poorly implemented, were pleased with Defense's decision to end the initiative, though they were concerned about overall job losses for contractors.

"We welcome Secretary Gates' acknowledgement that the Defense Department's savings assumptions associated with insourcing have been vastly overstated and based on incomplete analyses at best," said Stan Soloway, president and chief executive officer of the Professional Services Council, a trade group.

Defense insourcing guidance required officials to compare the labor costs of civilian and contract support. But a recent court ruling found the Air Force did not conduct a proper cost analysis while insourcing a function that a contractor had previously conducted.

The Defense Department hasn't provided any data to support the argument that government employees are a less expensive alternative to contractors, said Robert Burton, a procurement attorney and partner at the law firm of Venable, LLP in Washington, D.C. Unless the department intends to eliminate functions those contractors now are performing, any savings associated with the cuts are unlikely, he said.

"I've been in this business for over 30 years, and I don't recall any government initiative that has so negatively impacted small businesses," he said. Burton was the top career federal procurement official in the White House Office of Federal Procurement Policy from 2000 to 2008. Prior to that, he spent more than 20 years as an acquisition attorney at Defense.

While Secretary Gates has said the department no longer will automatically replace contractors with civilian employees, thus ending its controversial insourcing program, Burton said he doesn't believe insourcing is dead.

"I don't see any indication that [it] will be discontinued. I think these functions will be transferred to the federal government," Burton said. "We know for sure they're trying to get around it with temporary hires–they're hiring the small business contractor employees."

Burton cited one firm that had nine employees assigned to a service support contract with the Pentagon, and Defense hired seven of the employees and ended the contract. Burton declined to name the contractor saying the firm fears retaliation if it files a protest.

"Here we have small businesses in effect doing the recruiting for the federal government, putting in [*sic*] the time and resources into recruitment and training only to lose these employees to the government. This is devastating to small business," he said.

He cited recent data, including an analysis by James Sherk, a labor policy analyst at the conservative Heritage Foundation think tank, which shows some federal employees earn significantly more in salary and benefits than people in comparable private sector positions.

The Business Coalition for Fair Competition, an industry association that has opposed federal insourcing plans, called on the administration to issue an immediate moratorium for the program.

In an August 13, 2010, letter to OMB's Acting Director Jeffrey Zients, John Palatiello, the group's president, said the "shift to government performance of commercial activities not only hinders the private sector, including small and minority-owned business, but places additional costs to taxpayers during a lengthened period of a steep decline in the nation's economy, a staggering national debt and high national rate of unemployment."

WHAT IS THE U.S. FEDERAL GOVERNMENT'S PROGRESS ON IMPLEMENTING SARA?

The Services Acquisition Reform Act of 2003 (SARA), signed into law on November 24, 2003, as Title XIV of Public Law 108-136, is intended to provide agencies with an array of tools to improve the acquisition of services in four major areas (see 1-3).

Table 1-3 Services Acquisition Reform Act of 2003 Provisions	
Categories	**Provisions**
Acquisition workforce and training	• Civilian acquisition workforce training fund • Acquisition workforce recruitment flexibility • Maintaining architectural and engineering acquisition workforce expertise
Business acquisition practices	• Civilian Agency Chief Acquisition Officers (CAOs) • CAO Council • Advisory panel on acquisition laws and regulations • Extension of franchise fund programs • Contracting for architectural and engineering services • Telecommuting for federal contractors
Commercial item acquisition	• Incentives for performance-based contracts • Time-and-materials contracting for commercial services
Other procurement flexibilities	• Special "other transactions" acquisition authority • Public disclosure of noncompetitive contracts for Iraq reconstruction • Emergency procurement flexibility

Source: GAO

Stated simply, some progress has been made in each of the four categories, yet the overall state of the U.S. government's ability to effectively cost and efficiently obtain quality services at fair and reasonable prices remains a matter of significant concern to the Office of Management & Budget (OMB), the Government Accountability Office (GAO), the U.S. Congress, and many U.S. citizens.

Recent reports from the Commission on Wartime Contracting (CWC), GAO, and several department Inspector General (IG) offices indicate:

■ Lack of proper education and training of key government acquisition personnel in services contracting;
■ Shortage of key government acquisition talent, especially systems engineering;
■ Lack of empowerment of government contracting officers in managing services contracts;
■ Concern about the use of high-risk contracts (i.e., time-and-materials and cost-reimbursement contracts) for the acquisition of services;
■ Inadequate use of performance-based services contracts;
■ Inappropriate application of incentives and award fees on services and systems contracts;

- Concern about the quality and effectiveness of contractor purchasing systems for services in support of the U.S. government; and
- Excessive pass-through costs on services and systems contracts.

WHAT IS THE U.S. DEPARTMENT OF DEFENSE PLAN TO IMPROVE SERVICES ACQUISITION?

According to Under Secretary for Defense, Acquisition, Technology, and Logistics Ashton Carter, in a memo dated September 14, 2010:

> Contract support services spending now represents more than 50 percent of our total contract spending. In 2009, the Department spent more than $212 billion in contracting services, using more than 100,000 contract vehicles held by more than 32,300 contractors—with more than 50 percent of the spend awarded to about 100 contractors.
>
> This contractor support is critical to the Department. For professional services, for example, the Department depends upon three sources: the government workforces, the unique not-for-profit FFRDCs and UARCs, and for-profit professional services companies. Management mechanisms are in place for the first two, but far less [so] for the third.
>
> The Department's practices for buying such services are much less mature than for buying weapons systems. It is critically important that we have a cohesive and integrated strategy with regard to the acquisition of services. This substantial amount of spend demands a management structure to strategically source these goods and services.
>
> **Create a senior manager for acquisition of services in each component, following the Air Force's example.** In order to achieve efficiencies in services contracting commensurate with the scale of the Department's spend, new governance is necessary. *I am directing the CAEs of the military departments and the commanders and directors of the other DoD components to*

establish a senior manager for acquisition of services, who will be at the General Officer, Flag, or SES level. This senior manager will be responsible for governance in planning, execution, strategic sourcing and management of service contracts. The senior manager will be the Decision Authority for Category I service acquisitions valued at $250 million or less or as delegated and [will] collaborate with requiring activities which retain funding authority on service contract spend.

Adopt uniform taxonomy for different types of services. Today, the Department lacks a standard taxonomy for service contract spend that can be used among the components to understand the Department's aggregate spending and value of specific services contracting. Without a standard approach, the Department has no way of measuring productivity in more than 50 percent of its contracting investment. *I am directing, therefore, each component to use the following primary categories of service spend: Knowledge-based services; Electronics and Communications Services; Equipment Related Services; Medical Services; Facility Related Services; and Transportation Services. These are derived from, and consistent with, Product Service (PSC) categories contained in the PSC manual maintained by the General Services Administration, Federal Procurement Data Center, and Office of Management and Budget (OMB). This taxonomy will be used by each component to ensure basic consistency.*

Address causes of poor tradecraft in services acquisition.–

■ *Assist users of services to define requirements and prevent creep via requirements templates.* The Department has experienced significant increases in mission/requirements creep for services spending, particularly in knowledge management services, which has increased 400 percent in the last decade. These requirements often require the same function or service to be provided but are written uniquely among various commands so that competition is limited. *Therefore, I am directing two initiatives to address mission/requirements*

creep. First, the Services and DoD components should estab-
lish , through their senior managers for services, maximum
use of standard templates in developing Performance Work
Statements (PWS) to improve contract solicitations. Successful examples of the use of standard templates are
the Navy's SEAPORT acquisitions and DLA's use of
templates to acquire Headquarters support services.
Second, I also expect market research to be strengthened in
order to understand industry's capabilities and appropri-
ate pricing within the market in which we are buying. I
expect the military departments and the DoD components
will achieve this by establishing dedicated market research
teams at the portfolio management level.

- *Enhance competition by requiring more frequent re-competes*
of knowledge based services. Although 89 percent of the
Department's services contracting spend was awarded
under competitive conditions, in 24 percent of those
cases only one bid was received. This suggests bona
fide competition (two or more bids) is not occurring in
the $31 billion represented by those cases. To improve
competition in services, *I will require the military depart-*
ments and DoD components to review the length of time that
services contracts remain in effect before re-competition occurs.
Single-award contract actions should be limited to three
years (including options) unless, by exception, it[*sic*] is
fully justified for longer periods by the senior manager
for services. Contract length should be appropriate
for the activity performed. Knowledge-based services
readily meet the three-year limit. Other services such
as Performance Based Logistics (PBL), LOGCAP, and
environmental remediation, as examples, may not. The
intent is that each service requirement will be reviewed
by the appropriate official and only those with a sound
business rationale will contain longer contract performance provisions. Multiple award IDIQ contracts may
by up to five years if on-ramp provisions are included
to refresh/update the competitor pool. In addition,
I expect Service component to align contract spend data,
to the maximum extent that is practical, to the functional/
requirements elements executing the spend. This will focus
all elements of the Department on the importance of
achieving improved results.

- In cases where "1-bid" proposals are received, *I will require fully negotiated pricing and cost data as appropriate. Further, I will require solicitations that receive only one bid, and that were open to industry for less than 30 days, to be re-advertised for a minimum additional period of 30 days.*

- *Limit the use of time and materials and award fee contracts for services.* Today, more than 20 percent of the Department's services acquisitions are written using Time and Material (T&M) or Cost Plus Award Fee (CPAF) contract types. At a time when the Department is driving toward more fiscal discipline, we spend about $24 billion in services using T&M contract types, which are the least preferred contract type for understanding costs. Similarly, CPAF contract types provide only limited motivation for cost discipline. The acquisition of services differs greatly from the acquisition of supplies and equipment. The contractor at-risk capital is typically much lower for most service acquisitions and must be factored into the contract decision process. *I will issue further detailed guidance for establishing a taxonomy of preferred contract types in services acquisition, but starting immediately, I expect services acquisitions to be predisposed toward Cost-Plus-Fixed-Fee (CPFF), or Cost-Plus-Incentive-Fee (CPIF) arrangements, when robust competition or recent competitive pricing history does not exist to build sufficient cost knowledge of those services within that market segment. I expect the cost knowledge gained from those contracts to inform the Should Cost estimates of future price and contract type negotiations. When robust competition already exists, or there is recent competitive pricing history, I expect components to be predisposed toward Firm-Fixed-Price (FFP) type contract arrangements. FFP should also be used to the maximum extent reasonable when ongoing competition is utilized in multiple award contract scenarios.*

- *Require that services contracts exceeding $1 billion contain cost efficiency objectives.* With large Department outlays of capital for services contracting, it is important that the Department incentivize, achieve, and share in cost improvements over the period of performance for support services acquisitions, including knowledge management services. In acquisitions of material and production end items, we expect the contractor to be on a learning or efficiency curve to drive costs down and value up. We should incentivize and expect similar cost improvements on high-value services contracts. *Beginning immediately, I will require services contracts valued at more than $1 billion to contain provisions in the contract to achieve productivity improvements and cost efficiencies throughout the contract period.*

Increase small business participation in providing services. Small businesses provide the Department with an important degree of agility and innovation, even in support services, and they do so with generally lower overhead structures. To strengthen and improve opportunities for small businesses in the acquisition of services, *I am directing the OSD Office of Small Business Programs to review acquisition plans for services acquisitions exceeding $1 billion, and to be members of the OSD peer reviews of services acquisitions. Additionally, when multiple award contracts are used for services acquisitions, specific tasks suitable for small businesses will be set aside and military departments and DoD components will seek opportunities to compete Multiple Award/IDIQ contracts among small businesses.*

SUMMARY

This chapter has provided an overview of the complex and dynamic sphere of U.S. government services contracting. The following key issues associated with U.S. government services contracting have been addressed:

- Services most commonly acquired by the U.S. government;
- Size and nature of U.S. government contract actions;
- Challenges in managing the U.S. government and industry multi-sector workforce and the role of insourcing;
- The U.S. government's progress in implementing the required improvements to services contracting enacted by the Services Acquisition Reform Act of 2003; and
- The U.S. Department of Defense plan to improve services acquisition.

Yet all of this is merely the tip of the iceberg when it comes to the topic of U.S. government services contracting.

The remaining chapters of this book are all designed and intended to provide a comprehensive and detailed understanding of the art and science of buying and selling professional services both by and to the U.S. government.

QUESTIONS TO CONSIDER

1. Does your organization have the appropriately educated and trained resources to effectively manage buying and/or selling professional services?

2. If you are a government prime contractor, do you have an approved purchasing system?

3. How effective is your organization in recruiting, hiring, training, and retaining key personnel to manage the buying and/or selling of professional services?

CHAPTER

BUYING AND SELLING LIFE CYCLE

By Gregory A. Garrett

INTRODUCTION

So, what makes buying and/or selling professional services unique? The answer is of course the people and their specialized education, training, certifications, and experience. In addition the very nature of what you are buying or selling, whether it is personal services or non-personal services; the location(s) of where the services must be delivered; how the services are priced/type of contract; whether the contract is for best efforts, level of effort, or performance-based, all affect how the services are bought, sold, and delivered.

In this chapter, a simple yet proven effective U.S. Government Services Contracting Buying and Selling Life Cycle is provided. The Buying and Selling Life Cycle will provide a structured approach to understanding how professional services are acquired by the U.S. government, sold to the U.S. government, and delivered/performed for the U.S. government. The U.S. Government Services Contracting Buying and Selling Life Cycle (see Figure 2-1) is composed of six distinct phases:

- Phase 1 – Requirements Determination
- Phase 2 – Solicitation Planning and Preparation
- Phase 3 – Opportunity and Risk Assessment
- Phase 4 – Proposal Development and Evaluation
- Phase 5 – Negotiations and Contract Formation
- Phase 6 – Contract Administration and Closeout

In each of the above stated six phases of the U.S. Government Services Contracting Buying and Selling Life Cycle, important actions are required by both the U.S. government agency (buyer) and the industry prime contractor (seller) to ensure that the work is properly planned and executed.

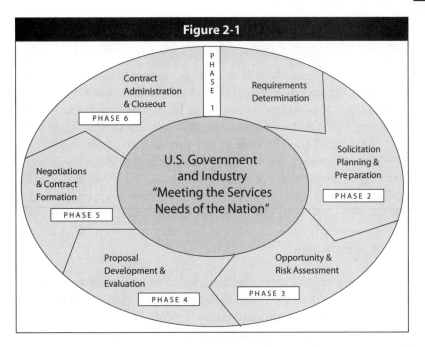

Figure 2-1

PHASE 1 — Requirements Determination

PHASE 2 — Solicitation Planning & Preparation

PHASE 3 — Opportunity & Risk Assessment

PHASE 4 — Proposal Development & Evaluation

PHASE 5 — Negotiations & Contract Formation

PHASE 6 — Contract Administration & Closeout

U.S. Government and Industry "Meeting the Services Needs of the Nation"

Increasingly, the actions between buyers and sellers required to build winning services contracts have become complex, lengthy, and dynamic. With the constant demands of customers for rapid response and best value, combined with widespread application of sophisticated technology in nearly every industry, government buyers have increasingly become more sophisticated in their source selection practices. This same availability of technology has also reduced the barriers to market entry in many industries so that new competitors arise on an almost daily basis. Buyers are looking for ways to reduce their costs and improve performance. Traditional sellers are finding they must cut services costs at every turn to compete with newer, smaller, and more nimble competitors. All these trends converge to make it essential that buyers and sellers, regardless of size or industry, work together using a structured approach to prioritize and focus scarce resources in order to maximize the opportunity for mutual success.

The U.S. Government Services Contracting Buying and Selling Life Cycle is just such a structured approach. It can be used in the government marketplace for domestic, multinational, or global opportunities. It also can be used to respond in a "reactive mode" to a buyer solicitation, such as a Request for Information (RFI), Request for Quotation (RFQ), or Request for Proposal (RFP). It is equally useful in a "pro-active mode" to generate an unsolicited offer to a buyer.

Whether your workplace is a large government agency, a small start-up company, or a global corporation, all are part of a virtual workplace that is no longer bordered by geography or time zone. Traditional face-to-face communication and interaction have been largely replaced by teleconference, e-mail, instant messages, and Webinars. The Buying and Selling Life Cycle provides a framework that is geography and time zone independent. It can be used effectively in single-location organizations where everyone is under one roof as well as in global corporations where employees will never meet each other in person and may not even have a face-to-face conversation.

Government contractors or sellers are driven by a profit motive and procure products and services to either increase revenues or reduce expenses. Although not driven by a profit motive, government buyers focus on the delivery of a specific program or service at a fair and reasonable price. A seller, even with the best technology or service in the world, will not win new business unless it can show the buyer how to apply its technology or services to increase the buyer's performance or reduce expenses. Sellers must demonstrate value to buyers by providing services that make business and life better, faster, and/or less expensive.

The foundation of the Buying and Selling Life Cycle is the focus on the customer's business problems or objectives. Simply stated, this process is all about creating mutually beneficial offers that solve the buyer's business problems or objectives and meet the seller's requirements for profitability and risk. Focusing on a customer's business problems or objectives is looking at business from the customer's perspective, which will drive both the buyer and the seller to create the best solution.

PHASE 1: REQUIREMENTS DETERMINATION

Requirements determination is the first services contract management challenge for a buyer. In a U.S. government department or agency, the challenge of requirements determination is typically supposed to be performed by the project/program manager responsible for the acquisition of specific professional services.

TWO

This make-or-buy or outsourcing decision requires consideration of many factors, some of which are strategically important. The decision to outsource creates a project that will be implemented in cooperation with an outside organization that is not entirely within the buyer's control. Market research is an essential element, which enables the buyer to more fully understand its purchasing options.

The relationship between buyer and seller is a legal, if not an economic, one of equals. The contract binds them to one another but does not put one under the other's managerial control. Sometimes the seller's economic position may be so powerful, however, that the terms and conditions (Ts and Cs) of the contract are ineffective in protecting the interests of the buyer.

For the seller, the contract presents an opportunity to succeed, but it also poses great risks. The seller may find that the buyer has specified its need inadequately or defectively; the seller's marketing department may oversell its services or capabilities; faulty communication may transpire between the two parties during contract formation; or more likely, some combination of all three of these problems may occur. In any of these cases, performance may be much more demanding than originally contemplated and may even be beyond the seller's capabilities. In addition, the buyer may wield great economic power, which effectively outweighs the contract Ts and Cs, which are designed to protect the seller from the buyer's potentially unreasonable demands.

All the communications breakdowns, misunderstandings, conflicts, and dispute that can occur within virtually every organization also can occur between organizations, often with greater virulence and more disastrous effect. Although a contract is intended to provide a remedy to an injured party if the other fails to fulfill its contractual obligations, it is not a guarantee. Legal remedies may be uncertain and, even if attained, may not fully compensate the injured party for the other party's failure. '

The outsourcing decision can be a critical one for any organization. After the decision to contract for goods or services is made, the buyer must plan carefully and implement the decision properly.

The U.S. government agency cognizant program manager should organize a multi-functional team or Integrated Project Team (IPT) to include all of the appropriate functional and end-user representatives, for example:

- Program Manager;
- Contracting Officer;
- Contracting Officer's Technical Representative;
- Cost/Price Analyst;
- Attorney;
- Budget/Financial Analyst;
- Small Business Advocate (if appropriate);
- End-User Customer Representative(s); and
- Others (as needed).

Together this IPT should determine (1) what professional services need to be acquired, (2) when the services need to be delivered, (3) where the services need to be performed, (4) how performance of the services will be evaluated, (5) what services evaluation criteria are most important, and (6) How much time, money, and resources the government agency will collectively dedicate to this effort?

It is not uncommon for U.S. government departments and agencies to struggle in developing their requirements and addressing these six key questions. Often a U.S. government agency will need to solicit more information from industry via a Request for Information (RFI), sources sought, industry exchange meetings, pre-solicitation industry conferences, etc., in order to fully develop its requirements. Chapter 3, provides a more detailed discussion of the art and science of requirements planning, including the tools, techniques, and best practices.

PHASE 2: SOLICITATION PLANNING AND PREPARATION

In the course of planning for the acquisition of professional services, the government buyer must:

- Conduct market research;
- Determine how to specify its services requirements or deliverables via a statement of work, performance work statement, or statement of objectives;
- Identify potential sources;
- Analyze the sources of uncertainty and risk that the purchase will entail;
- Develop performance-based standards, metrics, and incentives;

- Choose the methods for selecting a seller and for proposal evaluation, negotiation, and contract formation; and
- Arrange for effective administration of the contract.

Developing a statement of work (SOW), performance work statement (PWS), or statement of objectives (SOO) is one of the most difficult challenges in procurement planning. First, a buyer must understand its own requirements—quite a difficult task. Secord, a buyer must be able to communicate those requirements, typically in the form of either specific deliverables or some form of level of effort to others outside its organization, which is an even more difficult task, because developing and communicating performance-based requirements is one of the most critical functions in contract management.

Buyers may request bids, quotes, or proposals orally, in writing, or electronically through procurement documents generally called solicitations. Solicitations can take the form of a request for proposals (RFPs), a request for quotations (RFQs), and invitations for bids (IFBs).

Solicitations should communicate a buyer's needs clearly to all potential sellers. Submitting a high-quality solicitation is vital to a buyer's success. The better the solicitation from the buyer generally, the better the bids, quotes, or proposals, submitted by the sellers. Poorly communicated solicitations often results in delays, confusion, fewer bids or proposals, and lower-quality responses. Increasingly, U.S. government buyers are using electronic data interchange and electronic commerce via the Federal Business Opportunities (FBO) website (www.fbo.gov) to solicit offers from sellers of services worldwide.

Presale activities are the proactive involvement of a seller with prospective and current buyers. Presale activities include identifying prospective and current customers, determining their needs and plans, appropriately influencing customer requirements, and evaluating competitors. The most successful of these activities include proactive sales management and the extensive use of market research, benchmarking, and competitive analysis as proven tools and techniques to improve customer focus, gain insight, and provide advantage over competitors.

Clearly, seller selection or sourcing is one of the most important decisions a buyer will make. Contract success or failure will depend on the competence and reliability of one or more key sellers and their subcontractors. U.S. government procurement planners must identify potential sources of services, analyze the nature of the industry and market in which they operate, develop criteria and procedures to evaluate each source, and select one or more for contract award. No single set of criteria or procedures is appropriate for all procurements; thus, to some extent, original analyses must be made for each contract. In Chapter 4, the numerous tools, techniques, and best practices for solicitation planning and preparation for services contracts are discussed.

PHASE 3: OPPORTUNITY AND RISK MANAGEMENT

The U.S. government IPT (buyer) and the potential government prime contractor (seller) and their subcontractors should all conduct some sort of formal or informal opportunity and risk assessment of every services contract and related project. Clearly, every services contract and project present some potential positive outcomes or opportunities, including:

- On-time delivery;
- High-quality and professional services performance/provision;
- End-user/customer satisfaction;
- Follow-on business;
- On-time payment; and
- Fair profit.

Likewise, every services contract and related project contain some potential negative outcomes or risks, including:

- Late delivery;
- Poor quality services;
- End-user dissatisfaction;
- No follow-on business;
- Late payment;
- No profit/loss of money;
- Possible penalties;
- Termination; and
- Reprocurement costs.

For U.S. government contractors, making the bid/no-bid decision should be a multi-part process that includes evaluating the buyer's solicitation, understanding the competitive environment, and assessing the risks against the opportunities for a prospective contract. This step is critical to the services contract management process; however, far too many sellers devote too little time and attention to properly evaluating the risks before they leap into preparing bids and proposals.

Effectively managing risk is one of the keys to the success of sellers in today's highly competitive global business environment. Several world-class companies have developed tools and techniques to help their business managers evaluate the risks versus the opportunities of potential services contracts. The tools they use involve risk identification, risk analysis, and risk mitigation. In Chapter 5, the importance of opportunity and risk assessment is discussed in more detail, including numerous tools and techniques that have proven effective in U.S. government services contracts.

PHASE 4: PROPOSAL DEVELOPMENT AND EVALUATION

Bid or proposal development is the process of creating offers in response to oral or written solicitations or based on perceived U.S. government buyer needs. Bid and proposal development can range from one person writing a one- or two-page proposal to a team of people developing a multivolume proposal of thousands of pages that takes months to prepare.

When a government contractor develops a solution in more detail, it should take steps to ensure the solution is holistically compliant with the its technical, delivery, financial, and contractual requirements. A government contractor must also ensure that the design is consistent with the description in the proposal and the pricing developed. Finally, a government contractor needs to develop a delivery plan that addresses the fundamentals of who, what, when, where, and how the solution will be delivered.

As the services solution develops, the contractor will likely find gaps or potential adverse situations that could occur. These are risks that need to be addressed. For each of these risks, a contractor should develop a Risk Mitigation Plan using one or more strategies designed to avoid, transfer, share, or reserve the risk. These plans will become an important part of the review with company stakeholders later in order to obtain their authority to bid.

As a company's services solution takes shape, the company will develop one or more business cases. Ideally, the company will develop a government customer business case showing the costs and benefits of the solution in the government customer's financial terms. At a minimum, an internal business case on the profitability of the opportunity must be developed for review with a selling company's stakeholders in order to obtain their authority to bid.

Finally, a potential contractor needs to develop the proposal or government customer deliverable(s). Although the actual format will vary, major components of a government customer proposal typically include:

a) Executive Summary
b) Technical Response
c) Delivery Response
d) Pricing Response
e) Contractual Response.

The Executive Summary provides an overview of the offer and targets executive decision-makers in the customer's organization. The win strategy and the services solution architecture serve as the skeleton for the Executive Summary, which is augmented with key details from the Technical e, Delivery , Pricing, and Contractual Responses.

The Technical Response describes the products and services offered and explains how they solve the customer's business problems. The Delivery Response describes the specifics of how, when, and who will deliver and support the offer and may include items such as an Implementation Plan, Delivery Schedule, Transition Plan, Maintenance Plan, or Support Plan. Even if the Delivery Response is not delivered to the customer, a well thought out and realistic Implementation Plan should be developed for internal purposes to understand how the project will be delivered. Depending upon the scope and complexity of an offer, it may be appropriate to op- erationally view the Technical and Delivery Responses as a single deliverable for proposal development and review purposes.

The Pricing Response describes how an offer is priced and its price terms. The Contractual Response describes the terms and conditions under which the offer is made and typically includes topics such as internal commitments, warranty, payment terms, and liabilities. If financing is offered to the customer, this would typically be described in the Pricing Response, but may alternatively appear in the Contractual Response. Depending upon the scope and complexity of an offer, it may be appropriate to operationally view the Pricing and Contractual Responses as a single deliverable for proposal development and review purposes.

The type and number of Bid or Proposal Reviews are based on the scope and complexity of an opportunity and the time available. Bid or Proposal Reviews can be classified into two types: (1) internally focused reviews and (2) externally focused reviews.

An internally focused review, typically referred to as a Pink Team Review, is usually conducted by members of the Bid/Proposal or Capture Team reading what others on the team have written. The chief focus of an internal Pink Team Review is to ensure that the proposal is complete and accurate. Depending upon the complexity and scope of an offer and the time available, there may be multiple Pink Team Reviews. Due to specialization of resources, there will frequently be different review team members for the major sections of the proposal (e.g., Executive Summary, Technical Delivery, Pricing, and Contractual).

Externally focused reviews, typically referred to as a Red Team Review, are conducted by individuals who are not members of the Capture Team. These unbiased and impartial individuals will read what has been written from the customer's perspective. The chief focus of an external Red Team Review is to ensure the proposal makes sense and addresses specified customer requirements. Depending upon the scope and complexity of an offer and the time available, there may be multiple Red Team reviews. Due to specialization of resources and complexity of a proposal, there will frequently be different review team members for the major sections of the proposal (e.g., Executive Summary, Technical, Delivery, Pricing, and Contractual).

Source selection is all about the government buyer's evaluating the sellers' offers (bids, proposal, tenders, and/or oral presentations) and all of the seller's appropriate qualifications, including past performance, use of small business, financial strength, reputation, use of breakthrough technologies, etc. Selecting the right source, like selecting the right dance partner, is critical to ultimate business success. The key to source selection is to make the appropriate selection as efficiently, quickly, and cost effectively as possible. Source selection is typically driven by the people chosen to serve on the source selection team, the source selection process, the source selection evaluation criteria and weightings, and the source selection authority or key decision-maker.

For most strategic bids or proposals, sellers will have an opportunity to provide an oral presentation of their bid or proposal to a select group of the buyer. If the buyer does not offer this opportunity, the seller should request permission to provide such a presentation. This will give the seller a chance to review the bid or proposal and reinforce its win strategy with the buyer's key influencers and deci- sion- makers. Depending upon the scope of the bid or proposal, this may involve multiple presentations to multiple audiences. If the seller is not given the chance to provide an oral presentation, then the buyer will typically transmit numerous questions via email to the seller(s) requesting timely responses. Thus, the seller(s) will often reconvene a respective capture team to prepare appropriate responses to all of a buyer's questions. Chapter 6 provides a detailed process approach to developing and evaluating services bids and proposals, including numerous tools, techniques, and best practices.

PHASE 5: NEGOTIATIONS AND CONTRACT FORMATION

In U.S. government services contracting after a source is selected, the parties must reach a common understanding of the nature of their undertakings and negotiate the terms and conditions (Ts and Cs) of contract performance. The ideal is to develop a set of shared expectations and understandings. However, this goal is difficult to attain for several reasons. First, either party may not fully understand its own requirements and expectations. Second, in most communications, many obstacles prevent achieving a true meeting of the minds. Errors, miscues, hidden agendas, cultural differences, differences in linguistic use and competence, haste, lack of clarity in thought or expression, conflicting objectives, lack of good faith (or even ill will), business exigencies are all factors that can and do contribute to poor communication.

In any undertaking, uncertainty and risk arise from many sources. In a business undertaking, many of those sources are characteristic of the industry or industries involved. Because one purpose of a contract is to manage uncertainty and risk, the types and sources of uncertainty and risk must be identified and understood. Then buyer and seller must develop and agree to contract Ts and Cs that are designed to express their mutual expectations about performance and that reflect the uncertainties and risks of performance. Although tradition and the experience of others provide a starting point for analysis, each contract must be considered unique.

The development of appropriate Ts and Cs is an important aspect of contract negotiation and formation. Common Ts and Cs include period of performance, warranties, intellectual property rights, payments, acceptance/completion criteria, and change management. Some organizations spend a lot of time, perhaps months, selecting a source, but they hurry through the process of arriving at a mutual understanding of the contract Ts and Cs. A "let's get on with it" mentality sets in. It is true that contracts formed in this way sometimes prove successful for all concerned. However, when both sides are large organizations, difficulties can arise from the different agendas of the functional groups existing within each organization's contracting party. Chapter 7 provides a much more detailed discussion of the tools, techniques, and best practices related to negotiation and formation of government services contracts.

PHASE 6: CONTRACT ADMINISTRATION AND CLOSEOUT

Contract performance is essentially doing what it was said you were going to do. Contract administration is the process of ensuring compliance with contractual Ts and Cs during contract performance and up to and including contract closeout or termination.

After award, both parties must act according to the Ts and Cs of their agreement; they must read and understand their contract, do what it requires of them, and avoid doing what they have agreed not to do.

Best Practices

Best practices in contract administration require specific action on the part of both the buyer and the seller, including:

□ Reading the contract;

□ Ensuring that all organizational elements are aware of their responsibilities in relation to the contract;

□ Providing copies of the contract to all affected organizations (either paper or electronic copies);

□ Establishing system to verify conformance with contract technical and administrative requirements;

□ Conducting pre-performance (or kick-off) meetings with the buyer and seller;

□ Assigning responsibility to check actual performance against requirements;

□ Identifying significant variances;

□ Analyzing each variance to determine its cause;

□ Ensuring that someone takes appropriate corrective action and then follows up;

□ Managing the contract change process; and

□ Establishing and maintaining contract documentation (diaries and telephone logs, meeting minutes, inspection reports, progress reports, test reports, invoices and payment records, accounting source documents, accounting journals and ledgers, contracting records, change orders and other contract modifications, claims, and routine correspondence).

Periodically, buyer and seller must meet to discuss performance and verify that it is on track and that each party's expectations are being met. This activity is critical, as conflict is almost inescapable within and between organizations. The friction that can arise from minor understandings, failures, and disagreements can heat to the boiling point before anyone on either side is fully aware of it. When this happens, the relationship between the parties may be irreparably damaged, and amicable problem resolution may become impossible. Periodic joint assessments by contract managers can identify and resolve problems early and help to ensure mutually satisfactory performance.

After the parties have completed the main elements of performance, they must settle final administrative and legal details before closing out a contract. They may have to make price adjustments and settle claims. The buyer will want to evaluate the seller's performance. Both parties must collect records and prepare them for storage in accordance with administrative and legal retention requirements.

Unfortunately, contracts are sometimes terminated due to the mutual agreement of the parties or due to the failure of one or both parties to perform all or part of the contract. After a termination notice is received, the parties must still conduct the same closeout actions as are required for a completed contract. In Chapter 8, the importance and value of contract fulfillment, contract administration, and contract closeout are discussed in far more detail, and numerous tools, techniques, and additional best practices for services contracts are provided.

SUMMARY

In retrospect, this chapter provides a simple yet highly effective U.S. Government Services Contracting Buying and Selling Life Cycle. The Buying and Selling Life Cycle comprises six distinct phases, which each require the support and collaboration, to various extents, of the U.S. government department or agency (buyer), the government prime contractor (seller), and the respective suppliers and/or vendors (subcontractors). Buying and selling professional services requires some unique knowledge, tools, and techniques to achieve successful results. The remaining chapters of this book focus on providing greater detail on how to achieve success in U.S. government services contracting in each of the key six phases—for buyers, for sellers, and for subcontractors.

QUESTIONS TO CONSIDER

1. How well does your organization conduct requirements determination?

2. How effectively and efficiently does your organization plan and prepare solicitation documents?

3. How effectively does your organization conduct holistic opportunity and risk assessments of potential services contracts and projects?

CHAPTER

PHASE 1: REQUIREMENTS DETERMINATION

By Gregory A. Garrett

INTRODUCTION

One of the most critical challenges facing U.S government departments and agencies today is the need for the timely and cost effective acquisition and delivery of a wide range of professional services
to support the needs of our nation. The Office of Federal Procurement Policy (OFPP), which is within the Office of Management
and Budget (OMB), has promoted policies to improve the U.S.
government's acquisition of services for more than 30 years. By
memorandum in 2006, OFPP established annual goals for civilian
agencies to apply Performance-Based Services Acquisition (PBSA)
methods on 40 percent (measured in dollars) of eligible service
contract actions (including contracts, task orders, modifications,
and options) valued over $25,000. Likewise, the U.S. Department
of Defense (DoD) has a similar PBSA goal of 50 percent.

This chapter will provide a comprehensive discussion of the nature
of U.S. government services contracting requirements determination by examining the following key aspects:

- Establishing an integrated project team to determine requirements;
- Describing the nature of the services challenges/needs;
- Conducting market research to identify potential services
  solutions; and
- Drafting a Statement of Objectives (SOO) for the services
  required.

THE REQUIREMENTS DETERMINATION PROCESS FOR SERVICES

While the Federal Acquisition Regulation (FAR Part 11 – Describing Agency Needs) and its related supplements generally state how
a U.S. government agency should develop its purchasing requirements, it primarily focuses on acquiring products. It does not offer
a structured process approach with proven tools and techniques
to obtain quality services.

Figure 3-1 illustrates the requirements determination process for
services, which includes three critical elements: (1) key inputs; (2)
proven tools and techniques; and (3) desired outputs.

Figure 3-1 Requirements Determination Process for Services

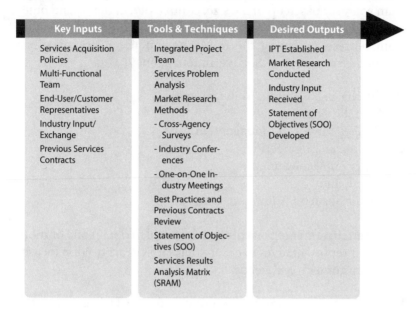

Key Inputs	Tools & Techniques	Desired Outputs
Services Acquisition Policies	Integrated Project Team	IPT Established
Multi-Functional Team	Services Problem Analysis	Market Research Conducted
End-User/Customer Representatives	Market Research Methods	Industry Input Received
Industry Input/ Exchange	- Cross-Agency Surveys	Statement of Objectives (SOO) Developed
Previous Services Contracts	- Industry Conferences	
	- One-on-One Industry Meetings	
	Best Practices and Previous Contracts Review	
	Statement of Objectives (SOO)	
	Services Results Analysis Matrix (SRAM)	

Key Inputs

The following are key inputs for the requirements determination process for acquiring services:

Services acquisition policies. The U.S. government has several key services acquisition policies that must be observed for acquiring services:

- Promote full and open competition to the maximum extent practicable.
- Specify services needs based upon market research.
- Include restrictive provisions only when required by the needs of the agency.
- Limit the use of time-and-materials (T&M) and cost-plus-award-fee (CPAF) contracts.
- Acquire commercial services pursuant to FAR Part 12 – Commercial Item Acquisition to the maximum extent practicable.
- State service requirements in terms of performance, insofar as possible.

Multi-functional team. The composition of the services acquisition team will vary based upon the size, complexity, urgency, and other agency factors. However, in most cases support will be needed from representatives of the following functional organizations within the respective U.S. government agency:

- Purchasing/Contract Management;
- Cost/Pricing;
- Budget/Financial Management;
- Technical/Engineering;
- Program Management;
- Legal; and
- Small Business Administration.

End-user/customer representative. It is vital to obtain one or more customer representatives to ensure that services acquisition focuses on the customer's real needs.

Industry input/exchange. It is critical for the U.S. government buyer to fully understand the nature and range of services available via information exchange with industry, preferably with the best-in-class companies.

Previous services contracts. It is equally important to draw upon the best practices of recent and similar services contracts by the agency or other U.S. government agencies.

Proven Tools and Techniques

The following are proven effective tools and techniques for determining requirements when acquiring professional services.

Integrated Project Team

Because of the mission-based and program-based focus of services acquisition that has resulted from acquisition reform and mandates for performance-based services acquisition, many more people play a role in acquisition teams today. In addition to contracting staff, for example, are those from program, financial, user, and even legal offices. All these skills and more can be required to create a true performance-based approach to an agency's needs.

It is important to recognize that integrated project teams are not a training ground. They are a field of operation for a team of people, who may vary in number, but who are among the best in their fields and have been trained in services acquisition. Composition of the integrated project team (IPT), from the numerous government functional areas is a critical success factor in performance-based services acquisition.

The members of the IPT must understand their roles and responsibilities. Regardless of its representation, the IPT is responsible for ensuring that the services acquisition

- satisfies legal and regulatory requirements;
- has performance and investment objectives consistent with the agency's strategic goals;
- successfully meets the agency's needs and intended results; and
- remains on schedule and within budget.

Successful IPTs typically have a number of features, including shared leadership roles, individual as well as mutual accountability, collective work-products, performance measures related to the collective work-products, and other characteristics.[1]

The Statement of Guiding Principles for the Federal Acquisition System states most simply: "Participants in the acquisition process should work together as a team and should be empowered to make decisions within their area of responsibility." (FAR 1.102(a)) Clearly defined levels of empowerment are critical to success.

In developing the services acquisition strategy, the key tools the IPT should use are consensus and compromise, without losing sight of three key questions:

1. What do I need?
2. When do I need it?
3. How do I know it's good when I get it?

If continuity is important, what can be done to keep an IPT focused and together? Added to empowerment and a shared vision, incentives are key. The most fundamental incentives are those that link program missions and team members' performance, and then tie performance to pay. If the IPT and the contractor have performance objectives, then the government team also should have performance objectives. Like contractor incentives, the government team's objectives should carry a value in terms of pay, recognition, and awards.

Keep in mind that these performance objectives should be program-based, not acquisition-based. Who cares if the contract is awarded in two months if it takes two years to get deliverables in the hands of the users? Incentives should be tied to the appropriate results.

Services Problem Analysis

Planning for a service acquisition should begin with business planning that focuses on the desired results or outputs. The first consideration is to determine the problem that the agency needs to solve. What results are needed? Will the results or solution meet the organizational and mission objectives?

Changes made to the Federal Acquisition Regulation in 2006 emphasize that acquisition planning must encompass performance-based considerations. FAR 7.105 (Contents of Written Acquisition Plans) specifically provides that

Acquisition plans for service contracts or orders must describe the strategies for implementing performance-based acquisition methods or must provide a rationale for not using those methods."

Moreover, the responsibility for performance-based strategies is tied to program officials:

> Agency program officials are responsible for accurately describing the need to be filled, or program to be resolved, through service contracting in a manner that ensures full understanding and responsive performance by contractors and, in so doing, should obtain assistance from contracting officials, as needed.[3]

Once the acquisition is linked to the agency's mission needs, the thoughts of the team should turn to what, specifically, are the desired results (outcomes) of contract performance. Is it a lower level of defaults on federal loans? Is it a reduction in benefit processing time? Is it broader dissemination of federal information?

Is it a reduction in the average time it takes to get relief checks to victims? What is the ultimate intended result of the contract and how does it relate to the agency's strategic plan? (Note that these are questions that a former solicitation—or someone else's solicitation—cannot answer.) These determinations are one of the tough tasks that the IPT must face.

The answers to these questions can normally be found, not with an exhaustive analysis, but through facilitated work sessions with program staff, customers, and stakeholders. By taking the process away from a mere paper review or an examination of the status quo, greater innovation and insight is possible. Once aired, those thoughts need to be captured in the statement of objectives. Note also that, to do this well, the IPT will need to seek information from the private sector during market research. Industry benchmarks and best practices from the best-in-class may help sharpen the IPT's focus on what the performance objectives should be.[4]

Market Research Methods

In the past it was not unusual for technical staff to conduct market research about marketplace offerings, while contracting staff conducted market research that focused on industry practices and pricing. A better approach is for the entire integrated project team to be a part of the market research effort. This enables the members of the IPT to share an understanding and knowledge of the marketplace—an important factor in the development of the acquisition strategy— and a common understanding of what features, schedules, and terms and conditions are key.

Cross-Agency Surveys/Collaboration

While many are familiar with examining private-sector sources and solutions as part of market research, looking to the public sector is not as common a practice. Yet it makes a great deal of sense on several levels.

First, there is an increased interest in cross-agency cooperation and collaboration. If the need is for help desk support, for example, many federal agencies have solved that problem and could potentially provide services through an interagency agreement or through an existing multiple-award contract vehicle. On the other hand, it could be that providing seamless services to the public might require two or more agencies to work together to acquire a solution.

Second, agencies with similar needs may be able to provide lessons learned and best practices. For example, the Department of Commerce COMMITS office has frequently briefed other agencies on the process of establishing a government-wide agency contract (GWAC) (see *www.contractdirectory.gov*). Another agency is now conducting public-sector market research about seat management implementation in the federal government. So it is important for the IPT members to talk to their counterparts in other agencies. Taking the time to do so may help avert problems that could otherwise arise during the acquisition.[5]

Industry Conferences

With regard to more traditional private-sector market research, it is important to be knowledgeable about commercial offerings, capabilities, and practices before structuring an acquisition in detail. This is one of the more significant changes brought about by acquisition reform.

Some of the traditional ways to do this include issuing "sources sought" type notices at FedBizOps.gov or www.fbo.gov, conducting "Industry Days," issuing Requests for Information, and holding pre-solicitation conferences. But it is also okay to simply pick up the phone and call private-sector company representatives.

Contact with vendors and suppliers for the purpose of market research is now encouraged. In fact, FAR 15.201(a) specifically promotes the exchange of information "among all interested parties, from the earliest identification of a requirement through receipt of proposals." The limitations that apply (once a procurement is underway) are that prospective contractors be treated fairly and impartially and that standards of procurement integrity (FAR 3.104) be maintained. But the real key is to begin market research before procurement is underway.

One-on-One Industry Meetings

While many may not realize it, one-on-one meetings with industry leaders are not only permissible (see Federal Acquisition Regulation 15.201(c)(4)) they are more effective than pre-solicitation or pre-proposal conferences. Note that when market research is conducted before a solicitation or performance work statement is drafted, the rules are different. FAR 15.201(f) provides, for example: "General information about agency mission needs and future requirements may be disclosed at any time." Since the requirements have not (or should not have) been defined, disclosure of procurement-sensitive information is not an issue. It is effective to focus on commercial and industry best practices, performance metrics and measurements, innovative delivery methods for the required services, and incentive programs that providers have found particularly effective. This type of market research can expand the range of potential solutions, change the very nature of the acquisition, establish the performance-based approach, and represent the agency's best step on the way to an improved partnership with industry.[6]

Best Practices and Previous Contracts Review

FAR Part 10 requires that as part of market research, an IPT should check *http://www.contractdirectory.gov* to see if there is an existing services contract available to meet agency requirements. FAR Part 10 also requires that a written market research report be placed in the contract file. The amount of research, given the time and expense, should be commensurate with the size of the acquisition.

Statement of Objectives

The SOO approach is described briefly in the Department of Defense *"Handbook for Preparation of Statement of Work (SOW),"* Section 5, for example:

The SOO is a Government prepared document incorporated into the RFP that states the overall solicitation objectives. It can be used in those solicitations where the intent is to provide the maximum flexibility to each offeror to propose an innovative development approach.

The SOO is a very short document (under 10 pages) that provides the basic, high-level objectives of an acquisition. It is provided in the solicitation in lieu of a government-written statement of work or performance work statement.[7]

The FAR now provides that the SOO shall include at a minimum the following:

- Purpose,
- Scope or Mission,
- Period and Place of Performance,
- Background,
- Performance Objectives (i.e., required results), and
- Any Operating Constraints

A short description of scope in the SOO helps the competitors grasp the size and range of the services needed. The Veterans Benefits Administration's scope statement follows:

> *The purpose of this [task order] is to provide the full range of loan servicing support. This includes such activities as customer management, paying taxes and insurance, default management, accounting, foreclosure, bankruptcy, etc., as well as future actions associated with loan servicing. This Statement of Objectives reflects current VA policies and practices, allowing offerors to propose and price a solution to known requirements. It is anticipated that specific loan servicing requirements and resulting objectives will change over the life of this order. This will result in VA modifying this order to incorporate in-scope changes.*[8]

The task of the integrated project teams was to "decide what problem needs solving." The basis for that analysis was information in the agency's strategic and annual performance plans, program authorization documents, budget documents, and discussions with project owners and stakeholders. That information constitutes the core of the statement of objectives.

In the case of the Veterans Administration, for example, the acquisition's performance objectives were set forth in this opening statement:

> *VA expects to improve its current loan servicing operations through this task order in several ways. Primary among these is to increase the number and value of saleable loans. In addition, VA wants to be assured that all payments for such items as taxes and insurance are always paid on time. As part of these activities, the VA also has an objective to improve Information Technology information exchange and VA's access to automated information on an as-required*

basis to have the information to meet customer needs and auditors' requirements.[9]

Services Results Analysis Matrix

As the information is developed, the integrated project team should begin capturing the information in a results analysis. The Department of Treasury guide, "Performance-Based Service Contracting," illustrates a six-column approach (see Table 3-1) using the following:

- Desired Outcomes: What do we want to accomplish as the end result of this contract?
- Required Service: What task must be accomplished to give us the desired result? (Note: Be careful this doesn't become a "how" statement.)
- Performance Standard: What should the standards for completeness, reliability, accuracy, timeliness, customer satisfaction, quality and/or cost be?
- Acceptable Quality Level (AQL): How much error will be accepted?
- Monitoring Method:
- Incentives/Disincentives for meeting or not meeting the performance standards.

The Treasury guide provides templates for help desk, seat management, systems integration, software development, and system design/business process re-engineering services.

The Department of Defense approach is very similar to the SRAM, that is, to document the desired outcomes, performance objectives, performance standards, and acceptable quality levels developed during the analytical process in a performance requirements summary (PRS). The PRS matrix has five columns: (1) performance objective, (2) performance standard, (3) acceptable quality level, (4) monitoring method, and (5) incentive.[10]

Table 3-1 Services Requirements Analysis Matrix					
Desired Outcomes	*Required Service*	*Performance Standard*	*Acceptable Quality Level*	*Monitoring Method*	*Incentives/ Disincentives*

Desired Outputs

Stated simply, the desired outputs of Phase 1: Requirements Determination for Services Contracts include:

- An integrated project team established by the U.S. government agency acquiring needed services;
- Appropriate market research conducted by the acquiring agency;
- Industry input/feedback to and members of the acquiring agency IPT to help it determine the agency's requirements;
- A statement of objectives developed by the IPT based on market research and industry input;
- Development of a *services requirement analysis matrix.*

Requirements Determination for Services (Best Practices)	
□ Review previous services contracts	□ Define (at a high level) desired services outcomes
□ Ensure senior management involvement and support	□ Decide what constitutes services success
□ Form an integrated project team (IPT)	□ Determine the current level of services performance
□ Define roles and responsibilities of IPT members	□ Take a team approach to market research
□ Develop rules of conduct for IPT members	□ Spend time learning from industry
□ Empower team members to look for innovative solutions to services needs	□ Talk to industry before structuring the services acquisition
□ Identify stakeholders and engage end-user/customer in requirements determination	□ Conduct one-on-one meetings with industry
□ Develop and maintain the knowledge base over the project life	□ Document market research
□ Incentivize the team: Establish a link between program mission and team members' performance	□ Write the services performance objectives into the SOO
□ Link services acquisition to mission and performance objectives	□ Make sure the government and the contractor share services objectives
	□ Develop requirements analysis matrix

SUMMARY

This chapter has provided a comprehensive process-oriented discussion of the nature of U.S. government services contracting requirements determination. This first phase of U.S. government services contracting presents a requirements determination process for services that includes key inputs, proven tools and techniques, and desired outputs. In addition numerous requirements determination best practices for services contracts are noted.

Chapter 4 builds on the desired outputs of the first phase of services contracting requirements determination by providing a process approach to planning and preparing successful solicitation documents.

QUESTIONS TO CONSIDER

1. Does your organization form integrated project teams to gather and develop purchasing requirements for services contracts?

2. How effectively does your organization conduct market research?

3. Does your organization develop a Statement of Objectives and Requirements Analysis Matrix when acquiring professional services?

ENDNOTES

[1] Gregory A. Garrett, *Performance-Based Acquisition: Pathways to Excellence*, NCMA, 2006.

[2] OFPP, *Seven Steps to Performance-Based Services Acquisition*, Rev. 2007.

[3] FAR 7.105

[4] Ibid, note 2.

[5] Ibid, note 2.

[6] Ibid., note 1.

[7] Department of Defense, *Handbook for Preparation of Statement of Work* Sec. 5, 2001.

[8] Ibid., note 2.

[9] Ibid., note 2.

[10] Department of Defense, *Guidebook for Performance-Based Services Acquisition*, 2000.

CHAPTER 4

PHASE 2: PROCUREMENT PLANNING AND SOLICITATION PREPARATION

By Gregory A. Garrett

INTRODUCTION

Once a U.S. government agency has decided to acquire professional services from industry and has determined its services requirements, then it must develop an appropriate procurement plan and prepare a solicitation document. Solicitation documents such as a Request for Quotation (RFQ), Request for Proposal (RFP), or Invitation for Bid (IFB) are commonly used by U.S. government agencies via the Federal Business Opportunities (FBO) website (*www.fbo.gov*) to communicate their purchasing needs and requirements to industry. Depending upon the nature of the services, size, complexity, urgency, location(s), and other factors, the services solicitation document and underlying procurement plan or business strategy may range from simple and routine to highly complex and unique.

As a result, there are a variety of different purchasing methods, solicitation actions, and pricing arrangements that should be considered in order to select the most appropriate means to obtain the services needed from the most qualified contractor(s) and subcontractors. Thus, this chapter will provide a process-oriented approach to the art and science of procurement planning that, in turn, drives the solicitation preparation.

PROCUREMENT PLANNING AND SOLICITATION PREPARATION PROCESS

Phase 2 of the U.S. Government Services Contracting Buying and Selling Life Cycle focuses on procurement planning and solicitation preparation. Figure 4-1 illustrates the key elements of U.S. government procurement planning and solicitation preparation, which includes key inputs, proven tools and techniques, and desired outputs. Phase 2 builds upon the outputs of Phase 1, which is discussed in Chapter 3.

Figure 4-1 U.S. Government Services Contracting

Phase 2: Procurement Planning and Solicitation Preparation Process

Key Inputs	Tools & Techniques	Desired Outputs
Integrated Project Team	E-procurement and Contracting Methods	Procurement Plan
Market Research Report	Services Evaluation Factors	Industry Participation and Feedback
Industry Feedback	Contract Type or Pricing Arrangements	Solicitation Document(s)
Statement of Objectives for Services	Incentives	
Services Requirements Analysis Matrix	Standard Forms	
	Draft Solicitation Documents	
	Pre-solicitation Industry Meetings/ Webinars and Comments	

Key Inputs

The following are key inputs to properly conducting U.S. government services contracting procurement planning and solicitation preparation:

- **Integrated Project Team (IPT)** The IPT typically includes representatives from the following functional areas:
  - Contract Management/Procurement
  - Cost/Price Analysis
  - Program Management
  - Engineering/Technical
  - Budget/Financial Management
  - Small Business Administration
  - Legal
  - Others
- **Market Research Report** A summary of all of the market research conducted, including Web-surveys, cross-government collaboration, review of sources sought, review of related Requests for Information (RFIs), etc.
- **Industry Feedback** Participation by companies in addressing specific U.S. government agency services needs via industry pre-solicitation conference, one-on-one industry meetings with the best-in-class companies, industry surveys, etc.

■ **Statement of Objectives (SOO)** A brief document developed by the government services acquiring agency that describes the outcomes or desired results of the services sought.

■ **Services Requirement Analysis Matrix (SRAM)** A six-column matrix that incorporates the key performance aspects and outcomes of the planned services (see Chapter 3 for the SRAM).

Proven Tools and Techniques

The following are proven effective tools and techniques that U.S. government agencies can use in conducting procurement planning and solicitation preparation for the acquisition of professional services.

e-Procurement and Contracting Methods

The two main approaches to contracting are *competitive methods,* such as purchase cards, imprest funds, auctions, Internet marketplaces, vertical exchanges, horizontal exchanges, Web portals, sealed bidding, private exchanges, two-step sealed bidding, and competitive negotiations and *noncompetitive methods,* such as purchase agreements and sole-source or single-source negotiations (see Table 4-1).

Table 4-1 Two Approaches to Contracting		
	Competitive	**Noncompetitive**
Simplified	• Purchase cards • Imprest funds or petty cash • Auctions • Net marketplaces • Vertical exchanges • Horizontal exchanges • Web portals	• Purchase agreements
Formal	• Sealed bidding • Private exchanges • Two-step sealed bidding • Competitive proposals • Competitive negotiations	• Sole-source negotiation • Single-source negotiation

Competitive Contracting Methods

The U.S. government prefers to purchase products and services using competitive contracting methods, ranging from simple to highly complex; all involve aspects of e-procurement.

Simplified Competitive Contracting Methods

Simplified competitive contracting methods include the following five arrangements:

- *Purchasing or procurement cards (P-cards)* A government organization's credit card commonly used to purchase low-price, off-the-shelf products and services. The degree of competition depends on the guidelines that the procurement organization will provide to the individuals empowered to use a P-card. Most organizations set predetermined spending limits on employee usage and track purchases to ensure that purchases are for business purposes only.

- *Imprest funds or petty cash* A small amount of money used to pay for small purchases of common products or services. Source selection depends on the company's or organization's purchasing guidelines.

- *Auctions* A widely practiced head-to-head bidding method, typically conducted face-to-face or via teleconferences, that is used to increase direct competition and that can be applied to the purchase of any product or service.

- *Net marketplaces* Two-sided Internet-based exchange where buyers and sellers negotiate prices, usually with a bid-and-ask system, with prices moving both up and down.

- *Vertical exchanges* A form of Internet marketplace for goods and services that are not specific to one industry.

- *Web portal* A public exchange, which may be vertical or horizontal, in which a company or group of companies lists products and services for sale and/or shares other business information.

Formal Competitive Contracting Methods

Formal competitive contracting methods are controlled bidding processes that keep pressure on competitors throughout the source selection process, with most of that pressure bearing on price. Thus, from the U.S. government buyer's point of view, competitive bidding is a highly effective technique for keeping prices low.

However, several disadvantages are associated with competitive bidding. First, it can be a costly process to administer because of the need to evaluate multiple formal proposals, and it can occupy a buyer's personnel for an extended period of time. Secondly, it can stifle communication between buyer and seller during contract formation because of the need to protect confidential information in competitors' proposals. This increases the risk of misunderstandings and disputes during contract performance. Third, the pressure to keep prices low can drive them below the point of realism, increasing cost risk and the attendant risk of poor seller performance and disputes. Competitive bidding, more so than other approaches, may create an adversarial relationship between buyer and seller, especially when the process takes on the characteristics of sealed bidding.

Nevertheless, competitive bidding can be effective, especially for purchasing commodities and common commercial services or for simple projects in which price is the most important factor. Most contracts for construction projects are still awarded through competitive bidding, as are most government contracts worldwide.

Sealed Bidding

Pursuant to FAR Part 14, competitive bidding usually takes the form of sealed bidding, in which price is the only criterion for selecting a source from a set of competing, prequalified sources. This technique entails soliciting, typically electronically, firm bids. The solicitation describes what the seller must do or deliver, the performance terms and conditions (Ts and Cs), and the deadline and location for submitting the bids. The bids usually state nothing more than the offered price. Sometimes bidders state their own Ts and Cs.

After the deadline passes, the buyer reviews the bids and evaluates them by comparing the prices offered. Buyers usually select the lowest bidder, but not always. The buyer may reject the lowest bids because they are too risky or because the bidder is not qualified. In the commercial world, the parties may negotiate after bid opening to reach agreement on details. Some buyers negotiate prices even after soliciting low bids, but this technique is ill-advised because bidders will anticipate the practice in the future and adjust their bids accordingly.

FOUR

To use sealed bidding, a buyer must have a specification that clearly and definitely describes the required product or service.

For bid price comparison to be meaningful, all bidders must be pricing the same requirements. Otherwise, the bids will not be truly comparable. In addition, the specification must be free of errors, ambiguities, and other defects. When a bidder thinks the buyer will change the specification during contract performance, he may buy in, anticipating the opportunity to increase the cost while negotiating for the change.

In addition because sealed bidding makes sense only for the award of firm-fixed contracts, performance cost uncertainty must be low. Otherwise, selecting the lowest bid will be a decision to select the proposal with the highest cost risk, which can have serious consequences. In a firm-fixed-price contract awarded by sealed bidding, an adversarial relationship is likely to develop between buyer and seller.

When using sealed bidding, the buyer must prequalify bidders or provide another way to ensure that the low bidder is competent to perform the work satisfactorily. Most buyers have a standard procedure by which potential sources can get on a bidder's mailing list or a qualified supplier's list. Many buyers will not entertain a bid from a source that is not prequalified by the quality and purchasing departments. Some buyers wait until after bids are reviewed and the low bidder is identified to determine a bidder's competence to perform, but this procedure is a wasteful one that frequently delays contract award.

Private Exchanges

Today many companies have developed private exchanges to procure goods and services from prequalified or preauthorized sellers. A private exchange is hosted by a single company and is located behind or inside a company's firewall. A private exchange typically operates using either a sealed bidding process or an e-auction process. More companies are using private exchanges to get the benefit of competition but are doing it in a controlled and secure electronic environment.

Two-Step Sealed Bidding

The two-step sealed bidding method requires sellers to first submit their technical proposal, typically electronically, and all other management and company qualification information, including past performance information. The buyer evaluates all the technical and other data– everything except pricing information– to determine whether the potential seller is a qualified supplier of the needed products or services.

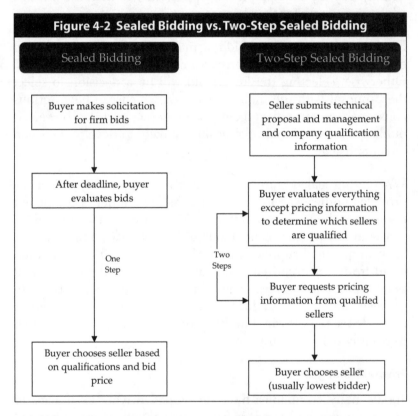

Figure 4-2 Sealed Bidding vs. Two-Step Sealed Bidding

The buyer then requests that the qualified sellers submit their respective pricing information for evaluation. Typically, the buyer then awards the contract to the qualified seller with the lowest price. Figure 4-2 compares sealed bidding and two-step sealed bidding.

Competitive Negotiations

Sometimes government buyers will use competitive negotiations pursuant to *FAR* Part 15, in which they solicit formal proposals from, and have discussions with, several competitors simultaneously. They may request a formal best and final offer *(BAFO)* before making a source selection decision. This approach is used commonly in government work and, in recent years, with increasing frequency in the commercial world at large.

In these competitions, technical considerations such as system design, are often more important than price, and the award is often made to someone other than the lowest bidder.

Even with electronic transmission of documents, competitive negotiations can be time-consuming, labor-intensive, and costly for both buyers and selling competitors. Competing businesses must often prepare voluminous proposals full of technical detail, make oral presentations, and prepare numerous proposal revisions and written responses to buyer inquiries. Proposal preparation costs can be high.

Competitive bidding and competitive negotiations have the common trait of merging source selection and contract formation. Combining these steps is accomplished through the buyer's solicitation (invitation for bids, tender, or request for proposals), which not only asks for proposals but also specifies what the buyer wants included as contract terms and conditions (Ts and Cs). The proposal, which is accompanied by other information intended to persuade the buyer that the firm submitting the proposal is the best qualified, is usually a promise to comply with the Ts and Cs in the buyer's solicitation.

If the source has not taken exception to any Ts and Cs in the solicitation and if the buyer is willing to accept all aspects of the proposal, selecting the best-qualified source is tantamount to accepting that firm's proposal. If the source has taken exception or if the buyer does not like all aspects of the source's proposal, the parties must negotiate to reach an agreement.

Noncompetitive Contracting Methods

Noncompetitive contracting methods, which may be used under specific circumstances, can be simplified or formal.

Simplified Noncompetitive Contracting Methods

When a buyer has selected a seller and wants to establish a successful, long-term contract relationship involving repetitive transactions, buyer and seller will commonly use simplified noncompetitive contracting methods to facilitate the contracting process.

These methods include oral contracts, oral contract modifications, and written agreements known as basic ordering agreements, purchase agreements, sales agreements, general agreements, master agreements, distributor agreements, and universal agreements, among others. These written agreements establish standard Ts and Cs by which the parties can reduce administrative costs and cycle time and increase customer satisfaction.

Formal Noncompetitive Contracting Methods

Noncompetitive contracting methods can be applied to either single-source or sole-source negotiation.

Single-Source vs. Sole-Source Negotiation

Single-source negotiation occurs when a buyer selects a single company or seller to provide products or services. In single-source situations, the buyer has the opportunity to select other sellers but has a preference for a specific seller. In contrast, sole-source negotiation occurs when there is only a single seller that can provide the needed product or service. Thus, a sole-source seller has a monopoly in its market and tremendous leverage with most buyers. Increasingly, buyers are reducing their use of competitive bidding and relying on negotiations with only one company as a means of awarding contracts. This process entails a more rigorous separation between source selection and contract formation than does competitive bidding.

Source selection is accomplished through relatively informal processes of inquiry. Market research provides a short list of potential sources. The companies on this list are usually contacted electronically and asked to complete questionnaires or to prepare information packages, or the buyer may simply use the Web and search for specific goods or services via supplier electronic catalogs without preparing a formal request for proposal. The buyer may visit the source to evaluate its facilities and capabilities in person or virtually via videoconferencing, Net-meeting, or video tapes.

The buyer may shorten the list to two or three companies to contact for more extensive discussions. When enough information is gathered, the buyer evaluates it and selects a single source for negotiation, leading to contract award. The parties may communicate several times before the source finalizes its proposal. When the source submits its proposal to the buyer, much of it will not be new but will merely confirm agreements reached during preliminary discussions.

After receiving a proposal, typically electronically, and conducting a preliminary analysis, a buyer may engage in fact-finding, seeking to understand all elements before deciding whether to bargain for better terms. With all the facts in hand, the buyer performs a thorough cost and technical evaluation of the proposal. During this evaluation, the buyer identifies every aspect of the proposal that must be modified through bargaining.

If the buyer decides to bargain, the negotiator develops a negotiation objective and presents it to company superiors for approval. If the objective is approved, the negotiator communicates with the source and bargains until the parties reach an agreement or a stalemate. The parties then prepare a document describing the Ts and Cs of their agreement and sign it to complete the source selection and contract formation processes.

Figure 4-3 compares competitive bidding, competitive proposals and negotiations, and single-source and sole-source negotiation.

Tools Techniques and Best Practices

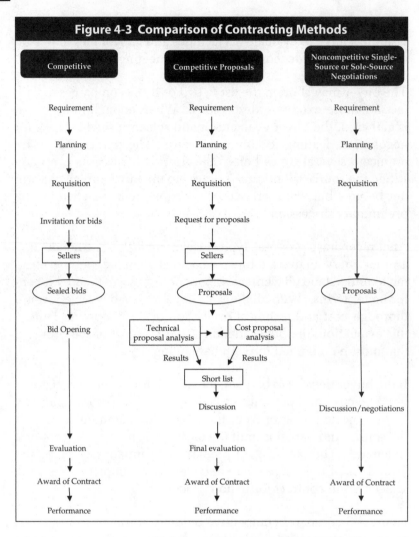

Figure 4-3 Comparison of Contracting Methods

These proven successful contracting methods may be used in either a paper/written (hard copy) mode or electronically. Competitive contracting methods are used most frequently in transactions for products and services globally. However, today most large-dollar, multi-year, complex contracts that integrate products, services, and solutions are awarded using noncompetitive contracting methods.

CONTRACT TYPE OR PRICING ARRANGEMENTS

Over the years some standard pricing arrangements for contracts have evolved. These arrangements fall into three categories: (1)

FOUR

fixed-price, (2) cost-reimbursement, and (3) time-and-materials contracts. These contract categories have developed as practical responses to cost risk, and they have become fairly standard formal arrangements. Incentives can be added to any of the contract types in these three categories and are discussed in detail below. Table 4-2 lists several types of common contracts in these categories.

These pricing arrangements, however, are manifested in the specific terms and conditions of contracts, hence, the contract clauses. No standard clauses for their implementation exist. Therefore, the contracting parties must write clauses that describe their specific agreement.

Table 4-2 Contract Categories and Types		
Fixed-Price	Cost-Reimbursement or Unit Price*	Time-and-Materials
Firm-Fixed-Price (FFP)	Cost-Reimbursement (CR)	Time-and-Materials (T&M)
Fixed-Price with Economic Price Adjustment (FP/EPA)	Cost-Sharing (CS)	Labor/Hour (L/H)
	Cost-Plus-Fixed Fee (CPFF)	
Fixed-Price Incentive (FPI)	Cost-Plus-Incentive Fee (CPIF)	
	Cost-Plus-Award Fee (CPAF)	

Fixed-Price Contracts

Fixed-price contracts are the standard business pricing arrangement. The two basic types of fixed-price contracts are firm-fixed-price (FFP) and fixed-price with economic price adjustment (FP/EPA). Firm-fixed-price contracts are further divided into lump-sum and unit-price arrangements.

Firm-Fixed-Price Contracts

The simplest and most common business pricing arrangements is the firm-fixed-price (FFP) contract. The seller agrees to supply specified goods or services in a specified quantity or using a level of effort (LOE) in return for a specified price, either a lump sum or a unit price. The price is fixed; that is, it is not subject to change based on the seller's actual cost experience. (However, it may be subject to change if the parties modify the contract.) This pricing arrangement is used for the sale of commercial goods and services.

Some companies include a complex clause in their FFP contracts, which may read in part as follows:

Prices and Taxes

The price of Products shall be ABC Company's published list prices on the date ABC Company accepts your order less any applicable discount. If ABC Company announces a price increase for Equipment, or Software licensed for a one-time fee, after it accepts your order but before shipment, ABC Company shall invoice you at the increased price only if delivery occurs more than 120 days after the effective date of the price increase. If ABC Company announces a price increase for Services, Rentals, or Software licensed for a periodic fee, the price increase shall apply to billing periods beginning after its effective date.

Note that this clause was written by the seller, not the buyer, and reflects the seller's point of view and concerns. Nevertheless, the pricing arrangement it describes is firm-fixed-price, because the contract price will not be subject to adjustment based on ABC Company's actual performance costs.

Clauses such as "Prices and Taxes" frequently form part of a document known as a universal agreement. The universal agreement is not a contract; it is a precontract agreement that merely communicates any agreed-to Ts and Cs that will apply when an order is placed by the buyer. After an order is accepted by the seller, the company's published or announced list prices become the basis for the contract price according to the terms of the universal agreement (this agreement is discussed below in "Purchase Agreements").

Firm-fixed-price contracts are appropriate for most commercial services transactions when cost uncertainty is within commercially acceptable limits. What those limits may be depends on the industry and the market.

Fixed-Price with Economic Price Adjustment (FP/EPA)

Fixed-price contracts sometimes include various clauses that provide for adjusting prices based on specified contingencies. The clauses may provide for upward or downward adjustments, or both.

Economic price adjustments (EPA) are usually limited to factors beyond a seller's immediate control, such as market forces.

This pricing arrangement is not a firm-fixed price, because the contract provides for a price adjustment based on the seller's actual performance costs. Thus, the seller is protected from the risk of certain labor or materials cost increases. The EPA clause can provide for price increases based on the seller's costs but not on the seller's decision to increase the prices of its products or services. Thus, there can be a significant difference between this clause and the "Prices and Taxes" clause discussed above.

The shift of risk to a buyer creates greater buyer intrusion into the affairs of a seller. This intrusion typically takes the form of an audit provision at the end of the clause, particularly when the buyer is a government.

EPA clauses are appropriate in times of market instability when great uncertainty exists regarding labor and materials costs. The risk of cost fluctuations is more balanced between the parties than would be the case under an FFP contract.

Cost-Reimbursement Contracts

Cost-reimbursement (CR) contracts usually include an estimate of project cost, a provision for reimbursing the seller's expenses, and a provision for paying a fee as profit. Normally, CR contracts also include a limitation on the buyer's cost liability.

A common perception is that CR contracts are to be avoided. However, if uncertainty about costs is great enough, a buyer may be unable to find a seller willing to accept a fixed price, even with adjustment clauses, or a seller may insist on extraordinary contingencies within that price. In the latter case, the buyer may find the demands unreasonable. Such high levels of cost uncertainty are often found in research and development, large-scale construction, and systems integration projects. In such circumstances, the best solution may be a CR contract, but only if the buyer is confident that the seller has a highly accurate and reliable cost accounting system.

The parties to a CR contract will confront some challenging issues, especially concerning the definition, measurement, allocation, and confirmation of costs. For example, the buyer may decide that the cost of air travel should be limited to the price of a coach or business-class ticket and should not include a first-class ticket. The buyer will specify other cost limitations, and the parties will negotiate until they agree on what constitutes a reimbursable cost.

Next, the parties must decide who will measure costs and what accounting rules will be used to do so. For example, several depreciation techniques are available, some of which would be less advantageous to the buyer than others. Which technique will the buyer consider acceptable? How will labor costs be calculated? Will standard costs be acceptable, or must the seller determine and invoice actual costs? What methods of allocating overhead will be acceptable to the buyer? How will the buyer know that the seller's reimbursement invoices are accurate? Will the buyer have the right to an independent audit? If the buyer is also a competitor of the seller, should the seller be willing to open its books to the buyer?

If these issues remain unsettled, the buyer is accepting the risk of having to reimburse costs it may later find to be unreasonable. This issue is the main problem with cost-reimbursement contracting, and it has never been entirely resolved.

Clearly, the CR contract presents the parties with difficulties they would not face under a fixed-price contract. First, the parties must define costs and establish acceptable procedures for cost measurement and allocation. Second, the buyer takes on greater cost risk and must incur greater administrative costs to protect its interests. Third, the seller faces greater intrusion by the buyer into its affairs. Nevertheless, many contracting parties have found a CR contract to be a better arrangement than a fixed-price contract for undertakings with high cost uncertainty.

Types of CR contracts include cost, cost-sharing, cost-plus-a-percentage-of-cost, and cost-plus-fixed fee.

Cost Contracts

The cost contract is the simplest type of CR contract. Governments commonly use this type when contracting with universities and nonprofit organizations for research projects. The contract provides for reimbursing contractually allowable costs, with no allowance for profit.

Cost-Sharing Contracts

The cost-sharing (CS) contract provides for only partial reimbursement of a seller's costs. The parties share the cost liability, with no allowance for profit. The cost-sharing contract is appropriate when the seller will enjoy some benefit from the results of the project and that benefit is sufficient to encourage the seller to undertake the work for only a portion of its costs and without a fee.

Cost-Plus-a-Percentage-of-Cost Contracts

The cost-plus-a-percentage-of-cost (CPPC) contract provides the seller with reimbursement for its costs and a profit component, called a fee, equal to some predetermined percentage of its actual costs. Thus, as costs go up, so does profit. This arrangement is a poor one from the buyer's standpoint, as it provides no incentive to control costs, because the fee becomes greater as the costs increase. This type of contract was used extensively by the U.S. government during World War I but has since been made illegal for U.S. government contracts for good reason. It is still occasionally used for construction projects and some service contracts in the private sector.

The rationale for this pricing arrangement was probably "the bigger the job, the bigger the fee"; that is, as the job grows, so should the fee. This arrangement is similar to a professional fee, such as an attorney's fee, which grows as the professional puts more time into a project. This arrangement may have developed as a response to the cost-growth phenomenon in projects that were initially ill-defined. As a seller proceeded with the work, the buyer's needs became better defined and grew, until the seller felt that the fees initially agreed to were not enough for the expanded scope of work. Again, while there was a place for CPPC in the past, today it is rarely used.

Cost-Plus-Fixed Fee Contracts

Cost-plus-fixed fee (CPFF) contract is the most common type of CR contract. As with the others, the seller is reimbursed for its costs, but the contract also provides for payment of a fixed fee that does not change in response to the seller's actual cost experience. The seller is paid the fixed fee on successful completion of the contract, whether its actual costs are higher or lower than the estimated costs.

If the seller completes the work for less than the estimated cost, it receives the entire fixed fee. If the seller incurs the estimated cost without completing the work and the buyer decides not to pay for the overrun costs necessary for completion, the seller receives a portion of the fixed fee that is equal to the percentage of work completed. If the buyer decides to pay overrun costs, the seller must complete the work without any increase in the fixed fee. The only adjustment to the fee would be in the event of cost growth, when the buyer requires the seller to do more work than initially specified.

This type of contract is on the opposite end of the spectrum from the FFP contract, because cost risk rests entirely on the shoulders of the buyer. Under a CR contract, a buyer might have to reimburse the seller for the entire estimated cost and part of the fee but have nothing to show for it but bits and pieces of the work.

CONTRACT INCENTIVES

The fundamental purpose of contract incentives is to motivate desired performance in one or more specific areas. Contract incentives are generally classified as either objectively based and evaluated or subjectively based and evaluated. Further, both classifications of contract incentives are typically categorized as either positive incentives (rewards – more money) or negative incentives (penalties – less money) or some combination thereof.

Incentives that use predetermined formula-based methods to calculate the amount of incentive, either positive or negative, in one or more designated areas are objectively based and evaluated. Facts and actual events are used as a basis for determination. Therefore, individual judgment and opinions are not considered in evaluation of performance. Objectively based and evaluated contract incentives commonly include the following designated performance areas:

- Cost performance,
- Schedule or delivery performance, and
- Quality performance.

Subjectively based and evaluated contract incentives use individual judgment, opinions, and informed impressions as the basis for determining the amount of incentive, either positive or negative, in one or more designated areas. These incentives can and often do contain some objective aspects or factors. However, subjective contract incentives are ultimately determined by one or more individuals making a decision based on their experience, knowledge, and the available information, that is, a total judgment. Subjectively based and evaluated contract incentives typically include the following:

- Award fees,
- Award term, and
- Other special incentives.

Figure 4-4 summarizes the link between rewards and penalties and contract incentives, which are described below.

Objective Incentives

Incentives Based on Cost Performance

Cost is the most commonly chosen performance variable. For fixed-price (cost) incentive contracts, the parties negotiate a target cost and a target profit (which equals the target price) and a sharing formula for cost overruns and underruns. They also negotiate a ceiling price, which is the buyer's maximum dollar liability. When performance is complete, they determine the final actual costs and apply the sharing formula to any overrun or underrun. Applying the sharing formula determines the seller's final profit, if any.

Figure 4-4 Contract Incentives			
Types of Incentives	Positive (rewards)	No Reward or Penalty	Negative (penalties)
Objective incentives			
Cost performance	Under budget	On budget	Over budget
Schedule or delivery performance	Early delivery	On-time delivery	Late delivery
Quality performance	Exceed requirements	Achieve contract requirements	Do not achieve requirements
Subjective incentives			
Award fee Other special incentives	Exceed requirements	Achieve award fee plan	Do not achieve requirements

Consider an example in which the parties agree to the following arrangement:

Target cost: $10,000,000
Target profit: $850,000
Target price: $10,850,000
Sharing formula: 70/30 (buyer 70%, seller 30%)
Ceiling price: $11,500,000

Assume that the seller completes the work at an actual cost of $10,050,000, overrunning the target cost by $50,000. The seller's share of the overrun is 30% of $50,000, which is $15,000. The target profit will be reduced by that amount ($850,000 – $15,000 = $835,000). The seller will then receive the $10,050,000 for the cost of performance plus an earned profit of $835,000. Thus, the price to the buyer will be $10,885,000, which is $615,000 below the ceiling price. The $35,000 increase over the target price of $10,850,000 represents the buyer's 70% share of the cost overrun.

Had the seller overrun the target cost by $100,000, raising the actual cost to $10,100,000, the seller's share of the overrun would have been 30%, or $30,000. That amount would have reduced the seller's profit to $820,000.

Basically, at some point before reaching the ceiling price, the sharing arrangement effectively changes to 0/100, with the seller assuming 100% of the cost risk. This effect is implicit in fixed-price incentive arrangements due to the ceiling price and is not an explicit element of the formula. The point at which sharing changes to 0/100 is called the point of total assumption (PTA), which represents a cost figure. Indeed, the PTA is often appropriately referred to as the high-cost estimate. Figure 4-5 depicts these relationships and outcomes in graph form. (Note that the graph shows a first-degree linear equation of the form $Y = A - BX$, with cost as the independent variable X, and profit as the dependent variable Y. B, the coefficient of X, is equal to the seller's share.)

The PTA can be determined by applying the following formula:

$$PTA = \left(\frac{\text{Ceiling price - Target price}}{\text{Buyer share ratio}} \right) + \text{Target Cost}$$

In the event of an underrun, the seller would enjoy greater profit. If the final cost is $9,000,000 (a $1,000,000 underrun), the seller's share of the underrun is 30%, which is $300,000. Thus, the price to the buyer would include the $9,000,000 cost and then $850,000 target profit plus the seller's $300,000 underrun share (total profit of $1,150,000). Thus, $9,000,000 actual cost plus $1,150,000 actual profit equals $10,150,000 actual price, reflecting precisely the buyer's 70% share of the $1,000,000 underrun [$10,850,000 target price minus 70% of the $1,000,000 underrun ($700,000) = $10,150,000].

Schedule or Delivery Performance Incentives

For many years, construction, aerospace, and numerous service industries have used schedule or delivery performance incentives to motivate sellers to provide either early or on-time delivery of products and services.

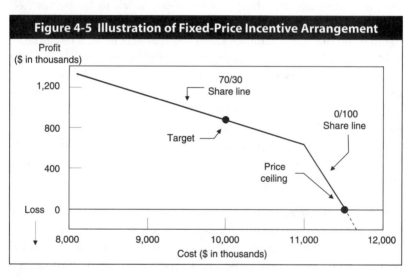

Figure 4-5 Illustration of Fixed-Price Incentive Arrangement

Liquidated damages are a negative incentive (penalty) for late delivery. Typically, a liquidated damages clause stated in the contract terms and conditions designates how much money one party, usually the seller, must pay the other party, usually the buyer, for not meeting the contract schedule. Often the amount of liquidated damages payable is specified as an amount of money for a specific period of time (day, week, month). A key aspect of liquidated damages is that the penalty is to be based on the amount of damages incurred or compensable in nature, but is not an excessive or punitive amount.

A proven best practice for buyers is to require negative incentives (or penalties) for late delivery and late schedule performance. Likewise, a proven best practice for sellers is to limit their liability for liquidated damages by agreeing to a cap or maximum amount and seeking positive incentives (or rewards) for early delivery and early schedule performance.

Quality Performance Incentives

Quality performance incentives are one of the most common topics in government and commercial contracting. Surveys in both government and industry have revealed widespread service contracting problems, including deficient statements of work, poor contract administration, performance delays, and quality shortcomings.

When a contract is based on performance, all aspects of the contract are structured around the purpose of the work to be performed rather than the manner in which it is to be done. The buyer seeks to elicit the best performance the seller has to offer at a reasonable price or cost by stating its objectives and giving the seller latitude in determining how to achieve them and incentives for achieving them. In source selecting, for example, the buyer might publish a draft solicitation for comment, use quality-related evaluation factors, or both. The statement of work will provide performance standards rather than spelling out what the seller is to do. A contract normally contains a plan for quality assurance surveillance and positive and negative performance incentives.

Few people disagree with the concept that buyers, who collectively spend billions of dollars on services annually, should use the performance-based approach, focusing more on results and less on detailed requirements. However, implementing performance-based contracting (using cost, schedule, and/or quality performance variables) is far easier said than done. The sound use of performance incentives is key to the success of the performance-based contracting approach.

Problems with Objective Incentives

While objective incentive schemes have some merit, they also involve some serious practical problems. First, they assume a level of buyer and seller competence that may not exist. Second, they assume effects that may not occur. Third, they create serious challenges for contract administration.

FOUR

To negotiate objective incentives intelligently, the parties must have some knowledge of the range of possible costs for a project. They also must have some knowledge of the likely causes and probabilities of different cost outcomes. If both parties do not have sufficient information on these issues, they will not be able to structure an effective incentive formula.

It is important that contracting parties share their information. If one party has superior knowledge that it does not share with the other, it will be able to skew the formula in its favor during negotiations. If that happens, the whole point of the arrangement, which is to equitably balance the risks of performance, will be lost. The buyer is usually at a disadvantage with respect to the seller in this regard.

An objective incentive assumes that the seller can affect a performance outcome along the entire range of the independent variable. However, this may not be true. For instance, the seller may actually exercise control along only a short sector of the range of possible costs, with some possible cost outcomes entirely outside the seller's control because of factors such as market performance. In reality, the seller's project manager may have little control over important factors that may determine the cost outcome, such as overhead costs. In addition, on some contracts short-term companywide factors, especially those involving overhead, may make incurring additional costs, rather than earning additional profit, more advantageous for the seller.

In addition, objective cost incentives are complicated and costly to administer with all the cost definition, measurement, allocation, and confirmation problems of CR contracts. The parties must be particularly careful to segregate the target cost effects of cost growth from those of cost overruns; otherwise, they may lose money for the wrong reasons. As a practical matter, segregating such costs is often quite difficult.

When using other performance incentives, the parties may find themselves disputing the causes of various performance outcomes. The seller may argue that the schedule delays are a result of the buyer's actions. Quality problems, such as poor reliability, may have been caused by improper buyer operation rather than seller performance. In short, the causes of performance failures may be difficult to determine.

One reason for using such contracts is to reduce the deleterious effects of risk on the behavior of the parties. Consequently, if a pricing arrangement increases the likelihood of trouble, it should not be used. The decision to apply objective incentives should be made only after careful analysis.

BEST PRACTICES

Actions to Improve the Use of Contract Incentives

These best practices should be followed when using incentive contracts:

- Think creatively. Creativity is a critical aspect in the success of performance-based incentive contracting.
- Avoid rewarding sellers for simply meeting contract requirements.
- Recognize that developing clear, concise, objectively measurable performance incentives will be a challenge, and plan accordingly.
- Create a proper balance of objective incentives—cost, schedule, and quality performance.
- Ensure that performance incentives focus the seller's efforts on the buyer's desired objectives.
- Make all forms of performance incentives challenging yet attainable.
- Ensure that incentives motivate quality control and that the results of the seller's quality control efforts can be measured.
- Consider tying on-time delivery to cost and/or quality performance criteria.
- Recognize that not everything can be measured objectively. Consider using a combination of objectively measured standards and subjectively determined incentives.
- Encourage open communication and ongoing involvement with potential sellers in developing the performance-based SOW and the incentive plan, both before and after issuing the formal request for proposals.
- Consider including socioeconomic incentives (non-SOW-related) in the incentive plan.
- Use clear, objective formulas for determining performance incentives.
- Use a combination of positive and negative incentives.
- Include incentives for discounts based on early payments.

□   Ensure that all incentives, both positive and negative, have limits.

FOUR

Subjective Incentives

Award Fee Plans

In an award fee plan, the parties negotiate an estimated cost, just as for cost-plus-fixed fee contracts. Then they negotiate an agreement on the amount of money to be included in an award fee pool. Finally, they agree on a set of criteria and procedures to be applied by the buyer in determining how well the seller has performed and how much of the fee pool the seller has earned. In some cases, the parties also negotiate a base fee, which is a fixed fee that the seller will earn no matter how its performance is evaluated.

The contract performance period is then divided into equal award fee periods. A part of the award fee pool is allocated to each period proportionate to the percentage of the work schedule to be completed. All this information is included in the award fee plan, which becomes part of the contract. In some cases, the contract allows the buyer to change the award fee plan unilaterally before the start of a new award fee period.

During each award fee period, the buyer observes and documents the seller's performance achievements or failures. At the end of the each period, the buyer evaluates the seller's performance according to the award fee plan and decides how much of the fee to award from the portion allocated to that period. Under some contracts, the seller has an opportunity to present its own evaluation of its performance and a specific request for award fee. The buyer then informs the seller how much of the available award fee it has earned and how its performance can be improved during ensuing award fee periods.

This arrangement invariably involves subjectivity on the part of the buyer; precisely how much depends on how the award fee plan is written.

Award Fee Arrangement Pros and Cons

The cost-plus-award fee contract is a cost-reimbursement contract with all its requirements for cost definition, measurement, allocation, and confirmation. For the buyer, the CPAF contract requires the additional administrative investment associated with observing, documenting, and evaluating seller performance. However, this disadvantage may sometimes be overemphasized, because the buyer should be performing many of these activities under a CR contract.

The disadvantages for the buyer are offset by the extraordinary power it obtains from the ability to make subjective determinations about how much of the fee the seller has earned. The buyer may, however, have difficulty establishing objective criteria for satisfactory service performance.

The power of subjective fee determination tends to make sellers extraordinarily responsive to a buyer's demands. However, the buyer must be careful, because that very responsiveness can be the cause of cost overruns and unintended cost growth.

The buyer's advantages are almost entirely disadvantages from the viewpoint of the seller, because the seller places itself within the power of the buyer to an exceptional degree. Subjectivity can approach arbitrariness or even cross the line. A seller may find itself dealing with a buyer that is impossible to please or that believes the seller cannot earn all the award fee because no one can achieve perfect performance.

Other Special Incentives

There is a growing recognition by buyers and sellers worldwide, in both the public and private sectors, that contract incentives can be expanded and that they are indeed valuable tools to motivate the desired performance. Increasingly, when outsourcing, buyers are motivating sellers to subcontract with local companies, often with special rewards for subcontracting with designated small businesses.

Likewise, many sellers are providing buyers with special incentives for early payment, such as product or service discounts or additional specified services at no charge.

Incentive Contracts

Cost-Plus-Incentive Fee Contracts

Cost-plus-incentive fee (CPIF) contracts allow overrun or underrun sharing of costs through a predetermined formula for fee adjustments that apply to incentives for cost contracts. Within the basic concept of the buyer's paying all costs for a cost contract, the limits for a CPIF contract become those of maximum and minimum fees. The necessary elements for a CPIF contract are maximum fee, minimum fee, target cost, target fee, and share ratio(s).

Fixed-Price Incentive Contracts

In a fixed-price incentive (FPI) contract, seller profit is linked to cost, schedule, quality, or a combination of all three. The objective is to give the seller a monetary incentive to optimize cost performance.

FPI contracts may be useful for initial production of complex new products or systems, although the parties may have difficulty agreeing on labor and materials costs for such projects due to a lack of production experience. However, the cost uncertainty may be great enough to warrant use of a CR contract.

Cost-Plus-Award Fee Contracts

Cost-plus-award fee (CPAF) contracts include subjective incentives in which the profit a seller earns depends on how well the seller satisfies a buyer's subjective desires. This type of contract has been used for a long time in both government and commercial contracts worldwide. The U.S. Army Corps of Engineers developed an evaluated fee contract for use in construction during the early 1930s based on its contracting experience during World War I. The U.S. National Aeronautics and Space Administration has used CPAF contracts to procure services since the 1950s. Other U.S. government agencies have also used these contracts extensively, including the Department of Energy and the Department of Defense. A small but growing number of commercial companies now use award fees to motivate their suppliers to achieve exceptional performance.

Cost-plus-award fee contracts are used primarily to procure services, particularly those that involve an ongoing, long-term relationship between buyer and seller, such as maintenance and systems engineering support. Objective criteria for determining the acceptability of the performance of services are inherently difficult to establish. The award fee arrangement is particularly well suited to such circumstances, at least from the buyer's point of view. However, this type of contract also is used to procure architecture and engineering, research and development, hardware and software systems design and development, construction, and many other services.

Time-and-Materials Contracts

In time-and-materials (T&M) contracts, the parties negotiate hourly rates for specified types of labor and agree that the seller will be reimbursed for parts and materials at cost. Each hourly rate includes labor costs, overhead, and profit. The seller performs the work, documenting the types and quantities of labor used and the costs for parts and materials. When the work is finished, the seller bills the buyer for the number of labor-hours at the agreed-upon hourly rates and for the costs of materials and parts.

Time-and-materials contracts are most often used to acquire a wide range of professional services, including telecommunications, construction, administrative, equipment repair, and maintenance services, when the cost in terms of effort required is uncertain.

Although T&M contracts appear to be straightforward, they may create some difficulties. This type of contract must be negotiated carefully, because each hourly rate includes a component for overhead costs, that is, both fixed and variable costs. Fixed costs are the costs that are incurred during a given period of operation, despite the number of work-hours performed. To recover its fixed costs, a seller must estimate how many hours will be sold during the contract performance period and allocate a share to each hour. If the parties overestimate how many hours will be sold during the period of performance, the seller will not recover all of its fixed costs. If the parties underestimate how many hours will be sold, the seller will enjoy a windfall profit.

Although the hourly labor rates are fixed, the number of hours delivered and the cost of materials and parts are not. Therefore, the buyer faces the problems of confirming the number of hours delivered and the cost of materials claimed by the seller. These problems are not as great as those under CR contracts, but they are not insignificant.

During the past few years the use of T&M contracts to acquire services has come under greater scrutiny in the U. S. government. U.S. government contracting offers are now required to complete a written justification for using or selecting a T&M pricing agreement for acquiring any services.

Further the U.S. government contracting officer must ensure the following aspects are required in all T&M contracts awarded:

- The contract must include a not-to-exceed (NTE) amount.
- The period of performance may not exceed three (3) years (base year plus option years).
- A determination and findings (D&F) must be completed, which describes why no other form or contract type is more suitable for the services contract.

In addition, the Office of Management and Budget has created a policy that describes all T&M, cost-reimbursement, and incentive contracts as high-risk contracting actions. Each agency is charged with establishing a goal to reduce their use of these contracts by 10% each fiscal year beginning in FY 2010.

Figure 4-6 provides a range of contract types keyed to performance measurement and risk.

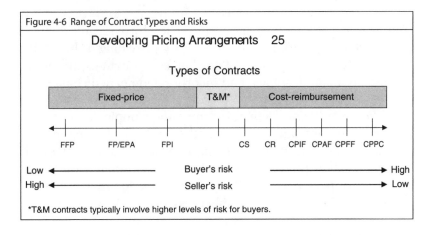

Figure 4-6 Range of Contract Types and Risks

CONTRACT TERMS AND CONDITIONS

Law and custom, company experience and policy, and project-specific analyses will determine the Ts and Cs a buyer will prefer. Governments and large companies usually have regulations or manuals that prescribe boilerplate terms and conditions clauses for the most common types of contracts.   All of the aforementioned contract types are discussed in the Federal Acquisition Regulation (FAR) Part 16, with respective contract clauses contained within FAR Par 52.

■ *Standard forms.* These forms may included standardized versions of contracts, standardized descriptions of procurement items, or standardized versions of all or part of the needed bid documents. Organizations doing substantial amounts of procurement should standardize and automate many of these documents.

■ *Request for Information.* Often buying organizations realize they need more input from prospective sellers before they can effectively state their performance-based requirements. As a result, many buying organizations submit a RFI to gather information before they prepare an RFP.

■ *Draft Request for Proposal.* On many important outsourcing requirements, buyers will use a draft request for proposal as a means to gather information from sellers, provide information to sellers, and improve their RFP by providing a draft RFP for review and comment. They key is to provide appropriate time to obtain feedback and incorporated needed changes.

■ *Solicitation Review.* Depending upon the complexity, urgency, dollar amount, and numerous other factors, a buying organization will typically conduct an informal or formal review of a solicitation prior to its actual submission or release to the public or to respective sellers. The solicitation review process will vary in range from simple to complex. A simple process may require just one or two people mere minutes or hours to review and approve the solicitation for submission. A highly complex, multiple review process usually involves potentially numerous internal functional experts and/or consultants and may require weeks or months to conduct a comprehensive solicitation review.

- *Understanding the Seller's Perspective.* An informed and professional buying organization will seek to understand the procurement opportunity and risk from not only its own perspective but also from the seller's perspective. The seller's perspective involves identifying potentially successful contract opportunities and capturing and performing such contracts. A potentially successful contract is one that can be performed at a price that will enable the seller to meet the needs of the buyer and earn a reasonable profit or gain another benefit, such as future business. In this case, the seller must:
    - Identify contract opportunities, such as revenue, basic gross profit, measured operating income, and future business;
    - Determine the potential profit or other business potential of the contract, the cost to pursue and win it, the chances of winning the contract, and the likelihood of successful contract performance; and
    - Define and assess the consequences of failure.

DESIRED OUTPUTS

The desired output of Phase 2: Procurement Planning and Solicitation Preparation is to develop an acquisition or procurement plan that describes how the remaining procurement processes–from solicitation planning through contract closeout–will be managed. The following are examples of questions to ask in developing a procurement management plan:

- What types of contracts will be used?
- If independent estimates will be needed as evaluation criteria, who will prepare them and when?
- What actions can the project management team take on its own?
- If standardized procurement documents are needed, where can they be found?
- How will multiple providers/suppliers be managed?
- How will procurement be coordinated with other business aspects such as scheduling and performance reporting?

A procurement plan may be formal or informal and highly detailed or broadly framed, based on business needs. Industry participation in the plan may include solicitation documents, such as a request for quotation (RFQ), a request for proposal, or an invitation to bid.

Tools Techniques and Best Practices

SUMMARY

In both the public and private business sectors, buyers are usually in a rush to get something they need, and they often want it badly. As a result, buyers often get what they want and they get it bad (services delivered late and/or over budget, services that fail to meet customer/user expectations, services that require more additional service than expected and/or more upgrades than planned, and services with a higher life cycle cost than expected).

Consequently, buyers must properly staff the first three steps discussed in this chapter in both quality and quantity of resources with realistic schedules that should be mutually developed. Buyers also should conduct market research; seek and obtain seller feedback via seller focus groups, meetings, conferences, or Web-based surveys; and use requests for information, draft solicitations, and the appropriate communications information technology, including Webinars, teleconferences, videoconferences, etc. Further, buyers must stop vendor-bashing suppliers and create real partnerships in order to maximize the opportunities for everyone involved in U.S. government services contracting buying and selling life cycle.

In this chapter, a process-oriented approach to the art and science of procurement planning is presented, which, in turn, drives the solicitation preparation and the entire services contracting life cycle.

Chapter 5 examines the opportunities and risk involved with U.S. government services contracting and offers numerous tools and techniques to mitigate risk and maximize business opportunities and successful delivery of needed services.

QUESTIONS TO CONSIDER

1. Does your organization spend sufficient time and resources conducting acquisition/ procurement planning for services contracts?

2. How well- educated and trained are your organization's contract management personal in planning and soliciting services contracts?

3. Does your organization have efficient and cost-effective policies, processes, methods, tools, and techniques to buy and/ or sell professional services?

CHAPTER 5

PHASE 3: OPPORTUNITY AND RISK ASSESSMENT

By Gregory A. Garrett

INTRODUCTION

This chapter explores how government contractors can identify and analyze opportunities and the risk involved with potential U.S. federal government services contracts. The key objectives of this Opportunity and Risk Assessment Phase of the U.S. Government Services Contracting Buying and Selling Life Cycle, introduced in Chapter 2, are (1) to understand opportunity and risk factors of services contracts, (2) to qualify the opportunities and risks of services contracts, (3) to gather competitive intelligence, (4) to develop a successful business strategy, and (5) to outline services contracting opportunities.

SERVICES CONTRACTING OPPORTUNITY AND RISK FACTORS

Most government contractors providing professional services quickly learn the numerous obstacles, challenges, and risk factors associated with U.S. federal government services contracting. However, the advantage is to learn these risk factors prior to their having a negative impact on the contracting company. The potential opportunity to win millions of dollars of business with one or more U.S. federal government agencies often clouds the business judgment of many company executives.

There are 12 proven best practices to reduce the wide range of business risk factors, which companies both small and large encounter as they become a U.S. federal government services prime contractor and/or subcontractor. Table 5-1 contains actions that have consistently proven to be effective in helping companies maximize their business opportunities while reducing the risk factors of doing business with U.S. federal government agencies.

FIVE

Table 5-1 Best Practices to Reduce Services Contracting Risk Factors	
Small Business	**Large Business**
1. Become a certified small business concern (in an appropriate small business category) pursuant to the Small Business Administration (SBA).	1. Create a separate business unit or business entity to segregate commercial business from business with the U.S. government.
2. Establish partnership agreements or contractor teaming agreements with two or more highly qualified government prime contractors.	2. Establish partnership agreements or contractor teaming agreements with two or more highly qualified government prime contractors.
3. Obtain two or more U.S. government contracting vehicles (GSA federal supply schedules, blanket purchase agreements, indefinite delivery contracts, etc.).	3. Obtain two or more U.S. government contracting vehicles (GSA federal supply schedules, blanket purchase agreements, indefinite delivery contracts, etc.).
4. Serve as a subcontractor to a proven successful large business.	4. Serve as a subcontractor to a proven successful small business.
5. Sell commercial items, products, and services only pursuant to FAR Part 12.	5. Sell commercial items, products, and services only pursuant to FAR Part 12.
6. Accept only fixed-price (FP) contract types, either firm-fixed-price (FFP) or fixed-price with an economic price adjustment (FP/EPA) from the government.	6. Accept only fixed-price (FP) contract types, either firm-fixed-price (FFP) or fixed-price with an economic price adjustment (FP/EPA) from the government.
7. Do not accept time-and-materials (T&M), cost reimbursement (CR), or labor/hour (L/H) contracts from the government.	7. Do not accept time-and-materials (T&M), cost reimbursement (CR), or labor/hour (L/H) contracts from the government.
8. Pursue small business set-aside opportunities.	8. Build close relationships with the a government agency's key program decision-makers related to your products and services.
9. Protect your intellectual property rights (patents, copyrights, trademarks, proprietary software, source codes, etc.).	9. Protect your intellectual property rights.
10. Read, understand, comply, and enforce contract terms and conditions.	10. Manage your supply chain effectively while ensuring full compliance.
11. Obtain and provide quality government contract training for your employees.	11. Obtain and provide quality government contract training for your employees.
12. Hire ethical, experienced, and successful advisors, consultants, and lawyers to assist your company.	12. Hire ethical, experienced, and successful advisors, consultants, and lawyers to assist your company.

The aforementioned best practices, if properly implemented, will help a company maximize business opportunities while reducing its risk factors. As a company's level of risk increases, so does the U.S. federal government's concern about its ability to successfully perform the contracted services. Consequently, as business organizational risk factors increase in quantity and severity , the more likely U.S. government agencies will increase their level of oversight, surveillance, audits, and investigations on government services contracts and subcontracts.

If a company fails to comply with critical U.S. federal government requirements, many mandated by public laws, significant civil and criminal penalties may apply to either individual(s) and/or the company. To paraphrase a well-known maxim, "Ignorance is *not* bliss in U.S. federal government services contracting." A company must quickly learn the rules of the game. And U.S. federal government services contracting is a complex game with hundreds of laws, thousands of pages of regulations, and continually changing requirements. Only the smart and strong survive and thrive in the U.S. federal services contracting marketplace.

The following graphic (Figure 5-1) summarizes the inputs, tools and techniques, and outputs covered in this chapter.

Figure 5-1 Opportunity and Risk Analysis Process

Input	Tools & Techniques	Output
Knowledge of your customer	**Qualify Opportunity & Risk**	Qualified Opportunity
Knowledge of your company	Opportunity-Risk Assessment Grid	Competitor Profile
Knowledge of your competitors	ORA Grid with Bid-No Bid Line	Win Strategy
	Elements of Opportunity	Offer Stakeholder Review Presentation Outline
	Elements of Risk	
	Opportunity Quantification Tool	
	Risk Quantification Tool	
	Gather Competitive Intelligence	
	Competitor Profile	
	Sources of Competitive intelligence	
	Develop Win Strategy	
	Sweet Spot-Sour Spot Analysis	
	Win Theme & Strategy Form	
	Customer Positioning Plan	
	Customer Contact Plan	
	Outline the Opportunity	
	Stakeholder Presentation Outline	

*This section is adapted from: *The Capture Management Life-Cycle: Winning More Business*, by Gregory A. Garrett and Reginald J. Kipke, CCH Inc., 2003.

INPUTS

As with all processes and approaches, the value of a great beginning cannot be understated. The three foundations or inputs of knowledge (see Figure 5-2) for success in the Opportunity and Risk Analysis step are

1. Knowledge of the customer.
2. Knowledge of competitors.
3. Knowledge of the potential contracting company.

The degree to which each of these inputs is mastered will greatly impact a company's ability to spot potential opportunities and get a jump on its competitors.

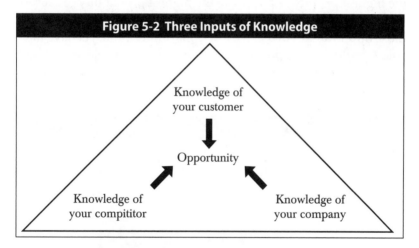

Figure 5-2 Three Inputs of Knowledge

TOOLS AND TECHNIQUES

Qualifying the Opportunity and Risks

The first action of this phase in the U.S. Government Services Contracting Buying and Selling Life Cycle is to qualify the opportunity and risks. *Webster's Dictionary* defines opportunity as "a set of circumstances providing a chance or possibility." *Webster's* defines risk as "the possibility of danger, injury or loss." In other words, elements of opportunity are those characteristics that increase the probability of success, and elements of risk are those characteristics that have the potential to negatively impact success.

Opportunity-Risk Assessment (ORA) Grid

There will often be more opportunities than a company has resources to pursue, so a company must prioritize and direct resources to those opportunities that have the highest probability of success and payback versus those that do not. Because comparing opportunities is essential for making choices, a methodology to assess and compare specific opportunities must be developed. An X-Y coordinate grid (see Figure 5-3), which plots opportunity on the Y-axis and risk on the X-axis can help. The grid is subdivided into quadrants in order to characterize different types of opportunity.

Quadrant A contains opportunities that have a high opportunity value and are also low risk. Quadrant A opportunities should be the highest priority as they have the highest probability of success with the best potential payback. In contrast, quadrant D contains those opportunities that have low opportunity value yet have high risk. Quadrant D opportunities are likely to be projects to avoid and not waste resources on by pursuing as they have a low probability of success and a low potential payback.

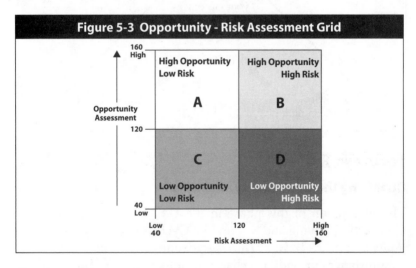

Figure 5-3 Opportunity - Risk Assessment Grid

Quadrant C opportunities have a low opportunity value but are also low risk while quadrant B opportunities are high opportunity value but also high risk. Opportunities in quadrants C and D should be considered marginal, and a company will want to focus on pursing those opportunities that fall into the upper left-hand corner of each of quadrant, while avoiding those that fall into the lower right- hand corner.

ORA Grid with Bid/No Bid Line

Placing a bid line on the grid (see Figure 5-4) illustrates this concept. Exactly where this line is placed on the grid will be based chiefly upon a company's resources and willingness to accept risk.

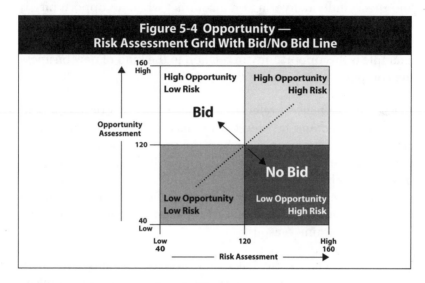

Elements of Opportunity and Risk

In order to plot specific opportunities, it is necessary to examine specific elements or characteristics that are typically used to assess opportunity and risk. While the specifics might vary from company to company, the elements of opportunity and risk, which are shown at Table 5-2, are common.

Table 5-2	
Elements of Opportunity	**Elements of Risk**
Corporate Direction Match	Customer Commitment
Competitive Environment	Corporate Competence
Revenue Value	External Obstacles
Potential Profitability	Opportunity Engagement
In-House Content	Solution Life Cycle Match
Future Business Potential	Period of Performance
Bid Resources	Delivery Schedule
Probability of Success	Resource Coordination
Collateral Benefit	Non-performance Penalties
Overall Strategic Value	Overall Feasibility

Elements of Opportunity

Corporate direction match refers to how consistent an opportunity is with a company's core business or corporate direction for new business. Companies have a much higher probability of winning and successfully delivering on a contract when an opportunity is consistent with their core business and strategic direction. One way to make this assessment is to honestly ask: "How perfect an example is this opportunity in relation to the kind of new business the company is seeking?"

Competitive environment refers to whether a company or its competitor is perceived and favored by the customer as a solution leader and supplier. Opportunities where the customer perceives a company as the leader and a favored supplier (for reasons other than price) are highly desirable. Customers hold this perception due to technology, reputation, past experience, industry commitment, and so on. Of course, the customer may perceive a competitor as the leader for the same reasons.

Revenue value refers to the dollar value of an opportunity. The intent is to distinguish small from large revenue opportunities. Obviously, this needs to be assessed in the context of the size of a company and the typical size and currency of new opportunities. Since exact pricing has yet to be developed, a company must develop a best estimate and focus only on near-term revenues, such as those likely to be generated in the first year of contract delivery.

Potential profitability refers to the likely margins on the business given the competitive environment and what it will take to obtain a services contract. Most companies have guidelines on profitability of new opportunities, which should serve as the basis to assess how rich or poor the margins are likely to be. Potential profitability should be estimated on the basis of near-term margins and not on margins on future business.

In-house content is the percentage of the products or services that will be provided by the company obtaining a contract. Frequently, opportunities require outside supplier products or services; however, ideally all or the vast majority of the products and services should come from within a company. A higher probability of success is attained from what a company knows best, which are its own products and services.

Future business potential refers to the degree to which an opportunity will impact additional business beyond the scope of a specific opportunity. For example, an opportunity may provide the means to gain a new account or to protect an existing one. A company should consider the degree to which specific identifiable future business is dependent upon winning and successfully delivering this sought-after business.

Bid resources refers to the resources required to bid and the impact that the pursuit of this opportunity will have on other opportunities being pursued. Opportunities do not exist in a vacuum, and all companies have resource constraints, so the opportunity cost of not pursuing or jeopardizing other opportunities must be assessed. Conversely, a company may have resources or assets that are idle that it wants to keep engaged and active to positively impact resource or asset utilization.

The *probability of success* refers to the likelihood that a company will obtain the business versus one of its competitors.

A *collateral benefit* is the degree to which pursuit of an opportunity will improve the existing skill level or develop new skills that will benefit other opportunities or future business. Since additional work typically improves existing skill levels, a company must consider the degree to which an opportunity will exceed the norm or have a wide-scale impact on a large population.

Overall strategic value refers to the overall need to win the opportunity, as assessed by the sales or key account manager. This takes into consideration all the opportunity elements, along with any other tangible or intangible aspects of the opportunity, that are relevant.

Elements of Risk

Customer commitment refers to the degree to which a customer has demonstrated a solid commitment to implement a solution offered in an opportunity. Typically this commitment is demonstrated either by a customer's budgeting for the implementation in a current or future business plan or identifying and assigning resources to support the implementation.

Corporate competence refers to a company's past experience or core competencies to deliver the solution required by an opportunity.

The more experience a company has in projects similar to the opportunity, the lower the risk. Conversely, if a similar project has never been successfully completed by any company in the past, then there is a tremendous risk with this opportunity.

External obstacls are the existing roadblocks that are beyond the control of either a customer or a company seeking to provide services. A good example would be a customer that is a regulated utility required to obtain approval from a state or federal authority before it can implement the opportunity. Another example might be a customer that has yet to secure the capital needed to fund the implementation during a period when capital is tightly constrained.

Opportunity engagement refers to the degree to which a company or its competitors are involved in establishing a customer's requirements. If a company does not help the customer develop its requirements, chances are one of its competitors did. The more involved a company is in establishing the requirements the more strength its products and services will have and the more weaknesses its competitors' products and services will have.

Solution life cycle match is the degree to which a company's solution involves the use of existing mature products versus new products or leading-edge technology. If a solution involves mature products available today, the risk associated with the solution is very low. On the other hand, if a solution involves many new products that have yet to be released or are based on leading-edge technology, the risk of encountering development delays and/or the products not functioning as planned increases.

Period of performance refers to the length of a contract. The longer the contract the greater the chance of significant changes. Personnel, customer environment, and business climate are a few examples of changes that can introduce risk impacting a project.

Delivery schedule refers to when delivery is required and who controls the schedule. The ideal situation is a flexible schedule that can be set by the selling company, which ensures the project will have adequate time to be successful. Conversely, if a customer has already fixed the delivery schedule and has also identified penalties for missing schedules, the selling company will assume a risk associated with missing deliveries. While delivery schedules are typically an issue when they are too short, in some situations a delivery schedule may be so far in the future that risks arise regarding whether the products to be delivered will still be manufactured.

Resource coordination refers to synchronizing the internal groups in a selling company or the external suppliers that must be engaged to deliver a solution. The larger the number of internal groups required, the more coordination required to ensure successful delivery and the higher the risk of a disconnect and delivery problem. Coordination of outside suppliers introduces even more risk as a selling company typically has more control over internal groups than external suppliers to resolve problems.

Non-performance penalties refer to customer-specified penalties for failure to deliver as promised. If a customer has not specified penalties or they can be negotiated, a company can minimize the risks. If a customer has specified monetary or other penalties that are non-negotiable, then the risk increases.

Overall feasibility is the assessment by a knowledgeable representative of the group in a company accountable to deliver the solution. A major factor to consider in assessing feasibility is past experience with a customer regarding its fulfilling obligations or addressing unforeseen problems equitably. If the project is extremely complex and a customer has a poor track record of supporting complex projects, the risk of the project's not being successfully implemented is high.

Opportunity – Risk Assessment Tool

Using the elements of opportunity noted above, a four -point scale can be used to assess each element(see Form 5-1). Since all elements do not have equal importance, this raw 1-to-4 score is multiplied by a weight to develop a weighted score. The weighted scores can then be totaled to derive a total weighted opportunity score that can then be plotted on the opportunity axis of the Opportunity-Risk Assessment Grid.

Form 5-1 Opportunity Quantification Tool						
Opportunity Element	**Score**				**Weight**	**Weighted Score**
	1	**2**	**3**	**4**		
Core Business / Corporate Direction	Counter to core business and corporate direction	Neutral to core business and corporate direction	Partially aligned to core business and corporate direction	Fully aligned to core business and corporate direction	6	
Competitive Environment	Competitor is clear leader and is favored by customer	Customer favors the competitor and is neutral to your company	No clear leader and customer has no supplier preference	Your company is clear leader and is favored by customer	5	
Revenue Value	Geater than $500K	Between $500K and $2.5M	Between $2.5M and $5M	Over $5M	4	
Potential Profitability	Profitabilty is Negative or Break Even	Profitability is between 0-50% of corporate requirements	Profitability is between 50-100% of corporate requirements	Profitability is over 100% of corporate requirements	4	
In-House Content	Less than 50% of content is from your company	Between 50-75% of content is from your company	Between 75-90% of content is from your company	Over 90% of content is from your company	4	
Future Business Potential	Little or no connection to future business	Possible link to future business	Likely link to future business	Assured or mandatory link to future business	3	
Resources to Bid	Will significantly drain resources working on other opportunities	Will drain some resources working on other opportunities	Will have little or no impact on resources working on other opportunities	Will use resources currently underutilized	3	
Probability of Success	Probability of success is near zero	Probability of success is less than 50%	Probabilty of success is over 50%	Success is almost certain	3	
Collateral Benefit	Little or no benefit to other projects or new company skills	Some benefit to either other projects or new company skills	Some benefit to both other projects and new company skills	Significant benefit to other projects or new company skills	3	
Overall Strategic Value	It is of low importance that your company win this business	It is somewhat important that your company win this business	It is of high importance that your company win this business	It is critical that your company win this business	5	
Total Weighted Opportunity Score						

Case Study: *IBM (Global Services)*

IBM has a long and well-deserved reputation for being proactive with its customers. The company has for many years taken great pride in its ability to understand its customers' challenges and business needs, thereby developing products, services, and/or solutions to satisfy its customers' needs. IBM also has a well-established business practice of evaluating both business opportunities and risks. Account executives and project managers always conduct a thorough opportunity and risk assessment for each project.

To help mitigate business risks IBM seeks not only to understand a customer's business situation, but to influence the customer's selection process for purchasing products and/or services. IBM Global Services, uses as its maxim "no blind-bids," which means IBM wants always to know the customer's needs, the risks, and the opportunities before a solicitation document (e.g., Invitation to Bid, Request for Proposal, etc.) is ever issued by a customer. At IBM opportunity and risk assessment is a proven best practice and an essential part of the company's business processes.

Case Study: *Boeing (Integrated Defense Systems)*

As companies become more successful in dealing with challenges, risk management becomes a structured process that is performed continuously throughout the business life cycle. Such is the case at Boeing Integrated Defense Systems, where designing, manufacturing, and delivering aircraft can take years and is a multi-billion dollar investment. Typically, Boeing evaluates risk categories and develops detailed risk mitigation strategies and actions to improve its business case by reducing or eliminating potential negative aspects.

Risk categories at Boeing include:

Financial Up-front funding and payback period based upon the number of planes sold;

Market Forecasting customers expectations on cost, configuration, and amenities based on a 30- to 40-year life of a plane;

Technical Required forecast of technology and its impact on cost, safety, reliability, and maintainability; and

Production Supply-chain management of a large number of sub-contractors without impacting cost, schedule, quality, or safety.

Using the same methodology for risk, as is shown below on Form 5-2, a Total Weighted Risk Score can be developed and then plotted on the risk axis of the Opportunity-Risk Assessment Grid.

Form 5-2 Risk Quantification Tool

Risk Element	Score				Weight	Weighted Score
	1	2	3	4		
Customer Commitment	Customer has assigned budget and personnel	Customer has assigned budget but not personnel	Customer has assigned personnel but not budget	Customer has not assigned personnel or budget	6	
Corporate Competence	Complete replication of past projects done by your company	More than 50% replication of past projects done by your company	Less than 50% replication of past projects done by your company	No replication of past projects done by your company	5	
External Obstacles	No obstacles exist which are outside control of customer	Some obstacles - customer is actively working to address each	Some obstacles - customer has plan to address each	Significant obstacles, customer has no plan developed to address each	4	
Opportunity Engagement	Your company developed requirements for the customer	Your company guided customer in devleopment of requirements	Your company provided comments after requirements were developed	Your company had no involvement in developing requirements	4	
Solution Life Cycle / Match	All requirements can be met by mature, released products	Less than 30% of products will be pre-released or new products	Between 30-70% of products will be pre-released or new products	70% of products will be pre-released or new products	4	
Period of Performance	Contract is for less than 6 months	Contract is between 6 months and 1 year	Contract is between 1 year and 3 years	Contract is over 3 years	3	
Delivery Schedule	Delivery schedule is flexible and will be set by your company	Delivery schedule to be negotiated by customer and your company	Delivery schedule is fixed, but no penalties for missed dates	Delivery schedule is fixed and penalties exist for missed dates	3	

Form 5-2 Risk Quantification Tool						
Risk Element	Score				Weight	Weighted Score
	1	2	3	4		
Resource Coordination	Need to coordinate less than 5 groups in your company	Need to co-ordinate 5 or more groups in your com-pany	Need to coordinate company groups and up to 2 outside sup-pliers	Need to coordinate company groups and 3 or more outside sup-pliers	3	
Non-Performance Penalties	No penalties for non-performance	Penalties to be negoti-ated between customer and your company	Fixed monetary penalties for non-perfor-mance with a limit	Fixed monetary penalties for non-perfor-mance with no limit	3	
Overall Feasi-bility / Risk	Project is feasible and risks are manageable	Project is feasible but risks require mitigation	Project has some ele-ments which are question-able but risks can be mitigated	Project has questionable feasibility and very high risks	5	
				Total Weighted Risk Score		

The Opportunity and Risk Quantification Tools, Forms 5-1 and 5-2, can be adapted and modified based on the particulars of a business and its past experience. The key to effective opportunity and risk qualification is to ensure the use of a consistent assessment methodology so opportunities can be compared and prioritized. Use of such a tool will prove invaluable towards improving sales representatives' productivity by directing them away from quadrant D opportunities (i.e., low opportunity with high risk) and focusing their energies on quadrant A opportunities (i.e., high opportunity, low risk) and the high-end quadrant B and C opportunities (i.e., low opportunity, low risk and high opportunity, high risk above the bid line).

COMPETITIVE INTELLIGENCE

The next step after an initial qualification of the opportunity and risks is to gather competitive intelligence. Basic information to be collected includes (1) competitors or competitive teams, (2) solutions the competitors may bid, (3) the strengths of competitor(s) or of its solution, and (4) the weaknesses of the competitor(s) or its solution.

Competitor Profile

Competitive intelligence information should be documented for future use and reviewed using a competitor profile template (see, Form 5-3).

	Form 5-3 Competitor Profile			
Rank	Competitor or Competing Team	Solution Being Bid	Strengths of Competitor and Solution	Weaknesses of Competitor and Strengths
1				
2				
3				
4				
5				

Sources of Competitive Intelligence

The term competitive intelligence is used to refer to information on competitors or competitive teams that is specific to an opportunity. This is in contrast to market intelligence, which is general information on competitors or competitive teams operating in the marketplace or industry. While, market intelligence should not be t discarded as an input, greater value comes from understanding competitors. Competitor information can and should be collected from a variety of sources, which not only increases the amount of intelligence gathered, but serves to validate information by confirming it from multiple sources. Care should be taken, however, to ensure that any and all competitive intelligence is gathered legally and ethically. For example, in addition to understanding a company's rules on soliciting information, it is equally important to understand a customer's rules regarding discussions with customer personnel and access to customer information that is part of the source selection process.

Some typical sources of competitive intelligence include:

Table 5-3 Sources of Competitive Intelligence
• Public press releases
• Public websites
• Public brochures
• Public advertisements
• Articles in trade publications
• Past bids to this customer
• Past bids to similar customers
• Customer list of companies requesting solicitation*
• Customer conversations*
• Customer events and meetings*
• Trade or Industry associations, and
• Competitive research or analysis

*Do not violate your disclosure rules.

DEVELOP A WIN STRATEGY

Having gathered competitive intelligence, the next step is to develop a Win Strategy. A Win Strategy is a collection of messages or points designed to guide a customer's perception of a company, its solution, and its competitors.

Sweet Spot and Sour Spot Analysis

Perhaps one of the best ways to graphically depict the elements of a Win Strategy is to use the concept of Sweet Spot and Sour Spot presented by Dr. David G. Pugh of the Lore International Institute in his article "A Bidder's Dozen: Golden Rules For Winning Work.. In Figure 5-5 the Sweet Spot and Sour Spot model depicts the relationship of a company's strengths and weaknesses to a customer's needs and the strengths and weaknesses of competitors. The Sweet Spot is where a company's strengths meet a customer's needs and coincide with a competitor's weaknesses. Conversely, the Sour Spot is where a competitor's strengths meet a customer's needs and coincide with a competing company's weaknesses.

The objective of a Win Strategy is to maximize the importance of a company's Sweet Spot to the customer and simultaneously minimize the importance of its Sour Spot. This will require considerable time and effort as competitors will obviously be trying to do the exact opposite. Win strategies that maximize the Sweet Spot are messages or points highlighting a company's strengths and amplifying or ghosting a competitor's weaknesses. Win strategies that minimize a company's Sour Spot are messages or points mitigating its weaknesses and neutralizing a competitor's strengths.

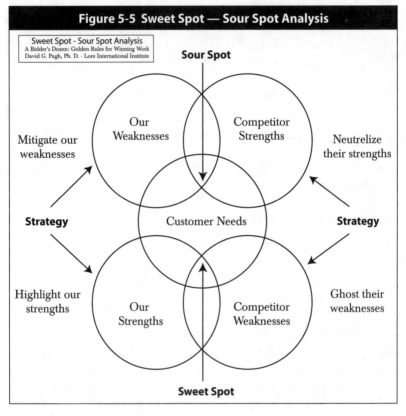

Figure 5-5 Sweet Spot — Sour Spot Analysis

Sweet Spot - Sour Spot Analysis
A Bidder's Dozen: Golden Rules for Winning Work
David G. Pugh, Ph. D. - Lore International Institute

Sour Spot

Our Weaknesses   Competitor Strengths

Mitigate our weaknesses   Neutrelize their strengths

Strategy   Customer Needs   **Strategy**

Highlight our strengths   Our Strengths   Competitor Weaknesses   Ghost their weaknesses

Sweet Spot

Changing customer perceptions requires repeating communication of a consistent message to numerous individuals in the customer organization. The most effective strategies are those that can be translated into straightforward themes or phrases that differentiate a company from its competitors. These themes or phrases can then be delivered to the customer in sales calls, executive contacts, proposals, presentations, advertisements, and all forms of communication over a period of time, thus changing perceptions.

Strategies should also focus on the points that are the most significant to a customer in terms of impact on its business problem or objective. The proverbial 80-20 Rule is a good guide to use in determining significance of requirements. Typically 20% of the requirements account for 80% of the value, and conversely, the remaining 80% account for only 20% of the value. Ideally, a company will want to position its Sweet Spot as part of the 20% that creates 80% of the value, and its Sour Spot as part of the other 80%, which has only minimal impact (i.e., 20%).

One successful technique to develop winning strategies is to gather a core team of individuals and hold a strategy session. During this session board and map the Sweet Spot and Sour Spot and develop strategies to address each. While this should be a small group, it is important to include a knowledgeable individual from each of the following areas:

- Sales or marketing,
- Manufacturing or supply chain,
- Engineering or technical support,
- Program management or product/service delivery,
- Contracting or legal, and
- Finance or business management

Win Theme and Strategy Form

A company must succinctly capture a Win Theme and a Win Strategy for review with stakeholders and later as a guide for the Capture Team. Form 5-4 is an example of a Win theme and strategy form that can be used for this purpose.

Form 5-4 Win Themes and Strategies
• Win Themes:
• Strategies to maximize our strengths:
• Strategies to minimize our weaknesses:
• Strategies to neutralize competitor's strengths:
• Strategies to ghost competitor's weaknesses:

Customer Positioning Plan

As part of executing a win strategy a company must proactively communicate its messages to the customer through various channels in addition to its response or proposal. A key channel for communication is the relationship and regular contact between key customers and individuals in the company, which can be referred to as customer positioning. As part of enhancing the impact of customer positioning, a company can seize opportunities for potential customer contact by identifying major events or planned meetings and orchestrating the participation and messages to be communicated by key individuals. It is vital to develop documented plans to address each of these.

Form 5-5, Customer Positioning Planner, can be used to match key customers with the appropriate contact in a contracting company to develop relationships. The planner shows the name, title, and role of each key customer along with a primary and secondary contact from the company pursuing a contract and the type and frequency of contact. Types of contact include phone calls, personal meetings, dinner, or entertainment. Frequency of contact includes weekly, bi-weekly, monthly, and as-needed. A company should match "like-for-like." For example, match the CEO of the company as the primary contact with the CEO of the customer's company, with the president of the company pursuing a contract as the secondary contact. This will allow executives in the contracting company to establish a regular schedule of contact with its key customers.

Form 5-5 Customer Positioning Planner									
		Role				Frequency of Contact *			
Customer Position	Customer Name	Decision Maker	Influencer	Primary Contact	Secondary Contact	Phone Call	Personal Meeting	Dinner	Entertainment

* Weekly, Bi-Weekly, Monthly, As-Needed

Customer Contact Plan

In addition, a Customer Contact Planner, Form 5-6, can be used to manage contacts between key customers and individuals in the company pursuing a contract at major events or planned meetings. This planner provides space to identify each event, the date, purpose of the event, specific objective(s) to achieve at the event, customer participants, and participants from the selling company. Examples of events to be managed include trade shows, sporting events, briefings, seminars, etc. Using this planner helps keep track of the major events requiring participation in order to effectively establish and build relationships with r key customers.

Form 5-6 Customer Contact Planner					
Customer:			**Prepared by:**		**Date:**
Date	**Event**	**Purpose**	**Objective(s)**	**Customer Participants**	**Your Company Participants**

PURSUING SERVICES CONTRACT OPPORTUNITIES OUTLINE

Having developed a Win Strategy, the next step is to outline the opportunities and develop material to review with stakeholders to solicit their buy-in to pursue the opportunity. While this should be customized to the selling company and its business, an outline of the basic information to document in some type of presentation for review is important.

Outline of Offer for Stakeholder Opportunity Review

The format and size of a presentation will vary depending upon factors such as the scope of the opportunity, the number and level of the stakeholders, and the resource commitment required. Whether standardized on viewgraphs or written in narrative format, it is important to document the opportunity in a form that can be shared and updated as the opportunity is pursued and more information is obtained. If using viewgraphs, match the size of the presentation to the opportunity. Presentations on smaller opportunities should be kept to one slide per category, while larger ones may require one or more slides per subject to provide an adequate review. Following are the components included in an outline offer for stakeholder review of an opportunity.

Introduction

All Stakeholder opportunity reviews should start with a clear declaration and review of the purpose, agenda, limit, and participants. This will ensure that everyone understands why they are there (i.e., the purpose), the topics that will be covered (i.e., the agenda), how much time is allotted for the meeting (i.e., the limit), and most importantly, the meeting participants and their respective roles (i.e., the participants). An easy way to remember this is to use a mnemonic "be a PAL to participants", where *P* is purpose, *A* is agenda, and *L* is limit.

The purpose of the stakeholder review (see Table 5-3, below) is typically (a) to review the opportunity, (b) to make a bid/no bid decision, (c) to solicit resource commitment, and (4) to establish escalation support. The agenda is typically the topics covered, in sequence, along with the presenters who will cover each topic. The limit is the time allotted to the meeting. The participants are the stakeholders listed with their name, title, and functional responsibility.

Unless all of the stakeholders and everyone who will work on pursuit of the opportunity knows the customer thoroughly, a customer profile should be prepared. While stakeholders may have a general familiarity with the customer, it is important to ensure that all the stakeholders have a common appreciation for the customer's business so they can truly evaluate the opportunity and risks. Additionally, the customer profile will be used as a reference document to introduce others to the opportunity.

Customer Profile

A customer profile should briefly cover three subjects: (1) customer business, (2) the contracting company's presence, and (3) competitor presence. Customer business refers to demographics of the customer's enterprise and includes information such as mission statement, market strategy, target markets, market share, annual revenues, number of employees or locations, and geography. The company presence refers to the pursuing company's existing business with the customer, which is typically expressed in terms of the quantities or values of past products and services purchased and the percentage of the customer's past purchases spent with the company. Competitor presence refers to the existing business the customer has with competitors and is expressed in similar terms.

FIVE

Opportunity Profile

An opportunity profile should briefly cover six subjects: (1) the problem, (2) the solution, (3) the contract, (4) the basic scope, (5) the optional scope, and (6) key dates. The problem refers to the business problem a potential customer is trying to solve or the objective it is trying to achieve, which should be articulated as concisely and directly as possible. The solution refers to how the company pursuing a contract will potentially solve the customer's business problem, including the major products and services to be used and any outside products and services required. The contract refers to the anticipated type and term or length of the contract that is anticipated. Basic scope refers to the minimum or obligated geography or locations to be involved and the estimated value and/or quantities of major products and services. Optional scope refers to geography, locations, and products or services, which the customer may or may not purchase. Key dates are the major milestones, such as bid response date, anticipated contract signing date, first delivery date, and end of contract date.

Competitor Profile

The competitor profile should briefly cover (1) competitors, (2) competitor solutions, (3) competitor strengths, and (4) competitor weaknesses. Competitors are the specific competitors or competitive teams, by name, pursuing a specific opportunity. Solution refers to the solution each competitor or competitive team may offer to solve the customer's business problem. Strengths and weaknesses refer to the specific strengths and weaknesses of the competitors or of their solutions. This information should have been obtained during the Opportunity Profile stage and documented on the Competitor Profile form presented above.

Win Strategy

The Win Strategy should briefly cover (1) theme, (2) Sweet Spot, (3) Sour Spot, and (4) Positioning Plan. The theme is the overarching message(s) to be conveyed to the customer in all communications of "how and why" the company will solve the customer's problem the best. Sweet Spot and Sour Spot refer to the specific messages designed to maximize and minimize, respectively, a company's strengths and weaknesses, which were developed during the Opportunity Profile stage. Positioning Plan refers to the specific plans developed to communicate these messages to the customer, including tactics such as executive visits, briefings, tours, etc.

Issues and/or Concerns

Issues and concerns should briefly cover (1) product/service gaps, (2) availability gaps, (3) resource gaps, and (4) contract issues. Service gaps are any major gaps between a company's services and a customer's requirements. Availability gaps refer to either the need to commit to requirements that have been identified as a future capability but have yet to be funded for development or the need to deliver a product or service prior to the currently planned release schedule. Resource gaps refer to shortages or mismatches in availability, skill set, or funding for required resources for either the response or the delivery. Contract issues are the terms, conditions, or liabilities that are outside the norm for a company seeking an opportunity of this type.

Response Requirements

Response requirements should briefly cover (1) (time line, (2) personnel resources, and (3) other resources. Time line refers to the key milestones and dates required to develop an offer and deliverable document for a customer, whether it be in response to a customer solicitation or is a proactive proposal. Personnel resources are the number and skill sets of individuals required to develop the response. Other resources refer to non-personnel resources required to develop the response and may include items such as lab equipment, travel and living accommodations, proposal production costs, and/or outside consultants. Together the personnel resources and other resources represent the resource commitment the stakeholders must approve to pursue an opportunity.

Bid/No Bid Decision

The bid/no bid decision should briefly cover (1) stakeholder commitment and (2) action items. Stakeholder commitment means obtaining a clear commitment from the stakeholders to (a) fully support development of the response, (b) agree to promptly assign resources, (c) agree to be a point of escalation to help resolve roadblocks, and (d) agree to meet again to review and approve the response prior to submittal to the customer.

Case Study: *NCR (Professional Services)*

More than 10 years ago, NCR Professional Services formalized their Bid/No Bid decision-making process to include a tool that enabled them to assess both the opportunities and risks pertaining to a possible contract in a more objective and quantifiable manner. NCR calls its bid/no bid decision-making support tool Project Opportunity and Risk Assessment (PORA). PORA allows NCR to identify opportunities and risks, assess probability, assess monetary impact, and determine the expected monetary value associated with the overall business scenario in a timely, cost-effective, and automated manner.

OUTPUTS

At the completion of the identify and analyze opportunities and risk step of the winning government contracts process a company should have:

- Qualified Opportunity,
- A Competitor Profile,
- A Win Strategy, and
- An Offer for Stakeholder Opportunity Review
- Outline.

After completing an analysis of the potential opportunities and risk associated with a U.S. government services contract, the next action of the contractor is to make an intelligent bid/no bid decision.

The primary objective of the bid/no bid decision-making process is to present the facts to company stakeholders in as unbiased and objective a manner as possible so they understand the opportunity and the risks. The future of a company depends upon consistently making the best decisions on how to prioritize opportunities and commit scarce resources. A secondary objective of this phase of the U.S. Government Services Contracting Buying and Selling LifeCycle is to ensure all company stakeholders not only understand and agree to pursue the opportunity, but more importantly are in alignment with the solution proposed and the Win Strategy. Alignment is defined by *Webster's* as "being in correct relative position to something else." This alignment is critical to ensuring that everyone on the team is heading in the right direction, conveying the correct message (internally and to customers), and is not unintentionally creating problems or wasting resources on activities that are inconsistent with the Win Strategy.

SUMMARY

In the public business sector, many government contractors are often zealous in bidding and winning a contract. As a result, many government contractors and subcontractors do not take the time to properly conduct pre-contract award phase activities, especially identifying and analyzing risk. Thus, many government contractors are too quick to develop a bid or proposal for an opportunity. Surprisingly, many companies win only 15% to 20% of the contracts they bid and/or propose, thus losing a significant amount of money on bids and/or proposals that they often had little real chance of winning. Furthermore, many companies pursue the wrong contracts, just because they believe they can win them. A company must realize that because it can win a contract does not mean it should even bid the contract. Some deals are truly too high risk, and there is little or no way to achieve excellence and profitability with integrity. For sellers a tough lesson to learn is that sometimes no business is better than bad business. No company should adopt a strategy of "we bid everything" unless it is trying to go out of business as quickly as possible.

QUESTIONS TO CONSIDER

1. How well does your organization qualify opportunities, gather competitive intelligence, develop win strategies, develop customer positioning plans, and obtain stakeholder buy-in to pursue opportunities?

2. How effectively does your organization walk away from poor opportunities?

3. Does your organization have documented processes or tools and techniques to qualify opportunities, gather competitive intelligence, develop win strategies, develop customer positioning plans, and obtain stakeholder buy-in to pursue opportunities?

CHAPTER

6

PHASE 4: PROPOSAL DEVELOPMENT AND EVALUATION

By Gregory A. Garrett

INTRODUCTION

This chapter explores the fourth phase of the U.S. Government Services Contracting Buying and Selling Life Cycle introduced in Chapter 2. It focuses on the development of successful proposals and government agencies' evaluation of proposals and selection of the best source/contractor(s). In order to obtain business with the U.S. government it is vital for a company to master the art and science of developing excellent proposals, which are written sales presentations. Most government contractors typically have a bid win rate of 30% (3 out of every 10 proposals submitted). However, best-in-class government contractors are often able to win contracts 50% of the time or more often. This chapter explains the process by which government contractors plan, write, review, edit, and submit winning proposals to U.S. government agencies and how those government agencies conduct their source-selection process.

DEVELOPING WINNING PROPOSALS

To develop winning proposals it is important to perform the following actions:

- Conduct a Capture Team Kickoff Meeting,
- Develop the Customer Solution,
- Develop Risk Mitigation Plans,
- Develop Business Case(s), and
- Develop the Proposal.

Figure 6-1 shows the Key Inputs, Proven Tools and Techniques, and Desired Outputs of the Proposal Development Process.

Figure 6-1 Proposal Development Process

Input	Tools & Techniques	Output
Select a Capture Team	Conduct a Capture Team Kickoff Meeting	Customer Solution
Draft a Preliminary Capture Project Plan	Execute the Capture Project Plan	Design
		Pricing
		Delivery Plan
Draft a Communication Plan	Capture Team Status Meetings	Risk Mitigation Plans
	Action Item Register	Business Cases
Review past lessons learned and best practices	Stakeholder Status Report	Customer Proposal
	Stakeholder Status Review Outline	Executive Summary
		Technical Response
	Develop Solution	Delivery Response
	Solution Architecture	Pricing Response
	Compliance Matrix	Contractual Response
	Solution Linkage Matrix	
	Delivery Plan	
	Develop Risk Mitigation Plans	
	Sources of Risk	
	Ways of Mitigating Risks	
	Risk Mitigation Plan	
	Risk Mitigation Plan Log	
	Develop Business Case	
	Business Case Scenarios	
	Business Case Models	
	Product/Service Profile	
	Customer Business Case	
	Common Business Case Terms	
	Develop Proposal	
	Attributes of Winning Proposals	

*This section is adapted from the book *The Capture Management Life-Cycle: Winning More Business*, by Gregory A. Garrett and Reginald J. Kipke, CCH Inc., 2003.

INPUTS

The inputs for the Proposal Development step are to (1) select a Capture Team, (2) draft a Preliminary Proposal Capture Project Plan, (3) draft a Communication Plan for the team, and (4) review Lessons Learned and Best Practices from past proposals .

TOOLS & TECHNIQUES

Capture Team Kickoff Meeting

Perhaps the single biggest factor in developing a winning bid is having a team of resources aligned and dedicated to the same goal. This alignment and dedication does not occur by itself; it requires planning and cultivation on the part of the Capture Manager and the Core Capture Team.

The first action is to assemble the team and conduct a Capture Team Kickoff. If all team members are in the same location, or if travel is appropriate, this session is best conducted face-to-face. While a face-to-face session is desirable, the kickoff can be conducted equally effectively by conference bridge or an intranet sharing application, such as NetMeeting. It is essential to maximize participation, so even if the session is held face-to-face, a conference bridge or an intranet sharing application can be used for anyone who cannot attend.

The following Capture Team Kickoff Checklist, Form 6-1, presents the recommended topics, sequence, and presenters for the session. For most topics on the agenda a reference document was developed during the Pre-Award Phase, so no special presentation materials are required for the session.

Checklist	Agenda Topics	Reference Documents	Discussion Leader
	Form 6-1 Capture Team Kickoff Checklist		
	Introduction		
☐	Purpose, Agenda, Limit		Capture Manager
☐	Introduce Team Members		
	Review Opportunity		
☐	Customer Profile		
☐	Opportunity Profile	Stakeholder Opportunity Review Package	Sales Leader
☐	Competitor Profile		
☐	Win Theme & Strategies		
☐	Issues/Concerns		
	Validate Capture Plan		
☐	Work Tasks	Work Breakdown Structure (WBS)	
☐	Resources	Organization Breakdown Structure (OBS)	
		Responsibility Assignment Matrix (RAM)	
		Team Leader Roles & Responsibilities	Capture Manager
☐	Timeline	Task List Schedule	
☐	Communication Plans	Customer Positioning & Contact Plans	
		Project Communication Plan	
		Change Request Plan	
		Alert-Jeopardy-Escalation Plan	
	Review Proposal Development Plans		
☐	Development Process		
☐	Production Requirements	Proposal Development Checklist	Proposal Manager
☐	Layout & Assignments	Proposal Production Checklist	
☐	Proposal Reviews	Proposal Layout with Assignments	
		Pink Team & Red Team Checklists	
	Action Items and Next Steps		
☐	Action Items	Action Item Register	Capture Manager
☐	Meeting Schedule		

As with all meetings, reviewing the purpose, agenda, and time limit for the meeting and introducing all participants is a good way to start. The Sales Leader should provide a review of the customer, opportunity, competitor profiles, win themes and strategies, and issues/concerns. The Stakeholder Opportunity Review Package is used as the presentation materials. Not only will this eliminate the need for a separate presentation, it will serve to communicate to the team the stakeholders' support for the opportunity.

The next step is to validate the capture project plan, which will include reviewing the deliverables, work tasks, resources, team structure, time line and communications plans. The objective during this portion of the session is to get feedback on the plans, which may be in the form of criticism; no feedback is personal. It is recommended that the Capture Manager lead this discussion as it will serve to establish his or her role as leader of the Capture Team. It also provides the opportunity for the Sales Leader to endorse this role at the close of the presentation.

The next topic should be a review of the proposal development plans by the Proposal Manager. This review should include the Proposal Development Process, Proposal Production Requirements, and Proposal Layout with Volume and Section Assignments, all of which should have been developed during the Capture Project Plan stage. If not all of the section Assignments have yet been made, they can be completed during the kickoff session or they can be assigned as an action item to the volume owners or this can be completed this at the next team meeting. If there are still open questions concerning either Proposal Development or Proposal Production, assign them as action items with an owner and due date. Reviewing the objective and format for Proposal Reviews can be delayed until a later team meeting to save time.

The last topic on the agenda should be to review any action items developed during the session, as well as to establish a schedule for team meetings.

CAPTURE PROJECT PLAN FINALIZATION AND EXECUTION

Capture Team Status Meetings

While each subteam (i.e., technical, delivery, pricing, contractual) will meet on its own to complete work tasks and resolve open items, a schedule of regular status meetings with the entire team should be established. Regular status meetings ensure the team is aligned and on-track as they show status on work tasks and action items, as well as provide a forum to exchange information with the team.

The frequency of regular status meetings should be gauged to the length of the bid development stage and the nearness to completion. Generally, it is appropriate to meet daily during the last 3-4 weeks, 2 to 3 times per week at 4-10 weeks from completion, and once per week if completion will take 10 weeks or more. In the event of a large team that is not well aligned or when a large, complex opportunity has many open items or changes, meetings may occur more frequently.

The key is to keep regular status meetings focused and brief. Status meetings are not working meetings or forums to resolve open items; they are a forum to share information and collect status on work completed. The more frequently a meeting, the shorter it should be as there is less to report since the last meeting. Daily meetings should be no more than 30 minutes, whereas once per week meetings should be no more than 60 minutes.

Form 6-2 provides a recommended agenda for regular status meetings and shows the recommended topics, sequence, time, reference documents, and discussion leader. The meeting begins with a roll-call of participants, followed by a poll for new agenda items and any team announcements. Each core team member should provide a brief update on work tasks focusing on work started, work completed, problems needing assistance, and issues that should become new action items. This should be followed by a review of the Action Item Register to collect status on open items, after which new agenda items the team has identified are discussed. Finally, the close should include reminders regarding upcoming events and   details of the next status meeting.

Action Items

One of the biggest challenges during bid development is to effectively and efficiently resolve open items. Open items may be the result of new information, a change, an unforeseen event, a work task that is running behind, or an unanswered question identified in the capture project plan. According to an old expression "bad news does not get better with age," and the same is true of open items; the longer they remain unresolved, the bigger the potential negative impact. The key to resolving open items is to identify them early as action items for resolution.

A solid action item requires four components to increase the probability of resolution. The first part is a clear and concise definition of the open item which is the issue or problem. The second part is a clear and concise definition of the expected outcome or result. The third part is an owner, identified by name, who agrees to resolve the action item. The fourth part is a due date by which the action item must be resolved.

Action Item Register

For each action item, the issue, required action, owner and due date must be documented on an Action Item Register (see Form 6-2). An action item has an open status, which will change to closed once resolved. Each action item should be assigned a unique tracking number for easy reference, and its status should be noted as either open or closed. Action items should also be assigned a severity level, such as high, medium, or low impact, so they can be prioritized for resolution and escalation if not resolved.

Form 6-2 Action Item Register							
Status	No.	Issue	Action Required	Owner	Due Date	Severity	Progress

The Action Item Register is reviewed at each status meeting to ascertain progress toward closure of each item. Each owner should report on the actions taken and provide a prognosis on resolution. Owners must understand that if items are not resolved by the due date or there is no prognosis of resolution, an Alert-Jeopardy-Escalation will be issued. This is an incentive for owners to resolve open items and to ensure there are no surprises later if an Alert-Jeopardy-Escalation is used.

Alert-Jeopardy-Escalation

Alert-Jeopardy-Escalation is a means to raise the visibility of an issue and obtain help when an open item has not been resolved. In fact, there will be some open items that can only be closed by an escalation, in which case an escalation must be issued early to provide stakeholders time to take action. By identifying action items and regularly reviewing the Action Item Register, the team can identify the need for an Alert-Jeopardy-Escalation in a timely manner, thus maximizing the time available for and increasing the probability of resolution.

Customer Questions or Missing Information

When the need to ask a customer questions arises or missing information is needed to develop a bid, the questions should be asked as early as possible so as not to delay work tasks or create last minute changes. A work task on the critical path should not be delayed due to a question or missing information. Instead, an assumption based on input from the Sales Leader and appropriate team members can be made and documented in a response. If the solicitation is competitive where all questions are shared with all bidders, questions should be reviewed carefully to ensure they do not telegraph a company's strategy or weaknesses to competitors.

Change Requests

There is a maxim that is true in life and especially true in the pursuit of opportunities: "the only constant is change." While change is inevitable, a team must understand that changes should not be incorporated into work tasks until a change request has been approved. The inclusion of unapproved changes can easily result in mismatches during handoffs, which jeopardize the integrity of a solution and likely will result in the need for re-work. Work tasks on the critical path should not be delayed due to potential or pending change requests; rather core team leaders should be engaged to decide on a course of action.

Stakeholder Status Report

An important aspect of ensuring continued stakeholder support is to keep them informed on progress. Either a broadcast voice mail or a regular email sent to all stakeholders is fine for smaller opportunities of short duration. On large, complex or long duration opportunities, a more formal means of reporting progress, such as a regular status report or a Stakeholder Status Review, is required.

Form 6-3 is an example of a status report that can be used on a regular basis to update stakeholders on progress. It has space to identify the capture manager, due date of response, customer, opportunity tracking number, opportunity name, date of the report, date of last report, and date of next report. It also provides an area to provide an assessment regarding a solution, proposal, and budget using a simple red, yellow, or green indicator. This provides a means to advise stakeholders if things are on-track (i.e., green), somewhat off-track (i.e., yellow), or completely off-track (i.e., red). There are also spaces provided to briefly highlight work tasks completed since the last report, work tasks due before the next report, and any outstanding jeopardies or escalations.

Form 6-3 Stakeholder Status Report											
Capture Manager:								Due Date:			
Customer:								Tracking #:			
Opportunity:											
Report Date:				Last Report:				Next Report:			
Solution Assessment	Red	Yellow	Green	Proposal Assessment	Red	Yellow	Green	Budget Assessment	Red	Yellow	Green
Work tasks completed since last report											
Work tasks due before next report											
Jeopardys or Escalations											

Stakeholder Status Review Outline

If there is a lengthy time between the Stakeholder Opportunity Review and the Stakeholder Approval Review, a Stakeholder Status Review is appropriate. The purpose of this review is to keep stakeholders informed on the status of the work (both completed and remaining), changes (involving customer, opportunity, competitors, or win strategy), and issues (including jeopardies and escalations and potential issues). Form 6-4 provides a recommended outline for a stakeholder status review showing the topics and sequence of material to review.

Form 6-4 Stakeholder Status Review Outline		
Category	**Subject**	**Suggested Topics or Contents**
Introduction	Purpose	Purpose is typically to (1) review status, (2) review changes, (3) review issues.
	Agenda	Agenda is typically the topics covered, in sequence, with presenters
	Limit	Identify time alloted for meeting
	Participants	List of stakeholders with name, title, and functional responsibility
Status	Work Completed	Update on response timeline showing status of work completed
	Work Remaining	Update on response timeline showing status of work remaining
Changes	Customer Profile Update	Update on changes in customer business, your presence, or competitor presence
	Opportunity Update	Update on changes in problem, solution, contract, basic scope, optional scope or key dates
	Competitor Update	Update on changes in competitors, solutions, strengths or weaknesses
	Win Strategy Update	Update on changes in win theme, sweet spot, sour spot or positioning plan
Issues	Jeopardies	Review of jeopardies and escalations
	Potential Issues	Review potential problem areas or areas of concern
Closing	Next Review	Set date for next review or stakeholder meeting
	Action Items	Review of action Items created during review

SOLUTION DEVELOPMENT

As the Capture Team develops a solution, including design, pricing and delivery plan, it is critical that the team remain tightly linked to ensure holistic compliance of the solution. Holistic compliance means that technical, delivery, pricing, and contractual aspects of the solution are consistent and linked with each other (see Figure 6-2) to (1) solve the customer's problem or meet its objective and (2) satisfy company requirements for profitability and risk.

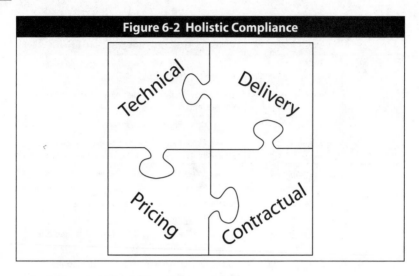

Figure 6-2 Holistic Compliance

Solution Architecture

Typically, a short time frame exists for responding to a customer solicitation; hence it will be necessary for work activities to occur concurrently. A solution must be communicated to the team in a summary form. One technique that is effective at achieving both needs is to create a solution architecture document. A solution architecture document is typically composed of one or more pictures or diagrams that show the solution, usually with a before and after view. This is augmented by a list of the products (e.g., hardware, software, version, release) and services comprising the solution. This document can serve as the basis for the detailed design and pricing to occur concurrently with development of the technical/delivery response. Additionally, this documentation can be used as an introduction for new team members, as well as to review the solution later during the stakeholder approval stage.

Compliance Matrix

When responding to customer solicitations, it is not uncommon to have customer requirements that cannot be fully met, and there is even the potential to have some that cannot be met at all. This is chiefly due to the fact that most customers solicit input from multiple suppliers and create a solicitation document by taking the best input from each supplier. A common technique used to identify gaps in the ability to meet customer requirements is through the use of a compliance matrix (see Form 6-5). A compliance matrix lists all the solicitation reference and functional requirements, along with an indication of whether compliance is full, partial, or none, and provides space for an explanation for partial compliance. Frequently, a customer will ask that a compliance matrix be included within a response. Even if it is not required for submittal to a customer, completing a compliance matrix as part of risk mitigation planning can help to clarify gaps and potential risk areas.

Form 6-5 Compliance Matrix					
Solicitation Reference	Functional Requirement	Compliance			Explanation
		Full	Partial	None	

Solution Linkage Matrix

Another common problem is ensuring linkage of the design, description, and pricing of a solution. This can easily occur when different team members perform separate roles, especially when a lot of changes exist. A solution linkage matrix (see Form 6-6) is a simple tool that can help ensure a solution is compliant and matches the solution described and priced. The solicitation references, functional requirements and the solution product or service that satisfies the requirement are listed. Then the accountable team members for the design, description (i.e., response), pricing, and overall linkage are identified. Typically, the overall linkage will be provided by either the Technical or Delivery Team leader.

Form 6-6 Solution Linkage Matrix						
Solicitation Reference	Functional Requirement	Solution Product/Service	Individual Accountable for Solution			
			Design	Description	Pricing	Overall Linkage

Delivery Plan

As part of developing a solution, a delivery plan that answers the who, what, when, where, how, and how much to deliver to the customer will need to be developed. Typical elements to consider in a delivery plan include program management; site inspections; engineering; ordering; manufacturing; transportation; warehousing; staging; installation; testing; acceptance; training; documentation; and operations, administration and maintenance (OA&M). The extent and detail of the delivery plan must be gauged to the scope of the solution offered and priced. For example, if the solution offer includes minimum delivery, the delivery plan may need to address only ordering, manufacturing, transportation, and acceptance.

RISK MITIGATION PLANS

Sources of Risk

In developing a solution and response, uncertainty regarding future events arises, which represents risks. Table 6-1 presents examples of common sources of risk.

Table 6-1 Sources of Risk			
Technical Risks	**Delivery Risks**		**Financial Risks**
Hardware Design Errors	Material Availability	Reliability	Changes in COGS
Software Design Errors	Personnel Availability	Maintainability	Changes in SG&A Expenses
Testing / Modeling	Personnel Skills	Operations & Support Equipment Availability	Changes in Interest Rates
Integration / Interface	Safety		Changes in Exchange Rates
Safety	Security	Transportation	Pricing Errors
Requirement Changes	Environmental Impact	Training Availability	Customer Financial Stability
Fault Detection	Communication Problems	Documentation Accuracy	Supplier Financial Stability
Operating Environment	Labor Strikes	Zoning-Regulatory Approval	**Contractual Risks**
Unproven Technology	Requirement Changes	Degree of Concurrency	Terms & Conditions
System Complexity	Subcontractor Stability	Number of Critical Path Items	Supplier Contracts

Mitigating Risk

Risk is mitigated through one of four fundamental strategies:

(1) Avoid the risk,
(2) Transfer the risk,

(3) Share the risk, or
(4) Reserve the risk.

Avoiding the risk means to avoid a scenario that can cause risk, such as staying away from requirements that a company cannot satisfy. To transfer the risk means shifting the risk to another, which can be accomplished by buying hazard insurance or hiring a subcontractor under a turnkey contract. Sharing the risk means spreading the risk, such as having a partner or other related projects to assume some of the risk. Reserving the risk means establishing reserve funds to cover all or a portion of the risk, somewhat like self-insurance.

Table 6-2, which summarizes various ways of mitigating or avoiding risks, was developed by John R. Schuyler and can serve as a good generator of ideas.

Table 6-2 Ways of Mitigating or Avoiding Risk	
Portfolio Risks	**Operational Risks**
Share risks by having partners	Hire contractors under turnkey contracts
Spread risks over time	Tailor risk-sharing contract clauses
Participate in many ventures	Use safety margins; overbuild and overspecify designs
Group complementary risks into portfolios	Have backup and redundant equipment
Seek lower-risk ventures	Increase training
Specialize and concentrate in a single, well-known area	Operate with redirect and bail-out options
Increase the company's capitalization	Conduct tests, pilot programs, and trials
Commodity Prices	**Analysis Risks (Reducing Evaluation Error)**
Hedge or fix in the futures markets	Use better techniques (I.e., decision analysis)
Use long- or short-term sales (price and volume) contracts	Seek additional information
Tailor contracts for risk sharing	Monitor key and indicator variables
Interest Rate and Exchange Rate	Validate models
Use swaps, floors, ceilings, collars, and other hedging instruments	Include evaluation practices along with project post-reviews
Restructure the balance sheet	Develop redundant models with alternative approaches and people
Denominate or index certain transactions in a foreign currency	Involve multiple disciplines, and communicate cross-discipline
Environmental Hazards	Provide better training and tools
Buy insurance	**Source:** Schuyler, John R. Decision Analysis in Projects: Summary and Recommendations. PM Network, October 1995.
Increase safety margins	
Develop and test an incident response program	

Tools Techniques and Best Practices

When considering a mitigation strategy, it is important to understand both the probability that an event will occur as well as the impact should the event occur. For risks with a high probability of occurrence and a high impact, consider an avoidance strategy. For risks with a low probability of occurrence and a high impact, consider a transfer strategy. For risks with a high probability of occurrence but a low impact, consider a sharing strategy. For risks with a low probability of occurrence and a low impact, consider a reserve fund strategy. These guidelines are summarized on the following grid, Figure 6-3.

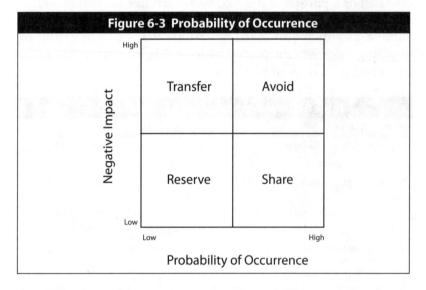

Figure 6-3 Probability of Occurrence

Risk Mitigation Plan

For each risk identified, a Risk Mitigation Plan, which can be completed using Form 6-7, should be developed and documented. The Risk Mitigation Plan form provides a space to identify the opportunity, opportunity tracking number, risk name (i.e., how the risk is referred to), an assigned risk number, the name of the person that developed the plan, the developer's title, and date the plan was prepared. There is a place to indicate the type of risk (i.e., technical, delivery, pricing, contractual) and a brief description of the risk along with its probability and impact. There is a space to show the mitigation strategy used (i.e., avoid, transfer, share, reserve) along with a brief description of the specific strategy. Finally, there is a place to identify the owner of the implementation of the mitigation plan and the owner's title.

Form 6-7 Risk Mitigation Plan			
Opportunity:		Tracking #:	
Risk Name:		Risk #:	
Developed by:	Title:		Date:
Type Risk ☐ Technical ☐ Delivery ☐ Pricing ☐ Contractual			
Briefly describe the risk its probability and its impact:			
Mitigation Strategy ☐ Avoid ☐ Transfer ☐ Share ☐ Reserve			
Briefly describe the migitation strategy:			
Mitigation Plan Owner:		Title:	

Risk Mitigation Planning Log

As a number of risks may arise , it is important to track and summarize them for stakeholders. Form 6-8 is a template of a Risk Mitigation Planning Log, which can be used for this purpose. It provides a space to list each risk, the risk number, the type of risk, who is developing the mitigation, the date (once it is developed,) and the strategy used.

Form 6-8 Risk Mitigation Planning Log											
		Type Risk						Strategy			
Risk Number	Risk Name	Technical	Delivery	Pricing	Contractual	Mitigation Plan Developed By	Date	Avoid	Transfer	Share	Reserve

Business Cases

Two business cases must be developed. An internal business case will show a company's revenues and costs associated with an opportunity, which is required to secure authority to bid. The other will be a customer business case to be included in the response to show the costs and benefits the customer will incur and realize by implementing a solution. Commercial customers purchase solutions to either generate revenues or reduce expenses, so a customer needs a business case to justify the expenditure within its company. It is beneficial to a potential contractor to prepare a customer business case to ensure that all benefits are identified, costs are not overstated, and to show the customer that the potential contractor understands its business problem.

Business Case Scenarios

For both business cases a clear set of assumptions regarding the size of the opportunity and the timing of the delivery must be developed. Most of the information that is needed should be available from the development of the solution (i.e., design, pricing, delivery plan); however, additional assumptions may be needed to produce a worst-case, most-likely-case, and best-case scenario. The worst-case scenario, assuming a winning bid, is the minimum solution a customer will choose to implement. The best- case scenario is the maximum solution a customer will choose to implement. The most-likely case scenario is between the two and represents how much of a solution the customer is most likely to implement. Factors to consider in each scenario include:

- Single versus multiple supplier awards,
- Minimum or maximum purchase requirements,
- Factors that could delay or accelerate the speed of delivery,
- Factors that could shorten or extend the life of the solution, and
- Factors that could increase or decrease the size of the problem.

Business Case Models

To simplify the work required to create each scenario, business case models can be used. It is likely that an overall solution can be broken down into a model solution composed of the typical products/services that would be delivered to solve one instance of the problem for a customer. There may be several sizes or types of problems to be resolved, so several solution models may be required. These solution models can help identify how many instances of each of the problems exist and how many solution models may be needed per year under a set of assumptions for each scenario.

Table 6-3 shows how to develop these estimates using one problem, which occurs 8,000 times over five years with one solution model. In the worst-case scenario, which might represent the minimum purchase under a multiple supplier award, solving 25% of the problems is assumed each year, in years one through three, for a total of 1,500 solution models. The best-case scenario, which might be the maximum delivery under a single award, assumes solving 50% in year 1 and increasing to solve 90% in year 5, for a total of 5,350 solution models. The most-likely-case scenario, which might be a modest delivery under a multiple supplier award, assumes 35% in year 1 increasing to 55% in the last 3 years, for a total of 3,850 solution models. The model becomes more realistic by introducing different size problems, multiple solution models, or different assumptions about the number of problems under each scenario.

Table 6-3 Business Case Models						
	Year					
Item	1	2	3	4	5	Total
Number of Problems	1,500	2,500	2,000	1,000	1,000	8,000
Worst Case Scenario						
Percent of problems solved	25%	25%	25%	0%	0%	
Number of solutions delivered	375.00	625.00	500.00	0	0	1,500
Most Likely Case Scenario						
Percent of problems solved	35%	45%	55%	55%	55%	
Number of solutons delivered	525	1125	1100	550	550	3,850
Best Case Scenario						
Percentage of problems solved	50%	60%	70%	80%	90%	
Number of solutions delivered	750	1500	1400	800	900	5,350

Product/Service Profile

A company may not have 100% of the solution to offer and may need to source product or service from a third party. The use of third parties introduces risk of their performance, which should be reserved by including a mark-up or margin on their products and services. The amount of third-party versus in-house products and services will significantly impact profitability and price competitiveness of a solution. When developing solution models, in-house versus third-party product and service amounts must be determined in each model. Then the units per year are used to populate a summary, which shows the percent of in-house versus third-party product and service for each scenario (see Form 6-9).

Form 6-9 Product / Service Profile				
Product / Service	**Year One**	**Year Two**	**Year Three**	**Total**
In-House Product				
Third-Party Product				
Product Subtotal				
% In-House Product				
In-House Service				
Third-Party Service				
Service Subtotal				
% In-House Service				
In-House P & S Total				
Third-Party P & S Total				
Product & Service Total				
% In-House				
% Product				

Customer Business Case

The customer business case can be developed using the same problem and solution models. Costs are the price for each solution model times the number of models delivered. The revenue increase or cost savings associated with solving each instance of each size problem multiplied by the number of problems solved are benefits. Alternatively, benefits are estimated by looking at the revenue increase or cost savings associated with the aggregate number of problems solved. The following factors are important in estimating customer benefits:

- Increased revenues from new products or services;
- Increased revenues from a larger volume of products or services;
- Increased revenues from introducing products or services earlier;
- Reduced personnel or contractor costs;
- Reduced space, utilities, or hardware/software support;

- Reduced insurance, interest, or cash flow requirements; and
- Depreciation/amortization on capital assets.

Common Business Case Terms

While the business cases should be developed by someone on the Pricing Team with financial training, Table 6-4 provides definitions of common business case terms used.

Table 6-4 Common Business Case Terms	
Item	**Definition**
Gross Sales	Total revenues at invoice value before any discounts or allowances
Discounts, Allowances and Returns	Price discounts, returned merchandise
Net Sales	Gross Sales minus Discounts, Allowances and Returns
Variable Costs	Costs associated with production that change directly with the amount of production, e.g., the direct material or labor required to complete the build or manufacturing of a product
Fixed Costs	Operating expenses that are incurred to provide facilities and organization that are kept in readiness to do business without regard to actual volumes of production and sales. Examples of fixed costs are rent, property taxes, and interest expense
Cost of Goods Sold (COGS)	Direct costs of producing finished goods for sale
Gross Profit Margin	Net Sales minus Cost of Goods Sold. Also called Gross Margin, Gross Profit or Gross Loss
Gross Profit Margin % or Ratio	Gross Profit Margin $ divided by Net Sales
Contribution Margin	Net Sales minus Variable Costs. Also called called Marginal Income. It is the amount of money available to cover fixed costs and generate profits.
Contribution Margin % or Ratio	Contribution Margin divided by Net Sales
Selling, General & Administrative (SG&A) Expenses	Administrative costs of running business
Depreciation	Amount of expense charged against earnings by a company to write off the cost of a plant or machine over its useful live, giving consideration to wear and tear, obsolescence, and salvage value
Amortization	Process of spreading the cost of an intangible asset over the expected useful life of the asset.
Operating Expenses	SG&A plus Depreciation and Amortization
EBITDA	Earnings Before Interest, Taxes, Depreciation and Amortization, but after all product / service, sales and overhead (SG&A) costs are accounted for. Sometimes referred to as Operating Profit.
EBITDARM	Acronym for Earnings Before Interest, Taxes, Depreciation, Amortization, Rent and Management fees.
Discounted Cash Flow (DCF)	Combined present value of cash flow and tangible assets minus present value of liabilities
Discount Rate	Interest rate used in calculating present value

PROPOSAL DEVELOPMENT

A solution it must be explained to the customer through a well-written response or proposal. The proposal payout with volume and section assignments defines who is responsible to write each of the responses. The Proposal Development Checklist defines the mechanics of how to develop assigned sections and share them. The Win Themes and Strategies defines the overarching message to be conveyed in the response and specific strategies to maximize strengths, minimize weaknesses, neutralize a competitor's strengths, and ghost a competitor's weaknesses.

Attributes of Winning Proposals

Before writing responses, team members should consider the following attributes of a proposal (see Table 6-12). This listing, designed for ease of evaluation and developed by David G. Pugh, Ph.D., of the Lore International Institute, will help to develop the right mindset.

Table 6-5 Attributes of a proposal designed with ease of evaluation in mind	
A Powerful Executive Summary	Powerful Proposal Design
Audience Designed	Double Exposure on a Single Page
1/3 Visuals, 2/3 Text, Ample White Space	Double or Message Column
Separately Bound	Themed and Captioned
Customer Focused	Emphatically Written
Strategy Driven	Active Voice and Personal Pronouns
Benefits Rich (Answers Why us? And So what?)	Effective Organization
Source: A Bidder's Dozen: Golden Rules for Winning Work, David G. Pugh, Ph.D. - Lore International Institute	

Why Proposals Lose Evaluation Points

Before describing the steps of the Bid Reviews stage, it is important to first understand why proposals lose evaluation points. The following pitfalls (see Table 6-6 were developed by the National Contract Management Association (NCMA).

Table 6-6 Why Proposals Lose Evaluation Points
Questionable or inadequate understanding of requirements or needs
Incomplete response to the solicitation; critical sections left out of the proposal
Noncompliance with specifications; misinterpretation of the specifications
Insufficient resources (time, funds, personnel, etc.) to accomplish the required services or tasks
Insufficient information about the resources required for satisfactory performance under the contract
Poor proposal organization; obstacles in correlating proposal content to the solicitation or requirements
Failure to show relevance of past experience to the proposed project
Unsubstantiated or unconvincing rationale for proposed approaches or solutions
Wordiness. Mindboggling wordiness.
Repeating requirements without discussing how they will be performed
Source: Building a Contract: Solicitations/Bids and Proposals - A Team Effort ? National Contract Management Association

Pink Team Reviews

The first step in the Bid Reviews stage is to conduct Pink Team reviews. The objective of Pink Team reviews is to ensure a proposal is complete and accurate. Due to the size of the response, the timing of when it is available for review, and the size of the opportunity, team, and content in each response, multiple Pink Team reviews are likely. For example, it is not unusual to have one Pink Team for the technical-delivery response, a separate Pink Team for the pricing-contractual response, and a third Pink Team for the executive summary.

The participants in the Pink Team reviews are the individuals who wrote the responses, while the reviewers are other team members, team leaders, a Sales Leader, Proposal Manager, and Capture Manager. Ideally, Pink Team reviews should be conducted face-to-face; however, a review can be equally as effective using technology, such as NetMeeting, videoconferencing, and teleconferencing, but it must be properly prepared. For small responses with few authors, a live Pink Team review session may not be necessary; responses may instead be distributed with reviewers forwarding their comments directly to the author by a specified deadline. This approach can also be used for larger responses to conduct a Pink Team review of the executive summary.

Responses should be distributed to the reviewers prior to the actual review session. This will allow for a shorter review session, while maintaining the quality of the review. The Pink Team reviews should be managed by the Proposal Manager. Also, it is important to ensure reviewers understand the purpose, format, time and location for the Pink Team reviews.

Pink Team Question Checklist

Form 6-10 is a Pink Team Question Checklist that reviewers can use as a guide for questions that should be considered during Pink Team reviews. The Pink Team review provides general questions to consider in reviewing all responses for organization, appearance, accuracy, and graphics. There are also specific questions to consider for the executive summary, the technical-delivery, and the pricing-contractual response.

Form 6-10 Pink Team Review — Questions Checklist			
Is the proposal complete and accurate?			✓
GENERAL	Organization	Is the proposal organized in a logical manner?	
		Does it have a clear table of contents? Is it logical?	
		Does the internal organization follow the table of contents?	
		Is the proposal a consistent document that appears to have been written by one person?	
	Appearance	How does the overall proposal look? Does it look professional?	
		Is it inviting to read? Is the proposal easy to follow?	
		Is the style consistent? Is the format consistent?	
		Is the proposal free of serious mistakes or typographical errors?	
	Accuracy	Is the solution presentation credible?	
		Are the facts correct? Are the data accurate?	
		Are the claims believable? Are the claims proven?	
		Is every claim supported? Is there an appropriate amount of supporting data?	
	Graphics	Are there enough graphics? Are there too many? Are they appropriate?	
		Are they well-designed to truly present information and key concepts at a glance?	
		Are they creative as well as accurate?	
		Are they correctly referenced in the text?	
EXECUTIVE SUMMARY		Does it give a sense of the overall proposal?	
		Does it present the customer problem/objective and the solution?	
		Is it an effective presentation of the company?	
		Is it sensitive to the customer's needs and requirements?	
		Does it sufficiently and clearly convey the win theme and strategies?	
		Was it worthwhile reading?	

Form 6-10 Pink Team Review — Questions Checklist	
Is the proposal complete and accurate?	✓
TECHNICAL / DELIVERY Is the customer problem or objective stated and analyzed?	
Does the proposed solution solve the problem or attain the objective?	
Is it clear? Too much detail? Not enough detail?	
Is this the best solution? Why? Are there alternative solutions?	
Are all customer specified questions answered?	
Are there any conflicting responses?	
Do the responses support the solution?	
Are all responses satisfactory to the team and properly represent your company?	
Is the delivery response complete and realistic?	
Will the delivery response satisfy the customer's requirements?	
PRICING / CONTRACTUAL Do all of the numbers add up?	
Are the detailed pricing pages consistent with the summary pricing pages?	
Has anything been "double counted"? Has anything been left out?	
Is there a logical flow of information that follows an outline?	
Are the terms and conditions explicit?	
Are all appropriate terms and conditions included? Are any missing?	

Proposal Deficiency Form

In order to ensure feedback is properly captured for the authors, deficiencies should be documented using a Proposal Deficiency Form (see Form 6-10). This form provides space to identify the proposal, proposal manager, deficiency owner (i.e., the author), who identified the deficiency, volume, section, solicitation reference, page number, brief description of the deficiency, and recommended action. There is also space to assign a deficiency number as well as to capture how and when the deficiency was resolved.

Form 6-11 Proposal Deficiency Form		
Proposal:	Volume:	Deficiency Number:
Proposal Manager:	Section:	
Deficiency Owner:	Solicitation Reference:	
Identified By:	Page Number:	Date Resolved:
Deficiency:		
Recommended Action:		
How Resolved:		

Proposal Deficiency Log

In order to ensure all deficiencies are closed, a summary of all deficiencies by their volume/section should be created, which can then be used as a checklist by the volume/section owner. The Proposal Deficiency Log can be used to collect and document all deficiencies in lieu of using an individual form for each deficiency. The Proposal Deficiency Log (see Form 6-11) provides space to identify the opportunity, proposal, volume/section, volume/section owner, deficiency number, solicitation reference, page number, deficiency, recommended action, deficiency owner, who identified the deficiency, and the date a deficiency was resolved.

Form 6-12 Proposal Deficiency Log							
Opportunity:				Proposal:			
Volume/Section:				Volume/Section Owner:			
Deficiency Number	Solicitation Reference	Page Number	Deficiency	Recommended Action	Deficiency Owner	Identified By	Date Resolved

Red Team Reviews

The second step in the Bid Reviews stage is to conduct Red Team Reviews. The objective of Red Team reviews is to ensure a proposal makes sense and solves a customer's business problem. If resources and time permit, reviewers can evaluate and score the responses as though they are the customer. Similar to the Pink Team review, there will likely be a Red Team for the technical-contractual response, another one for the pricing-contractual response, and a third for the executive summary.

Red Team reviewers should be individuals who are familiar with the customer's requirements as well as the subject matter within the response; however, they should not be individuals who were a part of the response team. However, peers or supervisors of the individuals who wrote the response are good candidates for Red

Team reviewers. Reviewers should mirror a customer by evaluating each section. As an example, stakeholders could review the Executive Summary. In addition to the responses, reviewers should have access to the solicitation, win themes and strategies, and relevant reference material in order to help them during their review.

Red Team Question Checklist

Reviewers can use as a guide for questions that must be considered during Red Team reviews a Red Team Question Checklist (see Form 6-12). This checklist provides general questions to consider in reviewing all responses for organization and emphasis, win themes and strategies, compliance and responsiveness, appearance and presentation, consistency and brevity, and visuals.

Form 6-13 Red Team Review - Questions Checklist		
Does the proposal make sense and solve the customer's problem?		✓
Organization and Emphasis	Do the content and organization of the response follow the content and organization of the customer request?	
	Are all of the main ideas up front?	
	Has the content of each section been previewed at the beginning?	
	Is summarized content at the end?	
	Are the paragraphs logical and easy to follow?	
	Does each paragraph have only one main idea?	
Win Theme and Strategies	Does the response effectively present the value of your company's solution?	
	Is it persuasive? Does it sell?	
	Does it follow the overall win theme ?	
	Are the win strategies reflected throughout the document?	
	Does the response emphasize the company's strengths?	
	Does the response mitigate the company's weaknesses?	
	Does the response ghost the competition's weaknesses?	
Compliance and Responsiveness	Does the solution solve the customer's problem or attain the objective?	
	Have all the customer's questions been answered?	
	Has every part of every question been answered?	
	Does the response address every customer request requirement?	
	Do the answers echo the customer's language?	
	Is the writing clear and to the point? What would make it clearer?	
	Do all the sentences make sense?	
	Are any statements vague or confusing or misleading?	

Form 6-13 Red Team Review - Questions Checklist		
Does the proposal make sense and solve the customer's problem?		✓
Appearance and Presentation	Is the response document professional?	
	Does it reflect the proper image of the company?	
	Do the pages have a clean, professional appearance?	
	Are all of the names and dates correct?	
	Do all of the cross-references have the correct page numbers?	
	Are all of the figures numbered consecutively?	
Consistency and Brevity	Do the writing styles match? Does the response seem as though one person wrote it?	
	Were consistent terms and abbreviations used?	
	Are your numbers consistent?	
	Have extraneous words, sentences, paragraphs, visuals, facts, or data been eliminated?	
	Has all of the boilerplate been customized for this customer and their its requirements?	
	Do any brochures or information sheets reflect a different format, give extraneous information, or appear to be placed in the document merely to add bulk?	
Visuals	Do visuals and text complement each other?	
	Are any visuals unnecessary?	
	Does the text make them redundant?	
	Are visuals appropriate for the technical level of the readers?	
	Are visuals simple, uncluttered?	
	Does each one have a clear message?	
	Do visuals stand by themselves?	
	Was each visual introduced before it appears?	
	Do the key visuals reflect the strategy?	
	Do they illustrate the major benefits for the customer emphasized in the bid?	

Red Team Evaluation Form:

The Proposal Deficiency Form and Proposal Deficiency Log from the Pink Team reviews also can be used to capture specific feedback by Red Team reviewers to document feedback to the authors. In addition, the reviewers should provide an overall evaluation of each volume by using the a Proposal Evaluation Form (see Form 6-14). This form identifies the opportunity, volume, and evaluator and asks the reviewer to assign a score of 1-to-5 for each category on the Red Team Question Checklist. Reviewers can then total the scores to provide an overall rating of each volume.

Form 6-14 Proposal Evaluation Form						
Opportunity:						
Volume:	Evaluator:					
	Excellent	**Good**	**Average**	**Poor**	**Terrible**	**Score**
Evaluation Factor/Subfactor	**5**	**4**	**3**	**2**	**1**	**Assigned**
Organization and Emphasis	☐	☐	☐	☐	☐	
Win Themes and Strategies	☐	☐	☐	☐	☐	
Compliance and Responsiveness	☐	☐	☐	☐	☐	
Appearance and Presentation	☐	☐	☐	☐	☐	
Consistency and Brevity	☐	☐	☐	☐	☐	
Visuals	☐	☐	☐	☐	☐	
					Totals	

Red Team Scoring Form

If the customer's specific criteria for evaluating a response is available, reviewers may score the responses as if they were the customer using Proposal Scoring Form 6-14. First, this form identifies the opportunity, volume, and evaluator. Next, it has the factors for the evaluation, maximum score, weighting (if any), and the weighted maximum score. Reviewers can then use the form to assign an evaluated and a weighted evaluated score.

Form 6-15 Proposal Scoring Form					
Opportunity:					
Volume:		Evaluator:			
Evaluation Factor/ Subfactor	**Maximum Score**	**Weight**	**Weighted Maximum Score**	**Evaluated Score**	**Weighted Evaluated Score**
Factor One					
Factor Two					
Factor Three					
Factor Four					
Factor Five					
Factor Six					
Factor Seven					
Factor Eight					
Factor Nine					
Factor Ten					
				Totals	

Red Team Do's and Don'ts

Table 6-14 is a compilation of recommended things Red Teams should and should not do in order to improve their effectiveness of.

	Table 6-7 RED TEAM DOs AND DONT's
Dos	Do organize and plan the proposal review process early in the proposal preparation.
	Do select the proposal review method that will do the most to increase win probability.
	Do consider using a running red team for a proposal that is to be written on a very tight schedule.
	Do consider dual Red Teams for major, must-win proposals.
	Do use a majority of outsiders and proposal professionals on Red Teams.
	Do make an early review of the proposal (sometimes called a Pink Team review) to ensure proper proposal structure and approach methodologies.
	Do have the proposal complete (including executive summaries, section/subsection introductions, and graphics) prior to Red Team review.
	Do hard edit a proposal prior to Red Team review.
	Do provide red team members with copies of both the solicitation and a comprehensive solicitation-to-proposal compliance matrix well before the proposal review.
	Do keep the Red Team members co-located during the proposal review.
	Do be specific in making comments and recommendations - general statements are usually useless.
	Do combine Red Team comments into a single volume.
	Do present proposal strengths and well-written areas during the Red Team debrief to the proposal team.
	Do remember that the proposal manager has total authority to accept or reject Red Team recommendations.
Dont's	Don't select any Red Team member who is not fully committed to work full time on the review and to stay and participate in making recommended fixes.
	Don't use a formal Red Team review if the review process delay will hurt the proposal effort.
	Don't ask a Red Team to score a proposal against the evaluation factors unless the proposal is complete.
	Don't ask the Red Team to pick between multiple approaches or solutions.
	Don't present minor issues during the Red Team debrief —concentrate the presentation on important issues.
Source: Focus on Basics - Using Red Teams Effectively, David H. Herond, Journal of the Association of Project Management Professionals, Fall 2000	

OBTAIN OFFER CERTIFICATIONS

Offer Certification Form

The third step of the Bid Reviews stage is to obtain offer certifications using Form 6-16, below, before proceeding to stakeholder approval and submittal of the response to the customer. The purpose of the offer certification is to ensure accountability by having each Team Leader sign that his or her portion of the solution is sound (i.e., doable and an appropriate solution for the company to offer), complies with all stated customer requirements, and verifies that the response has been reviewed and deemed accurate and complete. Additionally, the Sales Leader and Capture Manager should concur that they have reviewed the entire solution and responses and verify that the package meets the same criteria.

Form 6-16 Offer Certification Form			
Certifications			
Technical	Solution is certified as being technically sound and compliant with all stated customer requirements		
	Technical Response has been reviewed and is certified as being accurate and complete		
	Signature:	Name:	
		Title:	Date:
Delivery	Solution is certified as being delivery sound and compliant with all stated customer requirements		
	Delivery Response has been reviewed and is certified as being accurate and complete		
	Signature:	Name:	
		Title:	Date:
Pricing	Solution is certified as being financially sound and all pricing is certified as complete and accurate		
	Pricing Response has been reviewed and is certified as being accurate and complete		
	Signature:	Name:	
		Title:	Date:
Contracts	Solution is certified as being contractually sound and includes all appropriate terms & conditions		
	Contractual Response has been reviewed and is certified as being accurate and complete		
	Signature:	Name:	
		Title:	Date:
Concurrences			
Solution is concurred as being compliant with all stated customer requirements			
Entire response has been reviewed and is concurred as being accurate and complete			
Sales Leader	Signature:	Name:	
		Title:	Date:
Capture Manager	Signature:	Name:	
		Title:	Date:

Stakeholder Approval Review

Earlier in the process stakeholders who were part of a Stakeholder Opportunity Review to approve development of an offer were identified. In this last stage of the Developing Winning Proposals step these same stakeholders will be re-assembled to solicit their approval to submit the proposal to the customer.

Depending upon the size of the opportunity and potential liabilities additional approval from a senior executive, such as the company President or CEO, and potentially even the Board of Directors, may be needed. This is an important safeguard in companies to ensure that offers to enter into contracts with significant obligations are attained by individuals with the authority to bind the company. This information is generally identified in a Schedule of Authorizations or Approvals which should be available from a company's Chief Financial Officer (CFO) or General Counsel.

This approval will typically require an executive briefing document and approval package, which should have been identified as a work task in the Capture Project Plan. Details on the format of this package should be available from the Pricing Leader or the CFO, business management, or contracting stakeholder. These same individuals should be able to explain who should secure the approval and the time required for approval.

OUTPUTS

The key outputs of the proposal development process are the creation and review of the services proposal to be delivered to the U.S. government agency for its evaluation and source selection. Stakeholder approval is documented as required by a company's Schedule of Authorizations or Approvals.

Proposal evaluation, commonly called source selection, is about successfully implementing the plan to identify the right contractor to provide the desired services and/or solutions in a timely manner at fair and reasonable prices.

PROPOSAL EVALUATION PROCESS

Figure 6-4 Phase 4: Proposal Evaluation Process

Input	Tools & Techniques	Output
Bids or Proposals	Past Performance Evaluation Database	Selected Contractors who will Provde Timely Delivery of Quality Services, and/or Solutions at a Fair & Reasonable Price
Source Selection Plan	Source Selection Best Practices Checklist	
Evaluation Criteria	Total Cost of Ownership (TCO) Evaluation	
Evaluation Standards	Source Selection Decision Making Guidelines	
Weighting System	Evaluation of Oral Presentations by Sellers	
Screening System		
Source Selection-Process		
People		
Training		

INPUTS

Bids or Proposals. One or more proposals must be obtained in order to conduct source selection evaluation. Typically, most buyers will seek at least two or three bids or proposals from qualified or even pre-qualified sellers.

Source Selection Plan (SSP). As previously discussed, the SSP should include the following key elements: evaluation criteria, evaluation standards, weighting system, screening system, and source selection process.

People. The buyer must ensure that the appropriate quality and quantity of human resources are available to support the source selection evaluation process.

Training. The buyer must ensure the people involved in source selection evaluation are properly trained to conduct and document the evaluation process fairly, cost-effectively, and efficiently. If novices or trainees are used in the source selection evaluation process, then a coach or experienced mentor should be assigned to guide the trainees through the process and verify their quality of work.

TOOLS & TECHNIQUES

Following are a few of the many proven tools and techniques to help business professionals involved in the complex selection process to conduct their evaluation process more effectively and efficiently.

PAST PERFORMANCE EVALUATION

U.S. government buyers should always include past performance as an evaluation criterion/ factor in their request for proposal (RFP) and subsequent source selection process. The weighting of the importance of past performance will vary based upon numerous factors. Contractors with no similar past performance should not be assigned a negative rating nor should they receive a positive rating because they have no poor past performance. The key factors to consider regarding each contractor's past performance is the relevancy of the work and the currency of the past performance. Clearly, a contractor that has recently completed highly similar work and done so very well (on-time and within budget) and met or exceeded customer requirements, should receive an excellent past performance rating.

Federal Awardee Performance and Integrity Information System

When President Obama signed the 2010 Supplemental Appropriations Act on July 29, 2010, a provision of that law directed the General Services Administration (GSA) to make nearly all of the information in the recently-created Federal Awardee Performance and Integrity Information System (FAPIIS) database available to the public. Past performance reports are the only information exempted from this new public disclosure requirement.

On April 22, 2010, when FAPIIS originally went into effect, the regulatory history revealed many concerns about the potential for inaccuracies and misuse of sensitive information about contractors. (See 75 Fed. Reg. 14059, Mar. 23, 2010.) Despite the effort expended in addressing those concerns and the current Federal Acquisition Regulations clause's assurance that "only Government personnel and authorized users performing business on behalf of the Government will be able to view the Contractor's record, "(see FAR 52.209-9(b)(3)) contractors must prepare for the new reality that a significant amount of sensitive and potentially misleading information about their companies, teammates, and competitors is now publicly available. Contractors must be aware of the parameters of their self-reporting obligations and should monitor several proposals to expand the FAPIIS database that are presently under consideration.

FAPIIS Overview

The FAPIIS database includes data from the Past Performance Information Retrieval System (PPIRS) and the former Contractor Performance Assessment Reporting System (CPARS) relating to contractor performance, data from the Excluded Parties List System (EPLS) relating to responsibility determinations, and contractor self-reported information from the Central Contractor Registry (CCR), including, among other things, information concerning criminal, civil, and administrative actions and/ or settlements involving contractors and their business principals.

FAPIIS was created to satisfy requirements impost by Section 872 of the Duncan Hunter National Defense Authorization Act for Fiscal Year 2009 (Pub. L. 110-417). In accordance with Section 872(e) (1) of that Act, the FAPIIS database was only to be made available to contracting officers, certain other government personnel on request, individual contractors for the purpose of verifying the accuracy of information about themselves, and to the chairperson and ranking member of congressional committees.

By a single amendment to the Supplemental Appropriations bills, however, all of this highly sensitive and potentially misleading, incorrect, and/or outdated information must be made available to the public. The GSA has stated that it expects to open FAPIIS to the public by the end of the 2010, but regulations regarding the open version still must be approved by GSA officials. Federal Acquisition Regulation Case 2010-016 has been opened for the development of an interim rule. Contractors should review and consider commenting upon the interim rule once it is published.

Mandatory Self-Reporting in CCR

For every proposal relating to a government contract or grant opportunity with a value expected to exceed $500,000, companies must report certain criminal or civil violations, administrative actions, or settlements of such matters within the last five years. (See FAR 9.104-7(b); FAR 52.209-7(c).) This requirement applies to all such opportunities including those for commercial and commercial off-the-shelf (COTS) items. Moreover, there is no exemption for small businesses. Companies that hold government contracts for grants in excess of $10 million are deemed to have represented that the information they have entered into FAPIIS via the CCR website is "current, accurate, and complete as of the date of submission" of their offer.

(FAR 52.209-7(c), Information Regarding Responsibility Matters (APR 2010).)

The current FAR clause specifically requires contractors to report via CCR information regarding whether, within the last five years, the offeror or its principals have been the subject of a proceeding at the federal or state level resulting in (1) a conviction in a criminal proceeding; (2) a civil judgment of greater than $5,000 in damages with a finding of contractor liability; (3) an administrative finding of fault or liability with greater than a $5,000 fine or damages, restitution, or reimbursement greater than $100,000; and (4) a settlement of any such matter that could have led to the above results where the contractor admits liability. The requirement to report such events does not apply unless the contractor's or principal's underlying actions were related to the award or performance of a federal government contract or grant. Ld.

Proposed Expansions of FAPIIS Reporting

There are several legislative and regulatory proposals that would sweep more information into the FAPIIS reporting requirements. As noted in the preamble to the current FAR clause, information concerning state-level contracts will eventually be added to FAPIIS. Additionally, the government is considering a proposed rule that would (1) lower the threshold for triggering FAPIIS reporting from $500,000 to the simplified acquisition threshold and (2) include required reporting of violations of laws not related to federal contracts and grants. The Federal Contracting and Oversight and Reform Act of 2010 (S. 3323) would increase the period for retaining FAPIIS data from 5 to 10 years and require reporting of all administrative proceedings (not just those where there is a finding of fault or liability). In an apparently related development, there is an Advanced Notice of Proposed Rulemaking (75 Fed. Reg. 26916 (May 13, 2010)) that asks for input as to how the government could make contracts public but still protect contractors' proprietary information in anticipation of a potential future requirement to expand public availability of federal contracts.

Tips for Contractors

Contractors should be cognizant of the specific parameters of their reporting obligation and ensure that they provide accurate information but no more information than is required. Any information submitted by a contractor will be available to the public and may be used by so-called watchdog organizations or even competitors to cast the company or its leadership in a negative and potentially misleading light. Accordingly, contractors must monitor all information concerning their company and its principals in FAPIIS and take prompt action to correct any inaccurate or false information.

When contractor personnel update information in the CCR database, they should seek advice and guidance from counsel as new questions and issues arise and carefully evaluate what information falls within the requirements of the FAPIIS reporting regulation. Moreover, contractors must monitor the potential developments and expansion of FAPIIS to ensure that they comply with all pertinent reporting and certification requirements. Now that the database exists, lawmakers and regulators are likely to continue to expand FAPIIS's coverage, and contractors' compliance systems must evolve to meet the increasing demand for data and expansion of reporting requirements.

Source Selection: Seven Best Practices

Form 6-17 contains a checklist of seven proven effective source selection best practices.

	Form 6-17
Checklist	**Source Selection Seven Best Practices**
☐	Cycle-Time Targets – the buyer establishes a target of 90 days or less from issuance of the RFP to contract award
☐	Greater Pre-solicitation Efforts – the buyer actively encourages more definitive procurement planning, bidders conferences with prospective sellers, and circulation of draft RFPs to prospective sellers
☐	Proposal Page Limitations – the buyer provides that pages in proposals over a specified number will not be read but will be returned to the seller
☐	Reduced Number of Evaluation Factors – the buyers uses only essential evaluation factors
☐	Small Source Selection Teams – the buyer uses a small number of evaluators, each reading all of their specialization/section (technical, management, past performance, and cost) of the proposals
☐	Oral Presentations – the buyer requires the sellers to make oral presentations to the source selection team in the early stages of evaluation of proposals
☐	Limiting the Competitive Range – the buyer requires rigorous exclusion of marginal sellers from the competitive range

TOTAL COST OF OWNERSHIP EVALUATION

Total Cost of Ownership (TCO) is the latest buzzword, formerly known as Life Cycle Cost (LCC). No matter what you call it, TCO or LCC, there is a real, compelling need for buying organizations to spend some time and effort evaluating the potential product, service, and/or solution throughout its life cycle, from initial procurement through operational use, including support/maintenance/upgrades, to the end of the product/service life.

Source Selection Decision-Making Guidelines

The key to source selection is ultimately identifying the most qualified individual within a buying organization to serve as the lead decision-maker (LDM) or source selection authority (SSA). The LDM or SSA should be chosen based upon general business knowledge, experience within the industry, expertise in contract and supply-chain management, demonstrated leadership, and business integrity.

The LDA should use the evaluation criteria/factors, standards, weighting system, and screening system established in the source selection plan contained within the solicitation document and consider any rankings and ratings prepared by the source selection evaluation team/ board/ committee. The LDA should seek clear differentiators between proposals or bids that are consistent with the evaluation criteria and weightings established in the solicitation.

Unlike, U.S. government source selections, the final decision of the LDM or SSA should not be subject to bid protests.

Evaluation of Oral Presentations

Oral presentations are a powerful and effective tool for both buyers and sellers. Buyers should require sellers to provide oral presentations, as needed, especially for large, complex, and critical systems and/or professional outsourcing services. Buyers should pre-determine the weighting and key evaluation criteria factors for the basis of the evaluation of all oral presentations provided by the sellers.

DESIRED OUTPUT

The desired output of the Phase 4: Proposal Evaluation Process is the selection of a contractor who will provide timely delivery of quality services and/ or solutions at a fair and reasonable price.

SUMMARY

In the public business sector, government contractors' bid/proposal efforts should be guided by their opportunity and risk assessment and their business case. Government contractors should be focused on three key aspects: Can we win? Should we win? How do we win while achieving profitability with integrity? Developing and effectively communicating a win theme to the government buyer is essential. Further, selecting the right people, both internally and externally, to review a bid or proposal is very important to maximizing opportunities and minimizing risks. All too often bid or proposal reviews are merely a rubber stamp, which only adds time and money and offers little, real value to a bid or proposal.

By following the actions outlined in this chapter, a potential contractor can develop a solid solution to a government customer's business problem, which is good business for both the contractor and the U.S. government agency. More importantly, this is accomplished while optimizing scarce resources and results in a well-defined strategy and process to manage work tasks, manage change, minimize re-work, and maximize the probability of success.

On the opposite side, it is the responsibility of U.S. government agencies to efficiently and cost-effectively evaluate proposals they receive from contractors in a timely manner. Numerous tools, techniques, and best practices are available for conducting the proposal evaluation/ source selection for services contracts.

QUESTIONS TO CONSIDER

1. How effectively does your organization submit proposals which are win-win for a government customer and the contractor?

2. Does your organization have documented processes or tools and techniques to be used to develop proposals, review proposals, and obtain stakeholder approval?

3. What actions has your organization taken to improve your proposal development, proposal reviews, and approval skills for sales managers, capture/proposal managers and contract managers?

CHAPTER 7

PHASE 5: NEGOTIATIONS AND CONTRACT FORMATION

By Gregory A. Garrett

INTRODUCTION

Given the hundreds of billions of dollars spent each year by U.S. federal government agencies purchasing a wide variety of professional services, systems, and integrated solutions using government contracts, it is critical for government contractors to master the art and science of negotiation and contract formation. This chapter explores the fifth phase of the U.S. Government Services Contracting Buying and Selling Life Cycle introduced in Chapter 2. So, what is contract negotiation? According to I. William Zartman, author of *The Practical Negotiator*, "it is the process of unifying different positions into a unanimous joint decision, regarding the buying and selling of products and/or services." Further, Zartman states, "Negotiation is a process of making or reaching an agreement without rules about how decisions are made."[1] Based upon extensive experience and research, it is clear that many business professionals fear negotiating contracts.

So, why do many people fear negotiating contracts? The seven most typical responses include:

- It's too hostile and intimidating!
- I like to avoid conflict!
- I do not know enough about contracts!
- I do not know enough about the legal and/or technical aspects!
- I am not articulate enough!
- I do not want to develop a new challenging skill!

CONTRACT NEGOTIATION—A COMPLEX HUMAN ACTIVITY

Contract negotiation is a complex human activity. Successful contract negotiators must:

- Master the art and science, or soft and hard skills, required to become a master negotiator.
- Possess the intellectual ability to comprehend factors shaping and characterizing the negotiation.
- Be able to adapt strategies, tactics, and countertactics in a dynamic environment.
- Understand their own personalities and personal ethics and values.
- Know their products and services, desired terms and conditions, and pricing strategy.

■ Be able to lead a diverse multi-functional team to achieve a successful outcome.

If accomplishing all of the aforementioned tasks sounds easy, then you are either a highly skilled contract negotiator or somewhat na-ïve about what it takes to become a master contract negotiator.

CONTRACT NEGOTIATION APPROACHES

We all negotiate everyday—with our friends, our family, our business customers, suppliers, and/or team members. Some of us negotiate well on occasion with some of the parties in our lives. But most of us do not negotiate consistently well with all of the parties in both our personal and professional lives. The fact is there are two basic approaches to contract negotiations, (1) the intuitive approach and (2) the process approach.

The intuitive contract negotiation approach is usually characterized as non-structured, informal, and undocumented and yields inconsistent negotiation results. The intuitive contract negotiation approach is also affectionately known as the following:

■ The no-plan, no-clue approach,
■ Fly-by-the-seat-of-your-pants approach,
■ Ad hoc approach,
■ Think-out-of-the-box approach, or
■ Who needs a stinking plan approach?

The process negotiation approach is typically characterized as structured, planned, formal, and documented, yielding more consistent negotiation results. In the world of real estate, the old adage is that the three most important aspects are location, location, and location. Arguably, in the world of contract negotiations the three most important aspects are planning, negotiating, and documenting the deal.

CONTRACT NEGOTIATION—
THE ART AND SCIENCE OF THE DEAL

In contract negotiation, getting to yes means getting past no! As William Ury, co-author of the best-selling book *Getting to Yes* and author of *Getting Past No!*, states: "Getting around yes, but focusing on common interests not positions, is critical to achieve successful negotiation results.[2] Creating a joint prime contractor and subcontractor problem-solving environment is vital to developing a win-win contract negotiation situation. Remember, the right solution is truly a matter of perspective for both the prime contractor and the subcontractor. Like the game of chess, contract negotiation requires strategy, tactics, countertactics, and stressing one's flexibility and ability to adapt to changing situations while recognizing there is more than one way to achieve success. Unlike chess, contract negotiation provides an opportunity for both parties to meet or exceed their respective needs.

Contract Negotiation Objectives (Interests)

Clearly, contract negotiation is about a U.S. government agency acting as a buyer and a government prime contractor acting as a seller, an organization providing goods and/or services, and their respective representatives reaching a written agreement to document their relationship—who will do what, where, when, and for how much! Typically, a buyer's contract negotiation objectives include the following:

- Acquire necessary supplies, services, and/or solutions of the desired quality, on-time, and at the lowest reasonable price;
- Establish and administer a pricing arrangement that results in payment of a fair and reasonable price; and
- Satisfy needs of the end-user (customer).

Similarly, a contractor's contract negotiation objectives usually include the following:

- Grow profitable revenue (long-term vs. short-term);
- Increase market share within its respective industry;
- Deliver quality supplies, services, and/or solutions and achieve customer loyalty.

While each contract negotiation is unique and there may be some special objectives for certain deals, these contract negotiation objectives are relatively common for most government agencies, prime contractors, and subcontractors.

Figure 7-1 Getting Past No: Five Barriers to Cooperation		
The Goal: **Joint Problem Solving**	**Barriers to** **Cooperation**	**Strategy:** **Breakthrough Negotiation**
• People sitting side by side • Facing the problem • Reaching a mutually satisfactory agreement	• Your reaction • Their emotion • Their position • Their dissatisfaction • Their power	• Go to the balcony • Step to their side • Re-frame • Build them a golden bridge • Use power to educate
From: Getting Past No, by William Ury, 1993.		

Figure 7-1 illustrates the goal of most contract negotiations— creating a joint problem-solving environment to yield a win-win contractual agreement. Figure 7-1 also indicates five of the common barriers to cooperation that are frequently encountered during contract negotiations. Lastly, the last column of Figure 7-1 provides some of the unique terminology provided by William Ury in *Getting Past No*, which basically describes actions a negotiator can take:[3]

■ Step back and examine the big picture before you make any key decisions (Go to the balcony).

■ Look at the situation from the perspective of the other side/ party (Step to their side).

■ Re-evaluate the situation and determine if there are other alternative solutions (Re-frame).

■ Create a means to collaborate with the other side (Build them a Golden Bridge).

■ Provide new information or technology to enlighten the other side (Use power to educate).

CONTRACT NEGOTIATION—A PROCESS APPROACH FOR BUILDING SUCCESSFUL BUSINESS RELATIONSHIPS

Contract negotiation is the process by which two or more competent parties reach an agreement to buy or sell products and/or services. Contract negotiations may be conducted formally or informally and may involve many people or just two— a representative for the prime contractor and a representative for the subcontractor. Contract negotiation may take a few minutes or may involve many discussions over days, months, or years.

The desired result of the contract negotiation process is a contract. Contract formation is the process of putting together the essential elements of the contract and any special items unique to a particular business agreement (see Figure 7-2).

CONTRACT NEGOTIATION ESSENTIAL ELEMENTS

Figure 7-2 Essential Elements of Contract Negotiation

Key Inputs	Tools & Techniques	Desired Outputs
Solicitation (RFP, RFQ, etc.)	Oral Presentations	Contract or Walk Away
Bid or Proposal	Highly skilled contract negotiators	
Prime contractor's source selection process	Legal Review	
Subcontractor's past performance	Business Case Approval	
Previous contracts	Contract Negotiation Formation Process	
Competitor Profile	Plan negotiations	
Business Ethics/ Standards of Conduct Guidelines	Conduct negotiations	
Market and Industry practices	Document the negotiation and form the contract	

Source: World Class Contracting, Gregory A. Garrett, CCH, Inc., 2003.

KEY INPUTS

(The following section is a modified extract from World Class Contracting by Gregory A. Garrett, CCH Inc. 2003.)

Following is a brief description of the key inputs necessary to successful negotiation and contract formation.

- ***Solicitation.*** The solicitation is either an oral or a written request for an offer (Request for Proposal (RFP), Request for Quote (RFQ), Invitation for Bid (IFB), and so on) prepared by the government agency and provided to one or more potential government contractors.

- ***Bid or proposal.*** The bid or proposal is either an oral or a written offer by potential   contractors to provide products or services to the government agency, usually in response to a solicitation. It also includes all supporting documentation, such as delivery plans, assumptions, and cost/price models.

- ***Government's source selection process.*** Source selection is the process by which a government agency selects a contractor or source of supply for products or services. Government agencies typically apply evaluation criteria to select the best contractor to meet their needs. This source selection process is seldom an uncomplicated one because

- Price may be the primary determinant for an off-the-shelf item, but the lowest proposed price may not be the lowest cost if the subcontractor proves unable to deliver the product in a timely manner;
- Proposals are often separated into technical/delivery and pricing/contractual sections, with each evaluated separately;
- Multiple sources may be required for critical products;
- Bids or proposals may be simple, requiring only one person to evaluate the sources and select the best alternative or they may be complex, requiring a panel of experts. In fact, some proposal evaluations may require a consultant's assistance.

- *Source selection evaluation criteria.* Developing the evaluation criteria for source selection requires three prerequisites. First, the government agency must understand what goods or services it wants to buy. Second, the government agency must understand the industry that will provide the required goods or services. And third, the government agency must understand the market practices of that industry, which is provided by market research.

During requirements analysis and development of the specification or statement of work, the government agency gains an understanding of the required products or services. Understanding the industry means learning about the attributes of the goods or services in question and the firms that make them, including:

- What features do those goods or services have?
- What processes are used to produce or render them?
- What kinds and quantities of labor and capital are required?
- What are the cash requirements?

Understanding the market means learning about the behavior of prime contractors and subcontractors:

- What are the pricing practices of the market?
- What is the range of prices charged?
- What are the usual terms and conditions of sale?

After gaining an understanding of these issues, the government agency is ready to develop the evaluation criteria by selecting attributes for evaluation.

- ■ **Source selection attributes.** A consumer shopping for an automobile does not evaluate an automobile per se but rather selects attributes of the automobile, such as acceleration, speed, handling, comfort, safety, price, fuel mileage, capacity, appearance, and so forth. The evaluation of the automobile is the sum of the evaluations of its attributes.

  An automobile has many attributes, but not all are worthwhile subjects of evaluation. The attributes of interest are those that the consumer thinks are important for satisfaction. The attributes that one consumer thinks are important may be inconsequential to another.

  In most government procurements, multiple criteria will be required for successful performance for the following reasons: First, the U.S. government agency usually has more than one objective; for example, many government agencies look for both good quality and low price. Second, attributes essential for one objective may be different from those essential for others; for example, in buying an automobile, the attributes essential for comfort have little to do with those essential for quick acceleration.

  To complicate matters further, some criteria will likely be incompatible with others. The attributes essential to high quality may be inconsistent with low price; high performance, for example, may be incompatible with low operating cost. Thus, for any one source to have the maximum desired value of every essential attribute—for example, highest quality combined with lowest price—may be impossible. If so, the government agency must make trade-offs among attributes when deciding which source is best. These are considerations that make source selection a problem in multiple attribute decision-making, which requires special decision analysis techniques.

  As a rule, source selection attributes fall into three general categories relating to (1) the sources themselves, as entities; (2) the products or services they offer; and (3) the prices they offer. Thus, the government agency must have criteria for each category that reflect the agency's ideas about what is valuable. The criteria concerning the sources themselves, as entities, are the management criteria; the criteria concerning the products or services offered are the technical criteria; and the criteria concerning the prices of the products or services are the price criteria.

- *Contractor's past performance.* The past performance of a contractor is often a critical aspect of contract negotiation. Has the contractor delivered previous products and services on time? Has the contractor provided high-quality products and services?

  Past performance can be viewed as a separate evaluation factor or as a sub-factor under technical excellence or management capability. Using past performance history also reduces the emphasis on merely being able to write a good proposal.

- *Previous contracts.* Has the contractor provided products or services to this government agency in the past? If so, what did the previous contract say? How was it negotiated? Who negotiated it?

- *Competitor profile.* The competitor profile, developed during the Pre-Award Phase, provides a written summary of the contractor's competitors and their respective strengths and weaknesses compared to the contractor's.

- *Business ethics/standards of conduct guidelines.* Ethics is especially important in light of numerous recent cases of corporate greed, corruption, and violations of state, federal, or international laws. Every company should have mandatory business ethics policies, procedures, and well-defined standards of conduct. Even the appearance of conflicts of interests should be avoided. All business activities should be conducted in a professional and ethical manner.

- *Market and industry practices.* Knowing what competitors are offering (most-favored pricing, warranties, product discounts, volume discounts, and so on) is essential for a successful negotiation.

TOOLS AND TECHNIQUES

The following tools and techniques are used for negotiations and contract formation.

- **Oral presentations.** It is usually better to orally present a bid/ proposal to a customer than to merely submit it electronically (e-mail, FAX, CD-ROM) or in paper format. Oral presentations, when preformed by a skilled, knowledgeable, and persuasive individual, can help sell products, services, and/ or a solution to a prime contractor. Oral presentations also can address questions and clarify concerns that a government agency may have regarding a proposal.

- **Highly skilled negotiators.** Conducting contract negotiation is a complex activity that requires a broad range of skills. Providing negotiators with the best available training in contract negotiation is vital. Top negotiators help their organizations save money and generate higher profits.

Case Study: Northrop/Grumman

For more than 25 years, Northrop/Grumman has had an excellent reputation for building or developing highly skilled contract negotiators and negotiation teams. Northrop/Grumman has traditionally ensured that its sales managers, contract managers, and contract administrators receive appropriate and timely negotiation training via in-house professional seminars, university-based courses, and attendance at educational conferences and seminars. In addition, Northrop/Grumman has for many years developed and maintained a seasoned and highly-skilled major negotiations team, which is tasked with tackling the largest and most important contract negotiations.

- **Legal review.** A legal review should be conducted, if not as a regular part of the contract negotiation process, then at least for all key subcontracts.

CONTRACT NEGOTIATION PROCESS

The contract negotiation process is composed of three phases: (1) planning negotiations, (2) conducting negotiations, and (3) documenting the negotiations. Table 7-1 describes an effective, logical approach to planning, conducting, and documenting contract negotiations based on the proven best practices of world-class organizations.

Table 7-1 Contract Negotiation Process		
Plan the Negotiation	**Conduct the Negotiation**	**Document the Negotiation and Form the Subcontract**
1. Prepare	11. Determine who has authority	21. Prepare the negotiation memorandum
2. Know the other party		
3. Know the big picture	12. Prepare the facility	22. Send the memorandum to the other party
4. Identify objectives	13. Use an agenda	
5. Prioritize objectives	14. Introduce the team	23. Offer to write the contract
6. Create options	15. Set the right tone	24. Prepare the contract
7. Select fair standards	16. Exchange information	25. Prepare summary of negotiation results
8. Examine alternatives	17. Focus on objectives	
9. Select your strategy, tactics, and countertactics	18. Use strategy, tactics, and countertactics	26. Obtain required reviews and approvals
10. Develop a solid and approved team negotiation plan	19. Make counteroffers	27. Send the contracts to the other party for signature
	20. Document the agreement or know when to walk away	
		28. Provide copies of the contract to affected organizations
		29. Document lessons learned
		30. Prepare the contract administration plan

PLAN NEGOTIATION

The following ten actions should be performed to properly plan the negotiation:

1. *Prepare.* The lead negotiator must know his or her personal and professional strengths, weaknesses, and tendencies, as well as those of other team members. (Many self-assessment tools are available, including the Myers-Briggs Type Indicator® assessment, which can provide helpful insight on how an individual may react in a situation due to personal or professional tendencies.) Preparing a list of the strengths and weaknesses of team members is an important first step in negotiation planning (see Form 7-1).

Form 7-1 Team Members Strengths, Weaknesses and Interests	
Team Member	Team Member
Name	Name
Job Title	Job Title
Phone No.	Phone No.
Fax No.	Fax No.
E-Mail:	E-Mail:
Strengths 1	Strengths 1
2	2
3	3
Weaknesses 1	Weaknesses 1
2	2
3	3
Interests 1	Interests 1
2	2
3	3
Date Prepared:_____	Lead Negotiator:_____

2. ***Know the other party.*** Intelligence gathering is vital to successful negotiation planning. Create a checklist of knowledge about the other party to help the team prepare for negotiation (see Form 7-2). Listed below are a few suggested questions to discuss with team members to ensure understanding as much as possible about your own organization and the other contractor or government agency.

Form 7-2 Knowledge About the Other Party
Government and Contractor
☐ What is the government organization's overall mission?
☐ What is its reputation in contract negotiations?
☐ What is its current business environment in this agency?
☐ Who is the lead negotiator?
☐ Who are the primary decision makers?
☐ What are their key objectives?
☐ What are their overall contract objectives?
☐ What are their personal objectives?
☐ Who or what influences the decision makers?
☐ What internal organization barriers do they face?
Contractor Only
☐ When does the government agency need our products or services?
☐ How much money does the government agency have to spend?
☐ Where does the government agency want our products and services delivered?
☐ What benefits will our products and services provide?
☐ What is our company's past experience with this government agency?
Date Prepared:_____ Lead Negotiator:_____

3. ***Know the big picture.*** In the words of Stephen R. Covey, author of *The Seven Habits of Highly Effective People*, "begin with the end in mind." Keep focused on the primary objectives. Be aware that the ability of either party to be flexible on some issues may be limited because of internal policies, budgets, or organizational politics.

   One of the proven best practices to keep the negotiation focused is using interim summaries. The key is not to get caught up in small, unimportant details that derail the negotiation.

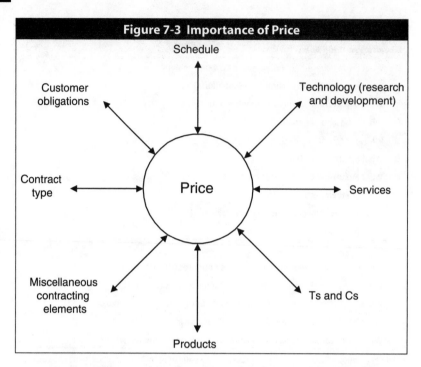

Figure 7-3 Importance of Price

4. **_Identify objectives._** Know what both the potential contractor and the other party want to accomplish (see Form 7-3). Successful negotiators know that nearly everything affects price (see Figure 7-3). Changes in schedule, technology, services, terms and conditions, customer obligations, subcontract type, products, and other subcontracting elements affect subcontract price.

A novice or apprentice negotiator is easily identifiable because he or she always wants to discuss price first. An experienced negotiator knows to agree to all the terms and conditions (Ts and Cs) first. Price is the last item a master negotiator will discuss and agree to. Master negotiators know what the big print giveth and the little print taketh away.

Form 7-3 Identification of Objectives	
Government Objectives	**Contractor Objectives**
Personal 1	Personal 1
2	2
3	3
4	4
5	5
Professional 1	Professional 1
2	2
3	3
4	4
5	5
6	6
7	7
Date Prepared:_____	Lead Negotiator:_____

5. ***Prioritize objectives.*** Although all terms and conditions are important, some are clearly more important than others. Prioritize objectives to help remain focused during negotiation (see 7-3) The various terms and conditions that affect cost, risk, and value are depicted in Figure 7-4.

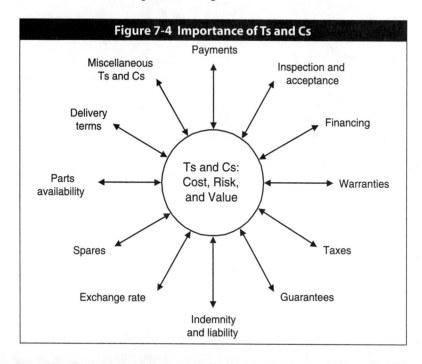

Figure 7-4 Importance of Ts and Cs

It is important for subcontract negotiators to understand and appreciate that all terms and conditions (Ts and Cs) contained in a deal have a cost, risk, and value associated with them and their specific wording. The exact wording of the deal is critical in contract negotiations.

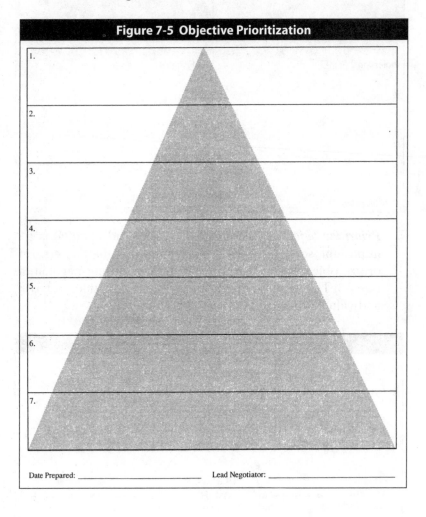

Figure 7-5 Objective Prioritization

Date Prepared: _____   Lead Negotiator: _____

Form 7-4 Objective Prioritization
1.
2.
3.
4.
5
6.
7.

Date Prepared:_____ Lead Negotiator:_____

6. ***Create options.*** Creative problem-solving is a critical skill of successful negotiators. Seek to expand options; do not assume that a single solution exists to every problem. Conducting team brainstorming sessions to develop a list of options to achieve negotiation objectives is a proven best practice of many world-class organizations (see Form 7-5).

Form 7-5 Create Options for Achieving Negotiation Objectives		
Government Objectives	**Possible Options**	**Contractor Objectives**

Date Prepared:_____ Lead Negotiator:_____

7. ***Select fair standards.*** Successful negotiators avoid a contest of wills by turning an argument into a joint search for a fair solution using fair standards that are independent of either side's will. Some standards to use in negotiation include:
   - Uniform Commercial Code;
   - United Nations Convention on Subcontracts for the International Sale of Goods;
   - American Arbitration Association standards;

- ISO 9000 quality standards;
- State, local, and federal laws; and
- Market or industry standards.

8. ***Examine alternatives.*** Prepare in advance alternatives to important negotiation issues or objectives. Successful negotiators know their best-case, most-likely, and worst-case (walk-away) alternatives for all major objectives (see Form 7-6).

Form 7-6 Objectives and Alternatives—Worst Case, Most Likely, and Best Case		
Objective:		
Worst Case	**Most Likely**	**Best Case**
(Plot your most likely position)		
Date Prepared:_____	Lead Negotiator:_____	

9. ***Select strategy, tactics, and countertactics.*** Negotiation strategies provide the overall framework that will guide how negotiations are conducted. Negotiation strategies can be divided into two types: win-lose and win-win.

Win-Lose Negotiaton

The win-lose negotiation strategy is about winning today, despite the potential long-term effect tomorrow and beyond. Common characteristics of the win-lose strategy include concealing one's own position and interests, discovering the other party's position and interests, weakening the other party's resolve, and causing the other party to modify its position or accept your position on all key issues. Although the win-lose negotiation strategy is not a politically correct approach, it is a commonly used negotiation strategy worldwide.

Win-Win Negotiation

The win-win negotiation strategy is about creative joint problem-solving, which develops long-term successful business relationships. The win-win negotiation strategy, however, may sometimes be difficult to accomplish. Among the obstacles to developing the win-win business environment are previous adverse government-contractor relations, lack of training in joint problem-solving and conflict resolution, and complex and highly regulated contracting procedures in some organizations, especially large companies and government agencies.

Winning or losing a contract negotiation is, indeed, a matter of perspective, which is based on a negotiator's knowledge, experience, and judgment. The only way to know whether a negotiation has been won or lost is to compare the results to the negotiation plan. Did you get what you wanted? Is what you got closer to your best-case, most-likely, or worst-case alternative? Clearly, without a contract negotiation plan, there is no basis against which to evaluate the negotiation outcome.   To achieve the desired contract negotiation results, you need not only a strategy, but also tactics and countertactics, which are a means to a desired end.

10. ***Develop a solid and approved team negotiation plan.*** The conclusion of contract negotiation planning should be a summary and documentation of all planned actions. If necessary, have the negotiation plan reviewed and approved by higher management to ensure that all planned actions are in the best interests of the organization (see Sample Form 7-7).

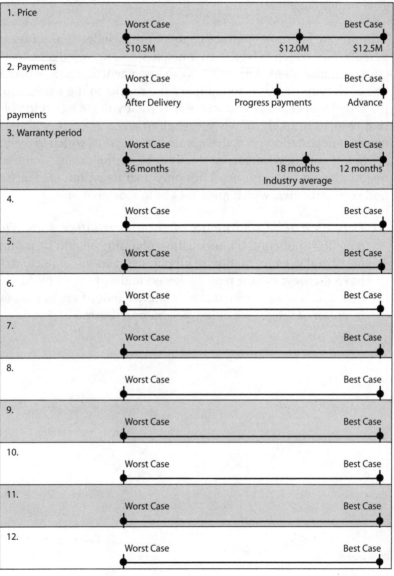

Form 7-7 Sample Negotiation Planning Summary

Possible Tactics and Countertactics

Objective	Planned Tactics — Government	Planned Countertactics — Contractor

Contract Price

Range
Best Case
Most Likely
Worst Case

Date Prepared:_____ Lead Negotiator:_____
Approved by:_____ Date Approved:_____

CONDUCT NEGOTIATION

The following activities are necessary to conduct the negotiation.

Determine who has authority. If possible, before the negotiation, determine who has the authority to negotiate for each party. At the start of the negotiation, establish (1) who has authority, (2) who the lead negotiator is for the other party, and (3) what limits, if any, are placed on the other party's authority.

Prepare the facility. Most government agencies want to conduct negotiations at their offices, which provides them with a sense of control. A contractor should try to conduct the negotiation at its location or at a neutral site, such as a hotel, conference center, via conference call, or NetMeeting.

Other key facility considerations include

- Size of the room;
- Use of break-out rooms;
- Lighting;

- Tables (size, shape, and arrangement);
- Seating arrangements;
- Use of audiovisual aids;
- Schedule (day and time); and
- Access to telephone, fax, e-mail/Internet, restrooms, food and drink.

Use an agenda. A proven best practice of successful negotiators worldwide is creating and using an agenda (see Form 7-8) for the negotiation. Provide the agenda to the other party before the negotiation begins. An effective agenda helps a negotiator to

- Set the right tone;
- Control the exchange of information;
- Keep the focus on the objectives;
- Manage time; and
- Obtain the desired results.

Form 7-8 Negotiation Agenda		
Contract		
Title		Date
Location		Time
Topics of Action		**Time**
❐ Introduce team members		_____
❐ Provide overview and discuss purpose of negotiation		_____
❐ Exchange information on key interests and issues		_____
❐ Quantity of products		_____
■ Quality of services		
■ Past performance		
■ Delivery schedule		
■ R&D, if any		
■ Training		
❐ Take a break		_____
❐ Review agreement on all key interests and issues		_____
❐ Agree on detailed terms and conditions		_____
❐ Agree on price		_____
❐ Review and summarize meeting		_____
Date Prepared:_____ Lead Negotiator:_____		

Introduce the team. Introduce the contracting team members or have team members make brief self-introductions. Try to establish a common bond with the other party as soon as possible.

Set the right tone. After introductions, make a brief statement to express team strategy to the other party. Set the desired climate for contract negotiation from the start.

Exchange information. Conducting contract negotiations is all about communication. Be aware that information is exchanged both orally and through body language, visual aids (pictures, diagrams, photographs, or videotapes), and active listening.

Focus on objectives. Never lose sight of the big picture.

Use strategy, tactics, and countertactics. Do what you say you will do, but be flexible in order to achieve objectives. Anticipate the other party's tactics, and plan countertactics, adjusting them as necessary.

Make counteroffers. A vital part of conducting negotiations is providing substitute offers, or counteroffers, when the other party does not accept an offer. All offers and counteroffers should be documented to ensure that both parties understand any changes in terms and conditions.

When offers and counteroffers are done right, they are part art and part science. A contractor should know the approximate range (monetary amount) a government agency intends to spend. In addition, a well-prepared contractor knows approximately what its competitors are likely to offer and their approximate price. Likewise, well- informed and prepared government agencies know what approximate range (monetary amount) contractors are likely to seek. When well-prepared government agencies and contractors enter into the exchange of offers and counteroffers, there should be a negotiation zone (see Table 7-2).

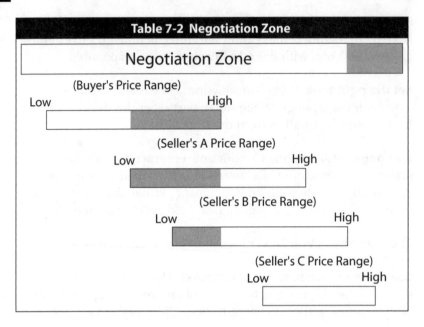

Table 7-2 Negotiation Zone

Given a competitive source business environment, contractors must ensure their initial offer is not so high that they will be eliminated from the competition. However, a contractor must also ensure that it maintains a healthy profit margin and still has room in its offer to give further price reductions if necessary to capture the business. Clearly, every contractor must perform a balancing act between the desire to win business versus the need to reduce/mitigate risks, while maximizing revenue and profit.

As illustrated in the Negotiation Zone (see Table 7-2), every government agency has a monetary range it expects to spend for the required products and/or services, which varies (low to high) based upon numerous variables typically contained within subcontract terms and conditions. Further, as depicted in Table 7-2, each contractor (A, B, or C) has a monetary range, typically described in its approved business case, within which it can make offers and counteroffers based upon its costs, risks, desired profit margin, and preferred terms and conditions.

Once both parties have made their initial offer, the fun really begins. How do you determine how much to move? Do you alter your terms and conditions in conjunction with changes in pricing? Do you offer a different type of pricing arrangement (e.g., from a fixed-price to a time & materials or cost-plus-fixed fee)? Should you refuse to move to force the other party to counteroffer? The answers to all of these questions is: it depends! This is why experienced, highly skilled master contract negotiators are a valuable asset to every organization involved in detailed, complex, and expensive contract negotiations.

Form 7-9 provides a simple, yet effective, means of documenting offers and counteroffers exchanged during subcontract negotiations. The number of offers and counteroffers typically exchanged are not as important as the value of the concessions made.

Form 7-9 Offers and Counteroffers Summary	
Government	**Contractor**
Offer	Counteroffer
Offer	Counteroffer
Offer	Counteroffer
Offer	Counteroffer
Date Prepared:_____	Lead Negotiator:_____

Document the agreement or know when to walk away. It is important to take time throughout the negotiation process to take notes on what was agreed to between the parties. If possible, assign a team member to record minutes. To ensure proper documentation, periodically summarize agreements on all major issues throughout the negotiation. At the end of the negotiation, summarize agreements both orally and in writing (see Form 7-10). If a settlement is not reached, document the areas of agreement and disagreement. If possible, plan a future meeting to resolve differences.

Remember: Do not agree to a bad deal; learn to say, "No thank you," and walk away.

Form 7-10 Negotiation Results Summary	
Contract Title	Date of Contract
Parties Involved	Date(s) of Negotiation
Brief Product/Service Description	Location
Agreed to Price	
Key changes from Approved Proposal	
Date Prepared:_____ Lead Negotiator:_____	

DOCUMENT NEGOTIATIONS AND FORM A WINNING CONTRACT

The following activities are conducted to document the negotiation and form a winning contract.

Prepare the negotiation memorandum (minutes or notes). Document what was discussed during the negotiation in a memorandum, minutes, or notes. After the memorandum is word-processed, spell-checked, and edited, have it reviewed by someone within the contracting organization who attended the negotiation and someone who did not. Then determine whether they have a similar understanding of the negotiation results.

Send the memorandum to the other party. As promptly as possible, provide a copy of the documented memorandum of the contract negotiations to the other party. First, email or fax it to the other party; then send an original copy by either overnight or second-day mail. Verify that the other party receives the negotiation memorandum by following up with another e-mail or a telephone call or send by registered mail, return receipt requested.

Offer to write the contract. The contractor should offer to draft the agreement so that the issues are in the contractor's own words. Today, most government contracts are developed using electronic databases, which facilitate reviews, changes, and new submissions.

Prepare the contract. Writing a contract should be a team effort with an experienced contract management professional at the lead. Typically, automated standard organizational forms, modified as needed, are used with standard terms and conditions that were tailored during negotiation. At other times, a contract must be written in full. Ensure that no elements of the subcontract are missing by using a checklist (see Form 7-11). After the initial contract has been drafted, obtain all appropriate reviews and approvals, preferably through electronic data.

Form 7-11 Essential Contract Elements Checklist		
Project Name	Prepared by (Print)	Date Prepared
Customer	Telephone/Fax	e-mail
❏ Deliverables and prices (provide a list of deliverables and their prices)		
❏ Deliverable conformance specifications		
❏ Requirements in statement of work (determine SOW requirements not listed as deliverables)		
❏ Delivery requirements (list delivery requirements, deliverable packaging and shipping requirements, and service performance instructions)		
❏ Deliverable inspection and acceptance		
❏ Invoice and payment schedule and provisions (include in subcontract tracking summary)		
❏ Representations and certifications		
❏ Other terms and conditions		

Prepare negotiation results summary. Prepare an internal-use-only summary of key negotiation items that have changed since originally proposed. Many organizations have found such a summary to be a valuable tool for explaining changes to senior managers.

Obtain required reviews and approvals. Depending on organizational procedures, products, services, and other variables, one or more people may be required to review and approve the proposed subcontract before signature. Typically, the following departments or staff reviews a contract: project management, financial, legal, procurement or subcontract management, and senior management. Increasingly, organizations are using automated systems to draft subcontracts and transmit them internally for the needed reviews and approvals.

Send the contract to the other party for signature. Send a copy of the contract to the other party via email or fax, and then follow up by mailing two original copies. With all copies include an appropriate cover letter with a return mailing address and time/date suspense for prompt return. Verify receipt of the contract by phone or email. Today, many organizations, as well as the laws of many nations, recognize an electronic signature to be valid.

Provide copies of the contract to affected organizations. The contract is awarded officially after it is executed, signed by both parties, and delivered to both parties. Ensure that all other affected organizations or parties receive a copy.

Document lessons learned. Take the time to document everything that went well during the contract negotiation process. Even more important, document what did not go well and why, and what should be done to avoid those problems in the future.

Prepare the contract administration plan. At the end of the contract negotiation process, follow a proven best practice by having the team that negotiated the contract help the team that is responsible for administering it to develop a contract administration plan.

The following Table 7-3 provides a checklist of proven effective contract negotiation best practices. How many of the actions listed do you and your organization both know and do? Knowing what to do is good, but doing it is better!

Table 7-3 Checklist of Government — Contract Negotiation Best Practices

The Government Should:

- ☐ Know what you want-lowest price or best value
- ☐ State your requirements in performance terms and evaluate accordingly
- ☐ Conduct market research about potential sources before selection
- ☐ Evaluate potential sources promptly and dispassionately
- ☐ Follow the evaluation criteria stated in the solicitation: management, technical, and price
- ☐ Use absolute, minimum, or relative evaluation standards to measure performance as stated in your solicitation
- ☐ Develop organizational policies to guide and facilitate the source selection process
- ☐ Use a weighting system to determine which evaluation criteria are most important
- ☐ Use a screening system to prequalify sources
- ☐ Obtain independent estimates from consultants or outside experts to assist in source selection
- ☐ Use past performance as a key aspect of source selection, and verify data accuracy
- ☐ Conduct price realism analysis
- ☐ Create a competitive analysis report
- ☐ Use oral presentations or proposals by subcontractors to improve and expedite the source selection process

The Government and Contractor Should:

- ☐ Understand that contract negotiation is a process, usually involving a team effort
- ☐ Select and train highly skilled negotiators to lead the contract negotiation process
- ☐ Know market and industry practices
- ☐ Prepare yourself and your team
- ☐ Know the other party
- ☐ Know the big picture
- ☐ Identify and prioritize objectives
- ☐ Create options-be flexible in your planning
- ☐ Examine alternatives
- ☐ Select your negotiation strategy, tactics, and countertactics
- ☐ Develop a solid and approved team negotiation plan
- ☐ Determine who has the authority to negotiate
- ☐ Prepare the negotiation facility at your location or at a neutral site
- ☐ Use an agenda during contract negotiation
- ☐ Set the right tone at the start of the negotiation
- ☐ Maintain your focus on your objectives
- ☐ Use interim summaries to keep on track
- ☐ Do not be too predictable in your tactics
- ☐ Document your agreement throughout the process
- ☐ Know when to walk away
- ☐ Offer to write the contract
- ☐ Prepare a negotiation results summary
- ☐ Obtain required reviews and approvals
- ☐ Provide copies of the contract to all affected parties
- ☐ Document negotiation lessons learned and best practices
- ☐ Prepare a transition plan for contract administration
- ☐ Understand that everything affects price
- ☐ Understand the Ts and Cs have cost, risk, and value
- ☐ Tailor Ts and Cs to the deal, but understand the financial effects on price and profitability
- ☐ Know what is negotiable and what is not

DESIRED OUTPUTS

Contract. The output from negotiations and contract formation may be the contract, which is both a document and a relationship between parties.

Or it may be best to—

Walk away. Do not agree to a bad deal. No business is better than bad business.

SUMMARY

Outsourcing is essential to business in the public sector. Many simple and smaller value business transactions are routinely accomplished using self-service electronic catalogs, procurement cards, or e-auctions. However, most large, complex business-to-business transactions still require more formal contract negotiation and formation. Clearly, less face-to-face or in-person interaction is required, in today's government business, because of the numerous advances in communication technologies—video conferences, 'Net meetings, teleconferences, emails, e-documents, electronic signatures, and electronic funds transfers. However, the need for highly-skilled contract negotiators who understand the process and have mastered all of the inputs, tools and techniques to achieve the desired outputs is more important now than ever before!

Negotiation and contract formation is vital to the success of prime contractors and subcontractors worldwide. When skilled contract negotiators follow a proven pro¬cess approach, successful business agreements are reached. Through effective contract formation practices, win-win contracts are developed and documented, yielding beneficial results for both parties.

Remember the words of Dr. Chester Karrass, author, consultant, and master contract negotiator, "You don't get what you deserve, you get what you have the ability to negotiate." The primary focus of this chapter is mastering the contract negotiation process by using a logical, organized, documented, step-by-step approach to building successful business relationships. The highly effective contract negotiation process discussed in this chapter has been taught to more than 25,000 business professionals worldwide via the National Contract Management Association (NCMA), The George

Washington University School of Business, The Keller Graduate School of DeVry University, Villanova University On-Line Masters Certificate Program in Contract Management, the University of California at Los Angeles, and the U.S. Naval Postgraduate School, to name just a few, with outstanding results. I hope that you will consider using the contract negotiation process, forms, and best practices discussed in this chapter.

The next chapter more closely examines the importance of managing services contracts after a contract has been awarded by the U.S. government.

QUESTIONS TO CONSIDER

1. Does your organization have a logical, documented, and proven successful contract negotiation process?

2. Do you consistently achieve your desired negotiation results?

3. Has your organization walked away from any potential bad deals in the past year? If so, how many and why?

4. What actions has your organization taken to help improve and/ or develop stronger negotiation skills for your sales managers, project managers, and contract managers?

5. How well do you document and share your negotiation lessons learned?

ENDNOTES

[1] Zartman, I. William, ed., *The Negotiation Process* (Beverly Hills: Sage Publications, 1978).

[2] William Ury, *Getting Past No* (New York: Bantam Books, 1993).

[3] Ibid.

CHAPTER 8

PHASE 6: CONTRACT ADMINISTRATION AND CLOSEOUT

By Gregory A. Garrett

INTRODUCTION

Phase 6 of the U.S. Government Services Contracting Buying and Selling LifeCycle focuses on successfully conducting contract administration and closeout. For more than three decades, U.S. government audits conducted by numerous agencies and watchdog groups have indicated the real and compelling need for improved post-award contract administration by government and industry. In both the public and private business sectors, contract administration is often an afterthought, usually insufficiently staffed in both the quality and quantity of resources (contract manager, project manager, technical managers, property managers, supply chain/subcontract managers, etc.). Typically, government and industry focus their time, attention, and key resources on soliciting, proposing, negotiating, and forming the contract—simply stated, getting the deal. As a result, there are often limited resources to manage, administer, and close out a contract.

While project management and earned value management have received significant focus and attention in recent years for the value-added capabilities they can provide, few organizations have focused much attention on post-award contract administration and closeout activities, which are equally vital to business success.

This chapter focuses on the importance of having the right people and processes in place to manage the growing number, value, and complexity of contracts in order to ensure that U.S. government agencies are able to obtain quality products, services, and/or solutions from government contractors and subcontractors.

CONTRACT ADMINISTRATION: PEOPLE AND WORKLOAD

As noted above, both U.S. government agencies and contractors are highly focused on awarding/receiving contracts and spending money. Yet both U.S. government agencies and government contractors currently experience a shortage of talent to effectively and efficiently manage the massive growth of U.S. government spending. Since fiscal year 2000 the U.S. government's spending has increased from $219 billion to more than $600 billion in FY 2010. In addition, the number of transactions or contracts awarded by U.S. government agencies during the same period of time has grown from 500,000 transactions in FY 2000 to over 10 million in FY 2010.

EIGHT

This tremendous spending growth during the George W. Bush administration was largely the result of numerous converging factors, including:

- Global War on Terrorism,
- Creation of the Department of Homeland Security,
- Significant Natural Disasters,
- Demographics—Aging of the Baby-Boomers,
- Rising Health Care Costs, and
- Economic Recovery Expenses Due to Recession.

Since the start of the Obama administration, U.S. government spending has gone to even higher levels, especially in the Department of Health and Human Services, Housing and Urban Development, Treasury, Labor, Education, Energy, Transportation, and Environmental Protection Agency, to provide for the growing demand for services, economic stimulus, and bailout of financial institutions Freddie Mac and Fannie Mae, automobile manufacturers; and others.

Thus, during the past decade U.S. government contracts have grown dramatically in:

- Number/quantity (up 14 times since FY 2000),
- Dollar amount/value – (up 3 times since FY 2000), and
- Complexity/integration of hardware, software, and professional services.

The number of people who are tasked to plan, negotiate, award, manage, administer, deliver/fulfill, and close out contracts and related projects, from both government and industry, has either remained the same or decreased in quantity. Additionally, both government and industry lack sufficient education and training to keep abreast of the dramatic increase in the complexity of the government's requirements and its increased spending.

From the U.S. government's perspective, the following job titles and/or roles are critical to its ability to acquire and manage products, services, and solutions obtained from industry to meet the needs of its respective agencies (see Table 8-1).

Table 8-1 Key Government People and/or Roles	
• Program Manager	• Contracts Specialist/Administrator
• Systems Engineer	• Government Property Manager
• Contracting Officer	• Budget/Financial Analyst
• Contracting Officer's Technical Representative	• Quality Assurance Specialist
• Lawyer	• Logistics Manager
• Cost/Price Analyst	• Others

During the past decade many of the people who performed these vital government acquisition positions have retired, transferred to other positions within government, moved to a position within industry, changed career fields, or some combination of the above.

From the industry or government contractor's perspective, the following similar job titles and/or roles are critical to the ability to win and successfully deliver on U.S. government contracts, subcontracts, and related projects (see Table 8-2).

Table 8-2 Key Industry People and/or Roles	
• Program Manager	• Logistics/Supply Chain Manager
• Systems Engineer	• Lawyer
• Contracts Manager	• Project Control Manager
• Subcontract Manager	• Business Development Manager
• Bid/Proposal/Capture Manager	• Account Manager
• Cost/Price Analyst	• Accountants/Financial Manager
• Contract Administrator	• Property Manager
• Buyers/Purchasing Specialist	• Others

Both U.S. government agencies and industry have heavily invested in numerous technology-based tools to improve their buying and selling, including software applications, hardware platforms, enterprise resource planning (ERP) systems, and other information technology (IT) related systems. However, many of these IT- and ERP-related investments have never achieved the promised results. Clearly, the U.S. government's buying and industry's selling of commercially available off-the-shelf products and services has been tremendously expedited by the expansion of the following:

- Internet-based business,
- Electronic Data Interchange (EDI),
- Electronic Funds Transfer (EFT),
- Electronic signatures,
- Electronic sales catalogs,
- Federal supply schedules (FSS),
- Government-wide acquisition contracts (GWACs),

- Blanket purchase agreements (BPAs), and
- Indefinite delivery indefinite quantity (IDIQ) contracts.

While a majority of the U.S. government's contracts are firm-fixed-price (FFP) and are used to acquire relatively simple commercially available off-the-shelf products and services, they typically comprise less than 50 percent of the dollars spent by some government agencies. Conversely, a minority of U.S. government contracts are cost-reimbursement or time-and-materials (T&M) contracts, which are typically used to acquire highly complex systems, integrated solutions, and a vast array of professional services. Yet these cost-reimbursement type contracts and time-and-materials (T&M) type contracts together often account for over 50 percent of the dollars spent by some government agencies.

What is driving the growing amount of money being spent by the U.S. government's acquisition of complex systems, integrated solutions, and professional services? The answer is the following converging factors:

- Increased threat of global terrorism,
- Evolving communication technologies,
- High services integration cost for hardware and software,
- Increased customer demands,
- Less government personnel with needed professional services expertise,
- Less government technical expertise to develop more detailed/defined requirements,
- Increased reliance on information technology platforms, related hardware, and software applications, and
- Other factors.

Type of Contract and Contract Administration

Why does the type of contract matter when it comes to contract administration? The answer is simple; when a firm-fixed-price (FFP) contract is awarded, the U.S. government has very low financial risk, because the contractor has agreed to perform the contract for a fixed amount of money. If the contractor can adequately perform the work for less, then it makes a higher profit. If, however, it takes the contractor more than the fixed amount to accomplish the work, then the contractor losses money. Thus, government agencies typically perform little contract administration on FFP contracts, because the contractor has the greatest financial risk.

Conversely, when a cost-reimbursement (CR) contract or a time-and-materials (T&M) contract is awarded, the U.S. government has higher potential financial risk. In the case of a cost-reimbursement contract, the government has agreed that the nature of the work is too difficult to adequately define at the start. Thus, on a cost-reimbursement contract the government is essentially purchasing a contractor's best efforts and promising to reimburse the contractor for all of its allowable, allocable, and reasonable expenses. Depending upon the type of cost-reimbursement contract, the contractor may receive an incentive fee, award fee, and/or fixed-fee, which is subject to specific Federal Acquisition Regulation (FAR) limitations.

In the case of a T&M contract the government has agreed that the nature of the professional services is too difficult to adequately define and scope out at the start. Thus, on a T&M contract the government is purchasing the contractor's best efforts for specific services in specific labor categories, plus related materials. In a T&M contract the time consists of a fully-loaded wrap-rate (direct cost, indirect cost, and profit) for each specific labor category on an hourly-rate basis. In a T&M contract the material consists of the total material costs, plus any related handling costs, but it does not typically include any profit, which is prohibited by FAR.

Since cost-reimbursement and T&M contracts place greater financial risk on U.S. government agencies, they are less preferred. Despite the fact that cost-reimbursement and T&M contracts are not preferred, they are and have been for many years the contracts upon which U.S. government agencies spend most of their money in buying systems, services, and integrated solutions. As a result, U.S. government agencies have struggled to provide the necessary contract administration support services and surveillance appropriate to help guide contractors, mitigate risks, and ensure successful programs.

CONTRACT ADMINISTRATION PROCESS

Contract administration can be straightforward or complex depending on the nature and size of a project. Administering a contract entails creating a contract administration plan and then monitoring performance throughout the many, varied activities that can occur during project execution. Key contract administration activities include ensuring compliance with contract terms and conditions; practicing effective communication and control; managing contract changes, invoicing, and payment; and resolving claims and disputes. Paying a contractor more money for doing more work than was originally agreed upon in a contract is both fair and reasonable. Likewise, an appropriate remedy is applicable if a contractor fails to properly perform work or fails to comply with the terms and conditions of a contract. Tailored project management and contract administration procedures are essential to ensure that both parties know what is expected of them at all times; to avoid unpleasant surprises and reduce risks regarding requirements, costs, or schedule-related issues; and to solve problems quickly when they occur.

However, government customers do sometimes consider contractors who effectively manage their contracts and actively pursue payment for contract changes to be nickel-and-diming them. Some contractors intentionally "low bid or underprice" an initial bid in order to get a contract on the bet that they can make enough follow-on sales to offset the initial loss and create a profitable long-term business relationship. Often government buyers are so motivated to reduce initial capital expenditures to fit their reduced budgets that they will essentially entice sellers into an initial low bid/buy-in business model.

Effectively managing the contract scope of work through proven project and contract management best practices is wise and financially prudent for both the government and industry. The government needs to ensure that it gets what it pays for and gets it when it needs it! Contractors need to ensure that they will provide the products and/or services as and when they agree to deliver them.

Post-award contract administration is the process of ensuring that each party's performance meets contractual requirements. On larger projects with multiple product and service providers, a key aspect of contract administration is managing the interfaces among the various providers. Because of the legal nature of the contractual relationship, the project team must be acutely aware of the legal implications of actions taken when administering a contract.

Effective contract administration is critical to effective project management because an organization's failure to fulfill its contractual obligations can have legal consequences. Thus, someone must oversee the performance of contractual obligations. That person is the contract manager, who must always be aware of the legal and financial consequences of an action or failure to act and who must take steps to ensure required actions are taken and prohibited actions are avoided. In a real sense, a contract manager is a project manager, and the principles of project management apply to his or her work.

Each party to a contract appoints a contract manager who monitors not only his or her own organization, but also the other party to ensure that both parties are keeping their promises. The contract manager must maintain these two perspectives throughout contract performance.

The post-award phase of the contract management process (see Figure 8-1) includes applying the appropriate contract administration and project management actions to the contractual relationships and integrating the output from these best practices into the general management of the project.

Figure 8-1 Post-Award Contract Administration Process

Key Inputs	Tools & Techniques	Desire Outputs
Contract	Project management discipline	Documentation
Project plans & schedules	Opportunity and risk management	Contract Changes
Work results	Contract changes management	Payment
Contract change requests	Contract analysis & planning	Completion of work
Invoices	Kick-off meeting or pre-performance conference	
	Contract claims and dispute resolution	
	Government Property management	
	Performance measuring & reporting (earned value management system)	
	Contract closeout checklists	

KEY INPUTS

Input to the post-award phase of the contract management process consists of the following items:

Contract

The contract document is the primary guide for project execution and administration of the contract.

Project Plans and Schedules

The project manager prepares appropriate plans to ensure the work is properly completed on time, on budget, and meets contractual requirements. Such planning can include a work breakdown structure (WBS), organizational breakdown structure (OBS), responsibility assignment matrix (RAM), schedules (Gantt charts, milestone charts, project network schedules, etc.), and an earned value management system (EVMS). In addition, the contract manager should develop a contract requirements matrix (see Form 8-1).

Form 8-1 Contract Requirements Matrix				
Deliverables				
Description	Contract Reference	Delivery Date or Services Date	Work Breakdown Structure Element	Other Reference

Work Results

The results of performing the contract requirements will affect contract administration.

Contract Change Requests

Contract change requests are a common element of most contracts. An effective process for managing contract changes must be in place to ensure that all requests are handled smoothly. Contract changes may be called amendments, modifications, change orders, supplemental agreements, add-ons, up-scopes, or down-scopes.

Contract changes are opportunities either to increase or decrease profitability for the seller. Changes are a necessary aspect of business for buyers because of changes in their needs.

Invoices

An efficient process must be developed for handling invoices throughout contract administration. Few areas cause more concern to sellers than late payment. Buyers can realize savings by developing an efficient and timely payment process because sellers are often willing to give discounts for early payment.

TOOLS AND TECHNIQUES

The following tools and techniques are used for contract administration.

Project Management Discipline

All work to be performed should be appropriately led, planned, scheduled, coordinated, communicated, tracked, evaluated, reported, and corrected, as necessary, using the basic guidelines of the Project Management Institute (PMI) *Project Management Body of Knowledge (PMBOK)*.

Contract Analysis and Planning

Before contract award, each party should develop a contract administration plan and assign the responsibility of administering the contract to a contract manager. To whom should the job be assigned? A project manager can do double duty as a contract manager. However, in most large companies, contract administration is a specialized function usually performed by someone in the contracting department, because doing the job requires special knowledge and training. Contract administration is an element of both contract and project management.

Kickoff Meeting or Pre-performance Conference

Before performance begins, the government and industry should meet (via teleconference, videoconference, Web meeting, or face-to-face) to discuss their joint administration of the contract (see Form 8-2). The meeting should be formal, agenda should be distributed in advance, and minutes should be recorded and distributed. Each party should appoint a person who will be its organization's official voice during contract performance. At the meeting, the parties should review the contract terms and conditions and discuss each other's roles. The parties also should establish protocols for written and oral communication and progress measurement and reporting and discuss procedures for managing changes and resolving differences. Government and contractor managers with performance responsibilities should attend the pre-performance conference or at least send a representative. Important subcontractors also should be represented. The meeting should be held shortly after contract award at the performance site if possible.

Form 8-2 Pre-performance Conference Checklist	
Project Name	
Prepared by (Print)	Date Prepared:
Customer	Contract
Contact Telephone/E-mail	

☐	Complete requirements analysis – verify and validate the requirements stated in the contract to ensure that the project, when completed according to the requirement statement, will meet the needs of both parties.
☐	Summarize contract requirements – complete a contract requirements matrix (see Form 8-1).
☐	Establish the project baseline – ensure that the baseline and specifications are established.
☐	Develop in-scope and out-of-scope listings – develop lists of items that the government and contractor consider within and outside the scope of the contract.
☐	List the contractor's assumptions about the government's requirements and understanding of the end-user's expectations.
☐	Establish preliminary schedule of meetings between the parties.
☐	Inform the team and other affected parties – brief the team members who will attend the meeting, ensuring they understand the basic requirements of the contract and the project.
☐	Review meeting findings with all affected people in your organization.
☐	Document who attended, what was discussed, what was agreed to, and what follow-up actions are required – by whom, where, and when.
☐	Prepare and send pre-performance conference meeting minutes to the other parties.

Performance Measurement and Reporting

During contract performance, the project manager, contract manager, and responsible business managers all must observe performance, collect information, and measure actual contract progress. These activities are essential to effective control of a project. The resources devoted to these tasks and the techniques used to perform them will depend on the nature of the contract work, the size and complexity of the contract, and the resources available. On large, complex contracts, the government often requires the contractor to apply an earned value management system (EVMS) to ensure that all aspects of cost, schedule, and technical performance are effectively integrated and successfully implemented.

Payment Process

Every contract must establish a clear invoicing and payment process. The government and contractor must agree to whom invoices should be sent and what information is required. Contractors must submit proper invoices in a timely manner, and the government is then required to pay all invoices promptly.

Contract Change Management Process

As a rule, any party that can make a contract can agree to change it. Changes are usually inevitable in contracts for complex undertakings such as system design and integration. No one has perfect foresight;– requirements and circumstances change in unexpected ways, and contract terms and conditions must often be changed as a result.

Dispute Resolution Process

No one should be surprised when, from time to time, contracting parties find themselves in disagreement about the interpretation of contract terms and conditions. Such disagreements typically are minor and are resolved without too much difficulty. Occasionally, however, the parties find themselves entangled in a seemingly intractable controversy. Try as they might, they cannot resolve their differences. If the dispute goes unresolved for too long, one or both of the parties may threaten, or even initiate, litigation.

Litigation is time-consuming, costly, and risky, and one can never be entirely sure of its result. Rarely is the outcome of litigation a truly satisfactory resolution of a dispute, and it sours the business relationships. For these reasons, litigation should be avoided. One goal of business managers and contract managers is to resolve disputes without litigation whenever possible.

For effective dispute resolution, one must

- Recognize that contract documents are not perfect,
- Keep larger objectives in mind,
- Focus on the facts,
- De-personalize the issues, and
- Be willing to make reasonable compromises.

When disputes become intractable, seeking the opinion of an impartial third party can sometimes help. When this approach is formal and the decision is binding on the parties, it is called arbitration. Many government agencies now include a clause in their contracts that make arbitration the mandatory means of resolving disputes.

Government Property Management

FAR Part 45 specifies the numerous government property management requirements for both government agencies and industry.

Contract Closeout Process

Contract closeout refers to verification that all administrative matters are concluded on a contract that is otherwise physically complete. In other words, the contractor has delivered the required supplies or performed the required services, and the government has inspected and accepted the supplies or services (see Form 8-3).

Form 8-3 Contract Closeout Checklist					
Project Name					
Prepared by (print)				Date Prepared	
Customer				Contract	
Contract Telephone/E-mail					
1.	□ yes	□ no	□ n/a	All products or services required were provided to the buyer.	
2.	□ yes	□ no	□ n/a	Documentation adequately shows receipt and formal acceptance of all contract items.	
3.	□ yes	□ no	□ n/a	No claims or investigations are pending on this contract.	
4.	□ yes	□ no	□ n/a	Any buyer-furnished property or information was returned to the buyer.	
5.	□ yes	□ no	□ n/a	All actions related to contract price revisions and changes are concluded.	
6.	□ yes	□ no	□ n/a	All outstanding subcontracting issues are settled.	
7.	□ yes	□ no	□ n/a	If a partial or complete termination was involved, action is complete.	
8.	□ yes	□ no	□ n/a	Any required contract audit is now complete	

OUTPUT

The following output functions result from contract administration.

Documentation

Documentation is essential to provide proof of performance, management of changes, justification for claims, and evidence in the unlikely event of litigation. The most important documentation is the official copy of the contract, contract modifications, and conformed working copies of the contract. Other important forms of documentation include:

- *External and internal correspondence.* All appropriate contract correspondence should be saved electronically by the contract manager and project managers, with separate files for external and internal correspondence. Each piece of correspondence should be dated and properly stored electronically.

- *Meeting minutes.* Minutes should be recorded electronically for all meetings between the seller and buyer. The minutes should state the date, time, and location of the meeting and identify all attendees by name, company or organization, and title. The minutes should describe all issues discussed, decisions made, questions unresolved, and action items assigned. Copies of the minutes should be provided to each attendee and to others interested in the meeting but unable to attend.

- *Progress reports.* Progress reports should be saved electronically and filed chronologically by subject.

- *Project diaries.* On large projects, the project manager and contract manager should keep a daily diary to record significant events. They should update their diaries at the end of each workday. The entries should describe events in terms of who, what, when, where, and how. Preferably, the diary should have daily entries and be kept in electronic form or in a bound book with pre-numbered pages. A diary supplements memory and aids in recalling events, and is useful as an informal project history when a new project manager or contract manager must take over. It can be of great assistance in preparing, negotiating, and settling claims, or in the event of litigation. However, a diary may become evidence in court proceedings, so a diarist should be careful to record only facts, leaving out conclusions, speculations about motives, and personal opinions about people or organizations.

■ *Telephone logs.* Another useful aid to memory is a telephone log, which is a record of all incoming and outgoing calls. It identifies the date and time of each call, whether it was incoming or outgoing, and if outgoing, the number called. It lists all parties to a call and includes a brief notation about the discussion.

■ *Photographs and videotapes.* When physical evidence of conditions at the site of performance is important, a photographic or videotape record can be helpful. This record will greatly facilitate communication and provides a description of the exact nature of site conditions. Whenever a contract involves physical labor, the project manager, contract manager, or other on-site representative should have a camera and film or a digital camera available for use. The purpose of documentation is to record facts and reduce reliance on human memory. Efforts to maintain documentation must be thorough and consistent.

■ *Contract changes.* As a result of changes in buyers' needs, changes in the technologies, and other changes in the marketplace, buyers need flexibility in their contracts. Thus, changes are inevitable. Sellers must realize that changes are not bad but are in fact good, because changes are often an opportunity to sell additional products or services.

Payment

Cash is important as sellers want their money as quickly as possible. The government should seek product and service discounts for early payment. Likewise, contractors should improve their accounts receivable management and enforce late payment penalties.

Completion of Work and Communication

The completion of work, the last step, is the contractor's actual accomplishment of the government's requirement for products, services, systems, or solutions.

Ensuring that the parties to the contract communicate with each other is important as a contract is a relationship. Because virtually every contract entails some degree of interaction between the parties, each must keep the other informed of its progress, problems, and proposed solutions, so that the other can respond appropriately.

Like all human relationships, contracts are dynamic. As performance proceeds and events unfold, the parties may find that they must modify their original expectations and plans to adjust to real events. As they do so, they must modify the contract terms and conditions to reflect the current status of their agreement. Changes are an inevitable part of contracting, because no one can predict the future with perfect accuracy. However, the parties should make changes consciously and openly, so that they remain in agreement about what they should be doing. Lack of communication can result in disputes over what each party's obligations really are.

An important part of communication and control is the effective management of changes. Effectively managing contract changes includes establishing formal procedures for modifying the contract and limiting the number of people entitled to make changes. It also entails establishing recognition and notification procedures in response to authorized changes. Finally, it requires establishing procedures for identifying, estimating, and measuring the potential and actual effect of changes on all aspects of contract performance. Form 8-4 provides a checklist of tips for successful contract administration.

Form 8-4 Checklist of Tips for Successful Contract Administration

- ☐ Develop and implement a project management discipline to ensure on-time delivery and flawless execution.
- ☐ Comply with contract terms and conditions.
- ☐ Maintain effective communications.
- ☐ Manage contract changes with a proactive change management process.
- ☐ Resolve disputes promptly and dispassionately.
- ☐ Use negotiation or arbitration, not litigation, to resolve disputes.
- ☐ Develop a work breakdown structure to assist in planning and assigning work.
- ☐ Conduct pre-performance conferences or a project kick-off meeting.
- ☐ Measure, monitor, and track performance.
- ☐ Manage the invoice and payment process.
- ☐ Report the progress internally and externally.
- ☐ Identify variances between planned versus actual performance – use earned value management.
- ☐ Be sure to follow up on all corrective actions.
- ☐ Appoint authorize people to negotiate contract changes and document the authorized representatives in the contract.
- ☐ Enforce contract terms and conditions.
- ☐ Provide copies of the contract to all affected organizations.
- ☐ Maintain conformed copies of the contract.
- ☐ Understand the effects of change on cost, schedule, and quality.
- ☐ Document all communication – use telephone, faxes, correspondence logs, and e-mails.
- ☐ Prepare internal and external meeting minutes.
- ☐ Prepare contract closeout checklists.
- ☐ Ensure completion of work.
- ☐ Document lessons learned and share them throughout your organization.
- ☐ Communicate, communicate, and communicate.

SUMMARY

Contract administration is an important aspect of successful business. Simply stated, contract administration is the joint government and contractor action taken to successfully perform and administer a contractual agreement, including effective changes management and timely contract closeout. The ongoing challenge is maintaining open and effective communication, timely delivery of quality products and services, responsive corrective actions to problems, compliance with all agreed-upon terms and conditions, and effective changes management. After a project is successfully completed, proper procedures are necessary to officially close out the contract.

Of course, the goal of nearly every contractor is to capture the government's follow-on business, which is far easier to do if the contract and related project were properly managed by both parties. Remember, achieving a true partnership between government and industry requires dedication and discipline by both parties, not just one!

Remember, too, the power of precedent. A contracting organization is always evaluated based on its past performance and the precedents it sets. The contract administration actions taken years ago affect an organization's reputation today. Likewise, in both government and industry the contract management actions that a party takes today form the organization's reputation for tomorrow.

QUESTIONS TO CONSIDER

1. How well does your organization select and staff post-award contract administration?

2. How effective is your organization in managing post-award contract changes?

3. On a scale of 1(low/poor) to 10 (high) how do you rate your organization's ability to efficiently and cost-effectively conduct contract administration and ensure successful contract results?

MANAGING SERVICE CONTRACTS IN THE DEPARTMENT OF DEFENSE: OPPORTUNITIES AND CHALLENGES

By Uday Apte, Geraldo Ferrer, Ira Lewis, and Rene Rendon

INTRODUCTION

The Department of Defense's (DoD) services acquisition volume has continued to increase in scope and dollars in the past decade. Between FY 1999 to FY 2003, DoD's spending on services increased by 66%, and in FY 2003, the DoD spent over $118 billion or approximately 57% of its total procurement dollars on services.[1] In recent years, DoD has spent more on services than on supplies, equipment, and goods, even considering the high value of weapon systems and large military items.[2] These services belong to a very broad set of activities ranging from grounds maintenance to space launch operations. The major categories include professional, administrative, and management support; construction, repair, and maintenance of facilities and equipment; information technology; research and development; and medical care.

As DoD's services acquisition volume continues to increase in scope and dollars, the agency must focus greater attention on proper acquisition planning, adequate requirements definition, sufficient price evaluation, and proper contractor oversight.[3] In many ways, these are the same issues affecting the acquisition of physical supplies and weapon systems. However, there are important differences between the production, acquisition, and delivery of services and manufactured goods. For example, services cannot be inventoried, require customer contact and joint production, and have customer-specific inputs. Moreover, intangibility in varying degrees makes it difficult to evaluate the quality and performance of a service operation.[4] The unique characteristics of services and the increasing importance of services acquisition offer a significant opportunity for conducting research in the management of the service supply chain within the Department of Defense.

SERVICE CHARACTERISTICS AND THEIR IMPLICATIONS FOR CONTRACTING

Service production differs from manufacturing in several ways. In many operational contexts, the key issues that are identified include the intangibility of service output, the difficulty of portability, and complexity in the definition and measurement of services (for example, see Fitzsimmons and Fitzsimmons[5]). Additionally, services often involve joint production between a buyer and a supplier. These characteristics create certain differences in the production and marketing of services. For example, the joint production aspect means that the productive system is often not buffered from the customer. The customer is often present and even participates in the production process, while simultaneously being a consumer. The resulting need for "customer contact" has been analyzed in the seminal work of Chase[6] to categorize different types of service firms and sectors. In this section the effect of some of the special characteristics of services on issues related to outsourcing of services and contracting for service delivery are examined.

Characteristics of Services

There is a growing body of literature on operations management in service firms. Special characteristics of service operations are discussed in textbooks[7] and in casebooks.[8]

Managing quality in service businesses, although similar in spirit to that in manufacturing, is somewhat different and relatively more challenging due to certain inherent characteristics of service operations. These include the intangibility of service outcome in some cases and the presence and participation of customers in the creation of many services. Intangibility of outputs results in difficulties in matching demand and supply since the output cannot be inventoried. This is, however, not meant to suggest that lack of inventory is a characteristic of services. In fact, as exemplified by a restaurant, managing the inventory of supplies (termed as tangible goods[9]) can be very critical to the success of a service enterprise.

The diversity of services makes generalizations that are helpful for managers of service businesses difficult. Lovelock[10] proposes five schemes for classifying services that offer insight for marketing and operations managers in different service businesses. Lovelock, Quinn, and Schmenner also provide suggestions for managing services business.[11] have also been proposed Chase's proposed theory of a customer contact approach to services holds that services that entail a high degree of customer contact have inherently smaller potential for efficiency due to the variability and uncertainty that customers introduce in the creation of services.[12] Apte and Mason propose that customer contact be conceptualized in two ways: first, in terms of propinquity, or a physical presence, involving a face-to-face contact between the customer and service provider, and second, in terms of a symbolic contact where the main purpose of customer contact is to exchange the information necessary in service creation and consumption.[13] It should be noted that a service activity, in general, requires a combination of both types of customer contact. With the progress of information technology, the symbolic portion of the contact is being increasingly automated. In many cases, information technology is also being used for redefining or reengineering services.

Closely related to the concept of customer contact is the service characteristic of co-production. Not only do customers have a presence during the service creation process, but they may have significant tasks to perform as well. Examples range from self-service at gasoline stations and salad bars to the shared responsibility for communication in diagnostic services and tailored financial services (including tax preparation). In some cases, a customer's participation in joint production is rather passive. But in other cases, such as financial planning or education, the participation may be very active and very significant in determining the quality of service production. Indeed, education is a major service sector for which an active role of the customer is absolutely critical. In the prototypical manufacturing case, customers' roles start after production has been completed. To the extent that this is not the case—for example, custom production of manufactured goods with customer-provided blueprints—the manufacturing business takes on more of the character of a service.

As noted above, many services have outputs that are intangible and difficult to measure.[14] For example, in services such as medical examinations or tax planning, output is quite intangible. Output of sales transactions involving manufactured goods can be metered rather easily with respect to the quantities involved. However, the delivered "quantity" of business consulting or medical services is rather more difficult to measure. In such cases, it is difficult for the buyer and the vendor to easily agree on exactly what output has been supplied. A serious confounding problem is that it is difficult to distinguish between the level of attributes of services and the quantity of services. For example, it may be hard to say whether medical advice is more correct, more thorough, more considerate of the patient, or simply more.

In textbook discussions of service operations, services are often described as being complex. A part of this complexity arises from the difficulties in measurement noted above. A second part arises from the joint production or custom character of many services, which in turn has two effects. First, the presence of the customer means that the service process cannot be separated from service output. The obvious consequence is a much larger set of attributes for customer evaluation. Moreover, the customer brings to the process a set of expectations and capabilities, as well as material inputs, that are specific to that customer. As a result, the output of the process as perceived by the customer may involve many customer-specific attributes. Participation in the production process is in itself a complex issue with some internal costs but possibly some consumption value as well. All these threads may be very difficult to untangle. For example, consider a class in a management course, with the students (possibly organized into groups) and instructors interacting in the course of a case discussion. It is nearly impossible in practice to measure the educational output received by any one student in an objective way, either in terms of quantity or attribute levels.

The special features of services lead to significant differences in the process of production, sale, and consumption of services. These in turn have implications for market structure, pricing, and contracting for services. Karmarkar and Pitbladdo present some key features regarding service contracting that are relevant to the development of a service quality model.[15] First and foremost, service operations are always post-contractual. Fixed-price contracts centered on output specifications can fail on two accounts. First, conceiving or verifying meaningful output specifications is difficult, and second, the variability of customer inputs and joint production makes fixed-price contracts risky for a firm even when the output specifications can be well defined. Alternatively, contracts based on process specifications, such as time and materials, may be unsuitable because they are risky for customers. These dual risks for firms/sellers and for customers/buyers can be addressed via stage-wise or contingent contracting, where the process is broken into stages and the price for a given stage is made dependent on the outputs of previous stages. For example, there may be a fixed fee for a diagnosis and a fixed fee for treatment which, however, depends on the outcome of the diagnosis. The uncertainty in customer inputs is resolved by the diagnosis before it materializes in terms of treatment cost.

Service Quality

Corporate experience indicates that customer satisfaction and high service quality lead to greater long-term profitability.[16] The topic of service quality, therefore, has received increasing attention during the last few decades. Deming[17] and Crosby[18] are notable examples of practitioner viewpoints on quality management. Gronroos provided one of the early research papers that explicitly dealt with service quality.[19] Adopting a customer's viewpoint, service quality is conceptualized by Parasuraman, Berry and Zeithaml as the difference between the service quality expectations of a customer and the quality of service delivery performance perceived by a customer.[20] Zeithaml, Parasuraman, and Berry provide a detailed discussion of their service quality model and the associated survey instrument, SERVQUAL.[21] Other research literature on service quality includes comprehensive collections of readings.[22] Chase and Bowen discuss service quality issues in terms of three elements of service delivery systems: (1) technology, (2) systems, and (3) people.[23] Apte, Karmarkar, and Pitbladdo provide a new framework for measuring and improving service quality.[24] In discussing the measurement and management of service quality, Collier examines the issues of definitions, standards and measurement, monitoring, and control of service quality.[25] The main conclusions of these researchers are:

- Customers find it more difficult to evaluate the quality of service as compared to the quality of goods.
- Customer evaluation of service quality involves comparison of a customer's expectations with actual service performance.
- Service quality evaluations are based on the outcome of a service as well as the process of service delivery.

The intangibility of service outcomes makes it difficult to clearly describe and quantify services and, therefore, to contract for services. Consider for example, the difficulty in writing a contact for an educational service involving academic lectures. How does one define a "pound of education" and how can one be sure when the contract is fulfilled satisfactorily. As Karmarkar and Pitbladdo explain, this is why in such cases we do not contract around quantities at all; rather we contract around process delivery.[26] In general, the more information intensive a service is the more difficult it is to develop clear and meaningful contracts. This difficulty is somewhat reduced in services where physical objects play a dominant role.

Intangibility of outputs also makes it difficult to define and measure quality. For example, even for a simple custodial service such as cleaning, it is not easy to define the desired level of cleanliness. The level of cleanliness needed for an office is certainly different from that for a hospital operating room. The desired time duration for maintaining a cleanliness status can also be an important matter in writing a contract for cleaning service. As research in service quality has found, customers typically evaluate the quality of service based on the outcome of a service as well as the customer's experience with the process of service delivery. For example, in a dining facility, not only must the food be tasty but the manner in which the food is served must also be courteous, prompt, and friendly. This means that the contracts for many services should not be based solely on outcomes but should include specifications on both the outcome and the customer's experience with the process.

Co-production requiring the presence and participation of customers in the creation of many services is an important characteristic of services. For example, in IT services such as software development, a customer's input in terms of desired specifications of a software system is critically important. However competent the software developer may be, the developed software will not be satisfactory if the specifications do not accurately reflect the true needs of the customer. Hence, contracts for services should ideally specify not only what the service provider should do but also what the customer should do. Otherwise, a satisfactory service outcome may not be realized.

Diversity of services also makes it difficult and undesirable to use the same contract vehicles or procedures for different services. For example, given the differences in medical services versus custodial services, it is important that the contracts for these services are customized to suit the life cycle needs of individual services.

Finally, services are complex and may involve multi-stage processes. This makes it important yet challenging to write contracts that are flexible enough to cover all relevant scenarios and eventualities. Moreover, if a contract cannot be satisfactorily defined, it may be desirable to deliver certain services using internal resources as opposed to outsourcing them.

SIZE AND STRUCTURE OF DoD's SERVICES ACQUISITION ENVIRONMENT

The DoD's procurement process is currently undergoing a transformation similar to the one experienced by private enterprises. This transformation is changing how the agency manages its procurement function to include its people, processes, practices, and policies. The DoD's procurement function is currently transforming from a transaction-oriented perspective to a strategic-oriented organization. No longer viewed as a tactical, clerical, or administrative function, the procurement function is gaining enhanced status as leading organizations understand the importance of achieving strategic objectives and the impact on competitive advantage. Specifically, the procurement transformation is taking place in three major areas: "moving from buying goods to buying services, moving from a command and control relationship to a partnering relationship between the government and contractors, and moving from a paper-based procurement system to electronic procurement."[27]

The transformation from buying goods to buying services is considered the driving force behind the procurement revolution. Gansler describes this transformation as a reflection of the changing role of government from a "provider of goods" to a "manager of the providers of goods and service…".[28] In addition, the method of procuring services is also changing. Traditionally, through the Request for Proposal (RFP), the government would dictate what the contractor was to do and how to do it. Through the use of detailed specifications and requirements, the contractor was directed how to perform the contracted effort. The procurement transformation is changing how the RFP is being developed. RFPs are now being written to communicate the performance objectives or end-results of what the contracted effort needs to achieve, not how the work is to be done].[29]

These two driving forces, the change in what the government is buying (services) and how the government is buying (performance-based contracts), are resulting in e government procuring solutions and knowledge, as opposed to specific supplies or standardized services.[30]

Growth and Scope of DoD Service Contracts

The federal government is the largest purchaser in the world. Every 20 seconds of each business day the federal government awards a contract with an average value of $465,000 .[31] In fiscal year 2004, federal government procurement spending totaled approximately $328 billion. Of that amount, approximately $99 billion was spent by the civilian agencies, with the remaining $228 billion spent by the Department of Defense.[32] Furthermore, the Department of Defense is the federal government's largest purchaser of services. As illustrated in Figure 9-1, since FY 1999 DoD's spending on services has increased by 66%, to over $118 billion in FY 2003, approximately 57% of total procurement value.

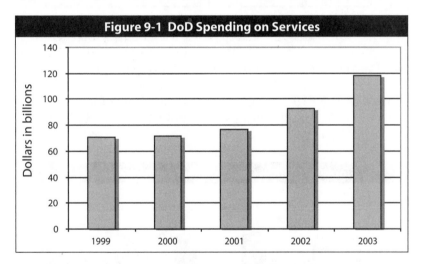

Figure 9-1 DoD Spending on Services

Source: Federal Procurement Data System-Next Generation (FPDS-NG)

Compared to other contract categories, the expenditure in services is the largest single spend category in the federal government. Figure 9-2 reflects the growth of services contracts in relation to the other contract categories. Between FY 1990 and 2000, procurement for services grew from $70 billion to $87 billion, where the procurement of supplies and equipment decreased from $102 billion to $77 billion in that same time frame.

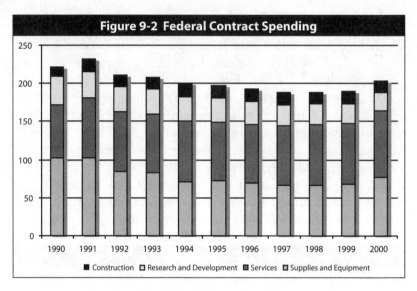

Figure 9-2 Federal Contract Spending

■ Construction ☐ Research and Development ■ Services ☐ Supplies and Equipment

Source: Contract Management: Trends and Challenges in Acquiring Services (GAO-01-753T) (2001)

Moreover, Figure 9-3 compares the procurement of services to the procurement of goods during the period FY 1998 and FY 2002 in the Department of Defense.

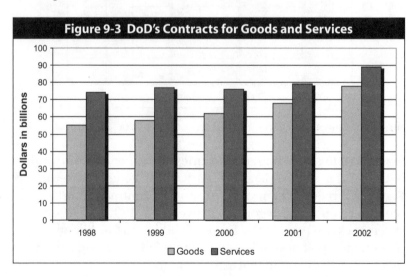

Figure 9-3 DoD's Contracts for Goods and Services

☐ Goods ■ Services

Source: Contract Management: High Level Attention Needed to Transform DOD Services Acquisition (GAO-03-935) (2003)

The DoD procures a variety of services in support of its mission. These services range from traditional commercial contracts such as IT support, custodial services, and grounds maintenance to mission-related services such as aircraft and engine maintenance and initial pilot training. In Figure 9-4 the major categories of services procured by the DoD and their values show that Professional, Administrative, and Management Support, and Construction, Repair, and Maintenance of Structure and Facilities are the types of services most often procured by the Department of Defense.

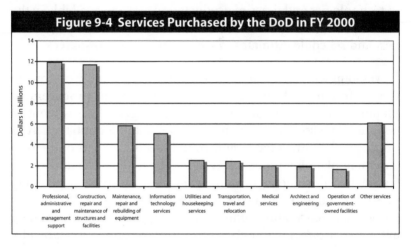

Figure 9-4 Services Purchased by the DoD in FY 2000

Source: Best Practices: Taking a Strategic Approach Could Improve DOD's Acquisition of Services (GAO-02-230) (2002)

SERVICES CONTRACT MANAGEMENT: AN OVERVIEW

The management of DoD's services contracts typically follows the traditional contract management process. This contracting process consists of the following phases:

- procurement planning,
- solicitation planning,
- solicitation,
- source selection,
- contract administration, and
- contract closeout.[33]

Each of these contracting phases will be discussed, along with key practice activities.

Procurement Planning

Procurement planning is the first contracting phase and involves identifying the business needs that can be best met by procuring products or services outside the organization. This process involves determining whether to procure, how to procure, what to procure, how much to procure, and when to procure. Key practice activities included within the procurement planning phase include determining the initial scope of work or the description of the product for acquisition, conducting market research to analyze the level of technologies and types of products and services available in the marketplace, determining funds availability, and developing initial cost and schedule estimates as well as manpower resources.

Developing an initial statement of work (SOW) and work breakdown structure (WBS) are also included in the procurement planning phase. Conducting an initial integrated assessment of contract-type selection, risk management, and an initial analysis of potential contract terms and conditions is also part of the procurement planning process.[34] It should be noted that many of the contractual documents developed in the procurement planning phase are initial draft documents, such as SOWs, WBSs, project scope statements, and funding and manpower estimates. These are initial draft documents simply because they are typically modified and revised as the acquisition program office becomes more knowledgeable of the business and technical aspects of the program. Industry, business, and technical knowledge are typically acquired through the use of market research activities, industry conferences, and requests for information (RFIs).

Solicitation Planning

The second phase of the procurement process is solicitation planning, which involves the process of preparing the solicitation documents needed to support an acquisition. This is a critical phase of the procurement process since it is during this phase that the work statements, specifications and other exhibits, standard terms and conditions, as well as special contract requirements are developed, revised, and finalized. Key practice activities within the solicitation planning process include using standard procurement forms and documents such as solicitation templates, model contracts, specifications and item descriptions, solicitation provisions, and contract terms and conditions .[35]

Solicitation

Solicitation is the third phase of the procurement process and is the process of obtaining bids and proposals from prospective sellers on how to meet the objectives of the project. The solicitation phase is critical to the overall acquisition strategy because it is this phase that executes the procurement planning strategy for a full and open competition or sole-source procurement. Some key practice activities within the solicitation phase include conducting market research and advertising to identify new sources of supplies and services for the purpose of developing a list of interested offerors. These offerors will receive the solicitation requesting the proposal. Another key practice activity in the solicitation phase includes conducting a pre-solicitation or pre-proposal conference to ensure that all prospective contractors have a clear, common understanding of the technical and contractual requirements of the acquisition .[36]

Source Selection

Source selection is the fourth phase of the contracting process and involves – receiving proposals and applying evaluation criteria in order to select the contractor. Key practice activities within the source-selection process include using evaluation criteria focusing on management, technical, and cost; tailoring the basis for award to either lowest cost/technically acceptable or best value; and taking into consideration an offeror's past performance in evaluating proposals.[37]

Contract Administration

Contract administration is the fifth phase of the contracting process and entails managing the relationship with the contractor and ensuring that each party's performance meets the contract requirements. During contract administration, the government's focus is on managing the contractor's cost, schedule, and performance. Key practice activities within the contract administration process include using an integrated team approach for monitoring the contractor's cost, schedule, and performance, and having an established process for administering incentive and fee-award provisions.[38] These incentives and award fees are tools used to motivate the contractor to meet specific performance standards.

Contract Types

The Federal Acquisition Regulation (FAR) identifies two major contract categories depending on the method of compensating a contractor: (1) cost-reimbursement contracts and (2) fixed-price contracts. In the fixed-price category, the contractor agrees to provide specified supplies or services in return for a specified price, either a lump sum or a unit price. The price is fixed and is not subject to change regardless of the contractor's actual cost experience. Only if the contract is modified is the price subject to change.[39]

There are various types of fixed-priced contracts such as firm-fixed-price (FFP), fixed-price with economic price adjustment (FP-EPA), and fixed-price-incentive (FPI). In the cost-reimbursement contract category, the contractor agrees to provide a best effort in performing the requirements of the contract, which are typically described based on broad specifications. In return, the contractor is reimbursed for all allowable costs up to the amount specified in the contract. Cost-reimbursement contracts include cost-sharing (CS), cost-plus-fixed fee, (CPFF), cost-plus-incentive fee (CPIF), and cost- plus-award fee (CPAF).

Closeout

The final phase of the contracting process is contract closeout, the process of verifying that all administrative matters are concluded on a physically complete contract. This involves accepting final deliveries, making final payment to the contractor, as well as completing and settling the contract and resolving any open items. Key practice activities within the contract closeout phase include using checklists and forms for ensuring proper documentation of closed contracts and maintaining a "lessons learned and best practices" database for use in future contracts and projects.[40] An important aspect of closing out a contract is conducting a final evaluation of the contractor's performance in terms of budget, schedule, and performance objectives. The government will use this final contractor evaluation in future contract competitions and source selections. The contract closeout phase is often forgotten and has been considered an administrative burden or relegated to a clerical or non-essential task.

DoD Policy on Contracting for Services

Since the beginning of the 1990s, DoD has seen a steady growth in the volume, complexity, and value of service contracts. Some of this growth results from an increase in the level of operations, some from the replacement of the civilian workforce by contractors, and some as a result of government policy dictating maximum use of contractors.

Compared with other federal agencies, the Department of Defense is often viewed as particularly aggressive in complying with the Office of Management and Budget's Circular A-76, Performance of Commercial Activities. The circular directs that the "longstanding policy of the federal government has been to rely on the private sector for needed commercial activities." A commercial activity is defined as "a recurring service that could be performed by the private sector and is resourced, performed, and controlled by the [government] agency through performance by government personnel, a contract, or a fee-for-service agreement."[41]

Accompanying this growth in outsourcing activity has been a downsizing of the DoD civilian and military acquisition workforce that is responsible for administering these contracts. Also, Congress has mandated a shift to performance-based service acquisition (PBSA). PBSA is intended to obtain higher levels of contractor performance at lower cost and to promote a partnership-oriented, long-term approach that allows the government—and the DoD in particular—to benefit from commercial best practices.[42] It is of interest that Circular A-76 mandates that, while actual performance of an activity may be outsourced, control remains with the government agency no matter what decision is ultimately made as a result of a competition between in-house and commercial providers.

The complexity of the monitoring process and the nature of the services outsourced make this contradiction even more difficult. A sanguine, yet now somewhat dated view of the agency's overall management challenges, has been provided by the DoD Inspector General:

> The seven audit reports that I am bringing to your attention today have a common theme, which is that eleven years of workforce downsizing, without proportionate workload reductions or productivity

increases, have created or exacerbated mission performance problems across a wide spectrum of DoD organizations and civilian personnel specialties. In an age when organizational agility is the watchword for successful businesses, DoD has been anything but agile, when it comes to managing human capital. This is partially due to restrictive personnel management laws and regulations, but also to previous reluctance to innovate and lack of strategic planning regarding the civilian workforce.[43]

In transaction cost analysis,[44] a distinction is made between the cost of delivering the service (production costs) and the cost of managing the relationship between a buyer and a seller (transaction costs). Circular A-76 directs a decision based entirely on production costs, while remaining silent on transaction costs. Yet from the point of view of both the taxpayer and the mission, the total cost should perhaps be the deciding factor.

The issue of control (also referred to as oversight or surveillance) transcends that of cost. The government agency that has outsourced an activity may simply not have access to the necessary personnel or budget to adequately exercise this control. Williamson emphasizes that, traditionally, a hierarchical (in-house) arrangement has lower transaction costs because it is easier to direct one's own employee to perform an activity. In contrast, specialist firms may have lower production costs because of experience or some type of economies of scale.[45] The challenge for government is to equitably consider all these factors when making a sourcing decision.

THE CHALLENGE OF OUTSOURCING SERVICES

Traditionally, DoD contracting practice has focused on goods, not services. This is in spite of the fact that services now account for over 55 percent of the dollar volume of DoD contracts.[46] A similar trend has been observed in other federal agencies.[47] Congress has mandated, through the National Defense Authorization Act of 2002, an improved management of the services contracting process.[48]

Outsourcing services on a large scale poses unique challenges for DoD. The department's employees, both those officially part of the acquisition workforce and those otherwise involved in the services acquisition process, are the focal point of any effort to increase the quantity and quality of outsourcing. Yet at the same time the number of those employees has been falling rapidly, and it is not unreasonable to claim that, in many cases, the necessary number of staff or skills are not present to ensure the adequate monitoring of the increased scale.

DoD has a responsibility to act as a knowledgeable client for the nation in its relationship with the private sector. As a knowledgeable client, its employees must be in a position to maintain a number of capabilities, including the following:

- An understanding of what services may or should be outsourced;
- An awareness of the capabilities and limitations of private sector firms in the appropriate area;
- The ability to tender for and competently evaluate competing bids from private sector firms;
- Where a service currently provided in-house is considered for outsourcing, the ability to evaluate competing bids from in-house and private sources according to the complex requirements set by the Office of Management and Budget; and
- The ongoing ability to develop, maintain, and improve the surveillance of contracted activity to ensure that value is obtained and to take corrective action where required.[49]

All of the above require an appropriate number of skilled personnel in a wide variety of fields. Expertise is needed in both contracting per se and in the technical or functional area that is being outsourced. Where outsourcing is viewed as a way to reduce government headcount (particularly that of civilian personnel), those remaining in the job need to have higher levels of expertise to conduct adequate surveillance of contracted activity. The GAO has emphasized the importance of improvements in monitoring (or surveillance) of DoD service contracts:

> According to DOD officials, insufficient surveillance occurred because surveillance is not as important to contracting officials as awarding contracts and therefore, does not receive the priority needed to ensure that surveillance occurs. ... Further, surveillance was usually a part-time responsibility and some personnel

felt that they did not have enough time in a normal workday to perform their surveillance duties .[50]

Addressing human capital issues in acquisition is not just a matter of the size of the workforce. It is also a capacity issue. While acquisition reforms have helped streamline smaller acquisitions, larger acquisitions, particularly for information technology, remain complex and technical. Yet agencies are at risk of not having enough of the right people with the right skills to manage these procurements. Consequently, a critical issue the federal government faces is whether it has today, or will have tomorrow, the ability to manage the procurement of increasingly sophisticated services. [51]

The occurrence of such phenomena is perhaps a natural outcome of the contradictory forces at work in outsourcing activities. While the emphasis is on reducing in-house personnel, outsourcing in itself may require a targeted increase in the number of government employees as well as some change in their qualifications to ensure that outsourcing is conducted according to regulations in a cost-effective, "best value" manner.

The Air Force is an example of an effective approach to the need for up-front planning of the in-house personnel requirements associated with outsourcing, as well as the inherently interdisciplinary mix of government personnel necessary for adequate contract surveillance .[52] However, the Air Force experience illustrates the difficulties of considering potential or actual contract management costs as part of the outsourcing decision.

A RAND Corporation study of 22 PBSA-inspired contracts at 15 Air Force bases concluded that information on the internal costs of outsourcing was "highly impressionistic" and that data on quality assurance costs, which should theoretically decline with a switch to PBSA, were ambiguous.[53] Even the actual expenditures on contracts were difficult to calculate and evaluate within the agency:

DOD is in the early stages of a spend analysis pilot. Although DoD is moving in the right direction, it has not yet adopted best practices to the same extent as the companies we studied. Whether DoD can adopt these practices depends on its ability to make long-term changes necessary to implement a more strategic approach to contracting. DoD also cites a number of challenges, such as its large and complex need for a range of services, the fragmentation of spending data across multiple information systems, and contracting goals for small businesses that may constrain its ability to consolidate smaller requirements into larger contracts. Challenges such as these are difficult and deep-rooted, but companies also faced them. For DoD to change management practices for the contracting of services will require sustained executive leadership at DoD as well as the involvement and support of Congress.[54]

Given the difficulties of capturing costs at many levels and for different activities, it is perhaps not surprising that DOD also suffers from major challenges in personnel management.

The Human Capital Issue

It is somewhat ironic, but not at all unexpected, that the downsizing of the DoD civilian workforce, and the increasing emphasis on moving military personnel into deployable positions, has resulted in increased concerns about who is minding the store. In its government-wide review of the acquisition function, the GAO emphasizes human capital as a cornerstone for an effective acquisition function, in particular, "valuing and investing in the acquisition workforce." Also, according to the GAO "integration and alignment" should form part of "strategic human capital planning."[55]

The emphasis on integration and alignment is particularly salient for DoD. What is being implied is that the in-house workforce needs to be developed and maintained in a manner commensurate with the workload requirements created by outsourcing. In an analysis of the Air Force's PBSA activities based on commercial practices for outsourcing of installation management, RAND Corporation noted that government personnel should have the ability to:

■ describe what service is desired and not how to perform the work;

- use measurable performance standards and quality assurance plans;
- specify procedures for reductions in fee or price when services do not meet contract requirements; and
- include performance incentives where appropriate.[56]

Yet Baldwin and Hunter also emphasize in the same report the need for more sophisticated statements of requirement, refinement and reduction of performance metrics, and, notably, widespread participation in the services contracting process. Such participation necessarily requires time and the application of expertise by qualified people. Particularly in an era of downsizing and with an aging workforce, recruiting and retaining suitable civil service personnel is a difficult process. Meanwhile, the military services must "grow their own" personnel in a closed environment that usually begins at the recruiting station and must balance a complex mix of occupational specialties, ranks, and attrition rates with the added complication of deployments that are impossible to forecast.

The FAR and other contracting regulations impose a host of responsibilities on acquisition and other government personnel for the entire services contracting life cycle. Not only must the agency head ensure that these responsibilities are carried out, but best practices must be used.[57] However, the policy-making agencies responsible for contracting rules have little connection to the organizations that set budgets or assign qualified people to the positions required to develop or monitor the contracts that result from those contracting rules.

In the private sector, this lack of communication may be less of a barrier, given the common sense of purpose imposed by the pursuit of profit.[58] However, it is reasonable to assume that increased contracting and decreased surveillance could lead to reduced quality performance. Some of the more extreme examples of this divergence in direction that have already led to widespread media attention include insufficient monitoring of contracts in Iraq by DoD, the Department of State, and other federal agencies[59] and the employment of illegal immigrants by contractors at military installations.[60]

The Department of Defense has responded to some of this divergence in policy by attempting to supplement or substitute on-site human expertise using a variety of methods. The first is to centralize, either on a national or regional basis, expertise in contracting or in a functional area, taking some responsibilities (and positions) away from individual installations. For example, the Army Contracting Agency and Army Installations Agency have been established as centers of excellence to direct and assist with the provision of the appropriate services.

The Department of the Navy has placed all shore installation management activities under regional commanders (such as Commander Naval Region Southwest) who then may establish detachments, as tenant activities, at specific installations as the perceived need may justify. Contracting itself has also been centralized in the Navy; all contracts above the simplified acquisition threshold (usually meaning small purchases such as office supplies that are carried out locally using credit cards) are undertaken by the Fleet and Industrial Supply Center (FISC) for that region. For example, the FISC in San Diego serves all Navy and Marine Corps installations in California and Nevada.

Another method DoD uses to "virtualize" expertise is to create Web-based sites where published direction, documents such as lessons learned, can be posted or chat rooms can be hosted. There are now a variety of such facilities in place. While these initiatives may appear laudable, questions remain. Centralization and regionalization are convenient vehicles for budget cuts, with the side effect of removing financial management flexibility from installation commanders. However, the Air Force seems to be resisting this trend, and Wing Commanders at installations are retaining a traditionally broad range of responsibilities, personnel, and budget under their chain of command.

Many types of services, and their contracts, do not lend themselves to codification or asynchronous communication. In such circumstances, the richness of face-to-face communication and the leveraging of experience acquired by long-term government personnel can be diminished or lost if human capital is not carefully managed. According to Nonaka and Takeuchi:

> ...frequent dialogue and communication helps create a "common cognitive ground" among employees and thus facilitates the transfer of tacit knowledge. Since members of the organization share overlapping in-

formation, they can sense what others are struggling to articulate.[61]

The shift from explicit, clerical-like functions to complex activities requiring a much more significant component of judgment is well represented by two shifts: (1) the majority of DoD acquisition is now for services rather than goods and (2) an increased emphasis is placed on PBSA. For example, the Air Force, which established a goal that at least half of all services acquisitions should be performance-based by 2005,[62] has also commented that what was previously viewed simply as purchasing within DoD has now evolved into a complex process that includes integrated supplier management, consideration of total ownership costs, cross-functional teams, and strategic sourcing strategies

Yet a RAND Corporation study of the Army shows that the remaining civilian acquisition personnel were not being used "as effectively as they should be," even with the recent loss of many military acquisition personnel to deployments.[63] The shift toward PBSA has significant implications for the government's in-house capabilities to perform outsourcing, but how these implications will be dealt with remains an interesting area for further study.

In its comprehensive review of the federal government's outsourcing process, the Commercial Activities Panel, a congressionally-chartered body chaired by the head of the GAO, emphasized that outsourcing policy be "consistent with human capital practices designed to attract, motivate, retain, and reward a high performing federal workforce." Similarly, the panel concluded that "the government faces continued and significant management, human resource, and professional development challenges, which affect the government's ability to manage the cost, schedule, and performance of in-house and contracted activities."[64] A significant increase in the volume, cost, and complexity of outsourced activity, declining numbers of experienced personnel, increased deployments, and widely rumored budget cuts do not point to a simple resolution of the challenges of contracting for services within DoD.

It is difficult in the best of times to undertake horizontal coordination between or within different agencies in Washington and translate them into improved cost-effectiveness in the field. Yet the integration of strategic human planning with other functions has been identified as critical to achieving desired mission outcomes.[65] DoD must also remain an attractive customer for the best-performing businesses and a knowledgeable client so that it can continue to act as an effective steward of public funds. PBSA, in the words of a RAND study, requires DoD to develop a "better understanding of how commercial firms do things."[66] Given the emerging environment, maintaining an effective capability within DoD to determine if and how services should be delivered, and how such services should be overseen, may pose a significant challenge.

CASE STUDY: PRESIDIO OF MONTEREY

The Presidio of Monterey (POM) has a complex history. Originally established as a fort (the Spanish meaning of *presidio*) under Spanish rule in 1770, POM began its life under the U.S. flag as a garrison for Marines in 1846. The site was inactive from 1856 until 1902 and hosted a variety of Army units until its official closure in 1944. Military training in the Monterey area continued five miles north of the city at Fort Ord (established in 1917), at 28,000 acres, one of the largest Army bases ever established. Fort Ord operated as a basic and advanced combat training center and until its closure under the Base Realignment and Closure (BRAC) process in 1994. After 1994, the POM continued to operate on its original 392 acres, which currently includes 180 buildings.[67] While language training in Japanese began in secrecy at the dormant POM beginning a few months before the attack on Pearl Harbor, in 1946 the site was officially reactivated as a foreign language training center, now known as the Defense Language Institute Foreign Language Center (DLIFLC or informally DLI). While DLI is part of the Army's Training and Doctrine Command (TRADOC), it has always had as its mission the training of military personnel from all of the military services. Additionally, a small number of civil servants from DoD and other federal agencies learn foreign languages at DLI, which graduates over 3,000 students annually in about 25 languages. While TRADOC is responsible for the funding and management of DLI, the functional sponsor is the Office of the Secretary of Defense (OSD).

When Fort Ord closed in 1994, the Army began transferring segments of the base to a variety of entities. A small portion of Fort Ord was retained for military use and designated as Ord Military Community (OMC). OMC includes DOD offices, housing, community facilities, and notably some POM and DLI organizations that could no longer be accommodated on the original POM site, given the growth of DLI. Some support, such as transportation and recreation, is also provided by POM to other DOD installations in the Monterey area. In a reversal of roles since the 1994 BRAC action, OMC is now a tenant activity of POM, which provides all administrative support such as contracting.[68]

Since the closure of Fort Ord, the end of the Cold War, and the attacks of September 11, 2001, DLI has both changed its mission and begun to grow rapidly. The focus has changed from the languages of the Warsaw Pact to those of the Middle East and Asia. In January 2006, DLI received additional funding of $362 million from OSD to further enhance the quantity and quality and instruction of over 200 classrooms and offices. This includes reducing average class size, hiring over 300 additional language instructors above the current complement of approximately 900, as well as adding about 250 additional support staff. A great deal of construction is also planned, extending until approximately 2012. POM, whose physical facilities have developed in the haphazard manner so typical of military bases, will evolve into a more campus-like facility designed around DLI's mission. Given the current expansion of POM and DLIFLC activity levels, a key challenge for both organizations will be agreeing on common levels of support and coordinating mission expansion and physical space requirements.[69]

Contracting Organization

Contracting for DLI and other activities supported by POM is provided by the Directorate of Contracting (DC), which falls under the POM Garrison Commander. Previously located on POM proper, the DC's offices relocated in early 2006 to the DOD Center, a large building at OMC, which served as the medical center for the previous Fort Ord. The DC is also functionally part of the Army Contracting Agency Southern Region (ACASR) headquartered at Fort Sam Houston in San Antonio, Texas. DLI is the largest single entity supported by the DC; its needs tend to directly or indirectly influence the remainder of the contracting activity carried out by the DC.

Furthermore, although DLI is the responsibility of TRADOC, POM and its associated physical infrastructure (land, roads, buildings, and utilities) are the responsibility of the Army's Installation

Management Agency (IMA) Southwest Region, also headquartered at Fort Sam Houston. POM is also responsible for management of two training facilities: Fort Hunter Liggett and Camp Roberts, both located about 80 miles southeast of Monterey near Paso Robles.

Accordingly, the DC has a number of reporting relationships within DoD, in addition to those with private bidders and contractors. Each of these relationships encompasses a specific mission, budgetary allocation, and regulatory framework. Additionally, the funding and activity levels may not necessarily be coordinated. The GAO has commented that among the military, the Army appears to have the greatest problem maintaining adequate levels of base operating support (BOS) funding, which can potentially contribute "to the degradation of many installation facilities and can adversely affect the quality of life and morale of military personnel."[70]

This situation represents a challenge where the base's mission (in this case, specifically, language training) is growing rapidly but, for example, the IMA or ACA is not in a position to fund the additional contracting workload associated with that growth. As noted above centralization of functional responsibilities within the different services imposes challenges. In the case of POM, the GAO's views on the subject may be particularly pertinent:

> Because the military services have often based future requirements estimates largely on prior expenditures, they do not necessarily know if BOS services were provided at appropriate levels. DOD and the military services have a strategic plan for installations and have multiple actions under way to address these problems, but they have not synchronized varying time frames for accomplishing related tasks. Until these problems are resolved, DOD will not have the management and oversight framework in place for identifying total BOS requirements, providing Congress with a clear basis for making funding decisions, and ensuring adequate delivery of services.
>
> While the Army's and Navy's creation of centralized installation management agencies can potentially create efficiencies and improve the management of the facilities through streamlining and consolidation,

implementation of these plans has so far met with mixed results in quality and level of support provided to activities and installations. Until more experience yields perspective on their efforts to address the issues identified in this report, GAO is not in a position to determine whether the approach should be adopted by the other services."[71]

One unique characteristic of the DC is its relationship with the two nearby cities of Monterey and Seaside. The legislation providing for the closure of Fort Ord in 1994 provided for a demonstration project (made permanent in 2003) that gave privileged contractor status, on a no-fee cost-reimbursement basis, to the Presidio Municipal Services Agency (PMSA) [originally known as the Joint Powers Authority (JPA)]. The PMSA is an inter-municipal consortium of the cities of Monterey and Seaside. The first JPA contract was signed in 1997, and the current agreement under the PMSA has been described as follows:

Under the expanded contract, which was signed in May 1999, the JPA maintains about 120 buildings at DLIFLC & POM and 35 buildings at the Annex. The buildings include such facilities as shopping malls, churches, a movie theatre, libraries, barracks, clubs, a sports center, and administrative buildings. As part of the contract, the building maintenance crews from the City of Monterey operate from facilities and shops at DLIFLC & POM, ensuring that support and services is[sic] immediately available.

Competing against national, commercial businesses, the City of Monterey was again awarded the contract through a competitive bid process in 2001. The contract is priced at $18 million over a 5-year period. Fire services are now contracted separately (see section above on Fire Protection Services at POM) and sewer maintenance is no longer part of the contract, as the City purchased the sewer system in July 2002.

Through this partnership and contract, the Army has realized a 41% reduction in expenses when compared with previous base operation costs and private con-

tracts. The City has also worked with the military staff
to reduce energy costs, by installing photocell timers
and HVAC controllers. Some $60,000 in energy costs
alone have been saved annually for one building."[72]

In 2000, the Army Audit Agency concluded that the use of PMSA
had resulted in a 41% cost reduction compared to previous military
and private services providers. POM has explained that "the local
municipalities have built-in incentives to reduce costs, improve
techniques, and streamline procedures as they are using their
resources up front until they are reimbursed" and that Monterey
and Seaside are "non-profit agencies with reasonable general and
administrative costs" with the necessary technical expertise in areas
such as traffic engineering.[73]

During the 2005 BRAC hearings, the Monterey model was cited as
an example of a technique for reducing BOS costs, and a number
of adjoining communities proposed similar arrangements that could
be utilized to preserve their military installations. It is of interest
that the PMSA uses the services of both cities' municipal work-
forces and also contracts with the private sector to carry out work
on the POM and OMC sites. Routine maintenance conducted by
PMSA for the Army currently costs approximately $5.3 million
in fiscal year 2004-2005.[74] The service supply chain model of the
contracting arrangements at POM is shown in Figure 9-5.

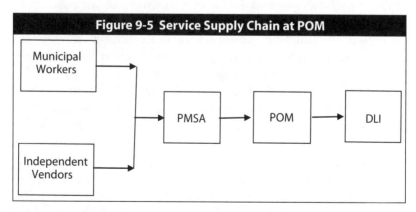

Figure 9-5 Service Supply Chain at POM

Contracting Activities

The DC is responsible for managing 53 contracts involving
approximately 500 contracting actions (such as new contracts,
renewals, and amendments) annually, representing a total value

of approximately $35 million, including $5.3 million contracted with PMSA.[75] However, as noted above, the creation of IMA and ACA have had a significant impact on the DC's staff, which has declined from 80 to 12. Additionally, funding is often inadequate to cover contracts in force and often is allocated by IMA or ACA on an incremental (less than yearly) basis.

Major contracts managed by the DC during FY 2006 included grounds and other infrastructure maintenance (mainly through the PMSA), supply or gas and electricity, custodial (janitorial) services, food services (which use contractor personnel in two POM dining halls), maintenance and dispatching of the motor pool (including buses), audio visual and IT services in support of the instructional mission, and fire protection for the POM from the City of Monterey, which is not covered by the PMSA.

For each contract, monitoring of contractor performance is the responsibility of the POM, DLI, or other organization that benefits from the contractor's services. For example, custodial services are monitored and contractor performance is reported to the DC by government employees within the Directorate of Public Works. These personnel are known by various titles such as technical personnel or quality assurance evaluators.

Efforts are underway to improve and standardize the training of these staff members so that they can carry out their duties in a consistent manner and ensure that the DC has the proper information on contractor performance in exercising its oversight responsibilities on behalf of the government. These initiatives are particularly important given the shortage of contracting staff. A related initiative by the DC to deal with the staffing problem is to reduce the total number of contracts through consolidation, which has a major impact on the administrative workload of both DC and user organization personnel.

POM staff are highly conscious of their role in supporting the mission, notably DLI's rapidly expanding instructional activities. However, there is concern about the long-term ability of POM to provide an acceptable level of service to DLI given the significant staff reduction. The problems can be deceivingly subtle. For example, as noted previously, DLI has received significant funding from OSD to improve the quality of instruction and the production of qualified linguists. However, much of the supporting infrastructure for this initiative will be provided through contracts. Requirements determination, market research, tendering, evaluation of proposals, correspondence with bidders, bid evaluation, contract award, and contract monitoring all require a variety of qualified personnel who may not currently be available. Additionally, agencies such as IMA, ACA or TRADOC may view DLI's expansion as an OSD-directed initiative that does not necessarily commit those organizations to assist POM.

CASE STUDY: TRAVIS AIR FORCE BASE

Travis Air Force Base is located approximately 50 miles northeast of San Francisco. Travis can be considered a small city unto itself, complete with airport, hospital, restaurants, and neighborhoods. As an Air Mobility Command (AMC) Base, Travis is home to the 60th Air Mobility Wing (AMW), which is the largest air mobility organization in the Air Force. Flying the Lockheed C-5 Galaxy cargo aircraft and the KC-10 Extender tanker aircraft, the 60th AMW fulfills its mission of global reach and flying support and humanitarian airlift missions anywhere in the world. Travis is also home to the David Grant Medical Center, the second largest medical treatment facility in the Air Force.

Contracting Support

Providing contracting support to Travis Air Force Base is the mission of the 60th Contract Squadron (CONS). The 60th CONS awards and administers over $320 million annually in contracts for construction, supplies, and services.[76]

In terms of services contracts, the 60th CONS manages service contracts that are traditionally found at most Air Force bases. These services include grounds maintenance, food services, custodial, and military family housing maintenance. Due to the unique mobility mission of Travis AFB and the medical mission of the adjacent David Grant Medical Center, the contracting squadron also manages some specialized services contracts, such as passenger terminal screening, professional medical staffing services, and falconry services.

Services Contracts

Travis AFB contracts with Pride Industries for many labor-intensive service contracts, such as grounds maintenance, food services, custodial, and military family housing maintenance. Pride Industries is also the contractor for the passenger terminal operations and pre-board screening. It is "the nation's largest employer of people with disabilities and provides a variety of outsourcing solutions to meet the manufacturing and service needs of companies nationwide" (Pride Industries). These contracts are based on a firm-fixed-price basis and use predominantly detailed specifications. Contracts based on detailed specifications focus on the contractor's complying with specific government requirements specified in the statement of work.

In supporting the David Grant Medical Center, Travis uses performance-based service contracts for nursing personnel supply, intensive care unit (ICU) services, natal services, and pediatric care. Performance-based service contracts are designed to focus on desirable performance results, including specific measurable objectives, and a quality assurance plan to ensure that contract requirements are met or exceeded.[77] Performance-based service contracts are based on a statement of objectives (SOO) developed by the government, which is included in the government's solicitation or request for proposal. The SOO identifies the end-results or desired performance results of the contract.

Organizational Processes and Tools

The 60th Contracting Squadron interfaces with the base organizations that own or manage the required services. For example, the 60th Civil Engineering Squadron owns the requirement for the grounds maintenance, custodial, and military family housing maintenance services. The Services Squadron owns the requirement for the food services, and the Medical Center owns the requirement for the medical services. These requirements owners represent the users for these specific services and, thus, are responsible for developing the statement of objectives or performance work statement (PWS), quality assurance surveillance plan (QASP), and the actual surveillance of the contractor's performance.

As the organization providing contracts support the requirements owners, the Contracting Squadron meets periodically with the functional managers and QAEs of those organizations to discuss any critical issues that may result in modifications to the contract statement of work, or quality assurance surveillance plan. Proactive and frequent communications are essential for a successful services contract. Travis AFB uses business requirement advisory groups (BRAGs) as the mechanism for conducting these communications. BRAGs are teams made up of cross-functional personnel that represent the functional organizations involved in the services contracts. These cross-functional teams plan and manage the service contracts throughout the services life cycle, including providing the market research, requirements determination, procurement and solicitation planning, as well as determining the performance surveillance strategy for the contract.

Each requirements organization provides quality assurance evaluators (QAEs) for controlling and managing the contractor's performance. The QAEs are considered experts within their specific function (grounds maintenance, custodial, housing maintenance, food services, medical services, etc) and are responsible for ensuring the contractor meets the requirements of the contract. The Contracting Squadron provides training to the QAEs and manages the base-wide quality assurance program. The contractor uses the PWS to ensure that it meets the performance objectives of the respective Statement of Objectives. QASP provides the quality assurance evaluator with an effective tool for assessing the contractor's performance. These surveillance tools include random sampling, 100-percent inspection, and periodic surveillance.[78] The QASP is used to ensure that the government receives acceptable contractor performance compared to the technical requirements of the contract.

CASE STUDY: NAVAL POSTGRADUATE SCHOOL

The Naval Postgraduate School (NPS) was established in Monterey, California, in 1952. Along with the U.S. Naval Academy and the Naval War College, NPS is often referred to as one of the Navy's flagship educational institutions. NPS awards accredited graduate degrees and offers short courses as well as distance learning programs. Current full-time enrollment is approximately 1,800. Students are military officers from all five U.S. Armed Services, U.S. government employees, and officers and government employees from approximately 60 nations.

NPS, like the Presidio of Monterey (POM), faces the challenge of determining the most effective manner to organize a complex educational mission while ensuring that adequate support for its physical facilities is in place, including service contracts. Following the closure of the nearby Fort Ord in 1991 (noted above) and its near-demise during the 1995 Defense Base Closure and Realignment (BRAC) process, NPS has undergone numerous changes in organizational structure and budgetary responsibilities, which have in turn significantly changed how service contracts are defined, competed for, and administered.

However, NPS and POM have not evolved toward shared support services, with a few minor exceptions such as medical care and military housing. Also unlike POM, NPS has not developed any innovative partnerships with the City of Monterey, although refuse collection and tree-trimming are provided to NPS by the city on a routine contractual basis.

Before the BRAC decision in 2005 to keep NPS open, the school's mission and functions were conducted in an essentially unitary style, much like a typical Air Force base. Support activities, military personnel, and civilian staff were the responsibility of the NPS President and (on a more frequent basis) the Chief of Staff, while the Provost (who is appointed by and responsible to the Secretary of the Navy, not the NPS President) had (and retains) authority over academic matters and faculty personnel issues.

Beginning in 2005, the Navy began to modify its installation management and contracting activities in order to reduce overhead costs and redirect notional savings toward operations. This was primarily achieved by separating mission and support functions, and then transferring responsibility to regional or national organizations that would provide the same services on a consolidated basis, assumedly ensuring a more uniform service level with fewer acquisition and acquisition-related personnel, consolidated service contracts covering a larger number of installations, and with the expectation of lower total contractual expenditures.

The changes had little impact on services contracting in support of the academic mission, which was left within the purview of NPS. However, the NPS Supply Department was closed, and all acquisition above the micropurchase (i.e., credit card) limit of $2,500

NINE

is now conducted by the Fleet and Industrial Supply Center-San Diego (FISC-SD). Purchasing agents in academic departments as well as the NPS Research Office now route their requisitions through FISC-SD, which is responsible for all Navy installations in California and Nevada.

Additionally, support functions such as facilities management and grounds maintenance, police, civilian human resources, legal services, and public affairs were transferred from NPS to a new entity, Naval Support Detachment Monterey (NSDM). NSDM functions as a local detachment of the Commander Naval Region Southwest (CNRSW), who is now considered the landlord for NPS and all other Navy units in the Monterey area. CNRSW, in turn, reports to the Commander Navy Installations Command (CNIC), a position established to "enable the Navy's Operating Concept through Enterprise alignment of all shore installation support to the Fleet, Fighter and Family" (see http://www.cni.navy.mil/cnic_hq_site/ AboutCNIC/index.htm). NSDM has a limited contracting capability, with four contracting officer positions that conduct contracting for the noted functions, particularly facilities management and construction. Larger construction contracts are issued by the Naval Facilities Engineering Command Southwest (NAVFAC Southwest) in San Diego, with local inspection and other liaison activities carried out by NSDM personnel, who absorbed the former NPS public works (facilities and grounds management) role.

In early 2006, further changes added to the fragmentation of service contracting responsibilities in the Monterey area. The remaining supply-related activities under NSDM were transferred to FISC-SD as part of a further regionalization initiative. Similarly, the NSDM Public Works organization became the Monterey detachment of NAVFAC Southwest. Finally, CNRSW currently plans to shift custodial and grounds maintenance contracts from NSDM to NAVFAC Southwest over the next few years. These are the largest ($1.2 million and $614,000, respectively) service contracts now administered by NSDM.

In summary, Navy units in the Monterey area, of which NPS and the Fleet Numerical Meteorological and Oceanographic Center are the largest, are now considered tenant activities of their new landlord, CNRSW. Further complexity has been added by centralization of service contracting at FISC-SW and the replacement of the locally-managed public works functions by NAVFAC detachments.

This challenging mix of organizational structures, comparable in some ways to the one now faced by POM, raises the issue of congruency in managerial decisions, budget allocation, and coherence of support versus mission needs. A final comment relates to the stewardship of NPS's academic mission, which has changed from being located in the Office of the Chief of Naval Operations (OPNAV) in Washington to the Naval Education and Training Command (NETC) in Pensacola, Florida, the latter being an organization that administers a large array of training and education facilities and has little expertise in graduate education. Notably, the U.S. Naval Academy is exempt from NETC oversight and continues to report to OPNAV, as did NPS in the past. It should be noted that NETC is currently being restructured and may become integrated into OPNAV. However, NPS appears to lack the clear mission sponsor role (which includes significant, dedicated funding) played by the Under Secretary of Defense for Intelligence in the case of the Defense Language Institute, and by extension, POM. How the various Navy and Army organizations in the Monterey area will continue to evolve their reporting relationships and consequent strategy for services contracting remains an open question.

SUMMARY

The establishment of centralized contracting organizations and the use of regional service contracts have been identified in this research as a current trend in DoD's approach to services acquisition. With the drawdown of the defense workforce and the consolidation of military installations, the Defense Department is attempting to achieve cost efficiencies by centralizing contracting organizations and awarding regional contracts for some military base support services.

An example of a centralized contracting organization includes the Fleet and Industrial Supply Center San Diego (FISCSD). FISC San Diego's regional contracts department provides a full range of acquisition and contracting support to all CONUS Navy installations west of the Mississippi River, unless otherwise assigned (see FISC San Diego website, https://www.navsup.navy.mil). Although the services being acquired are performed at geographically separated locations, in this case CONUS Navy installations west of the Mississippi River, the contracting support for these contracts (procuring contracting officers and contract administrators) are centrally located at FISC San Diego.

An example of a regional service contract includes a single contract awarded by the Air Force Space Command (AFSPC) to Phoenix Management Inc. for base logistics services at six military installations–Peterson AFB, Colorado (including Schriever AFB and Cheyenne Mountain); F.E. Warren AFB, Wyoming; Malmstrom AFB, Montana; and Vandenberg AFB, California. Although the logistics services will be provided at each of these six locations, only a single contract source selection was conducted and only one contract was awarded by the AFSPC Headquarters contracting office. It is also assumed that this logistics services contract will be centrally controlled at AFSPC Headquarters, but de-centrally executed at each of the military installations (Phoenix Management, Inc. website, http://www.pmiaus.com).

The centralization of contracting offices and the use of regional contracts will result in additional dynamics for the acquisition of services. The advantages of centralized contracting offices include better control of contracting operations, the development of consistent and standardized services requirements, and a decreased contract management workforce. Disadvantages of centralized contracting organizations include physical separation from the customer and the potential of non-responsiveness to a customer's requirements. For example, if the commander of a military installation has concerns or issues with the quality of a contractor's performance, the commander will typically have to contact the contracting organization, which is not only geographically separated from the commander's installation but may not consider the contractor's performance a critical priority.

The use of regional contracts provides a contracting organization with a means of applying a strategic approach to the acquisition of services. The advantages of regional contracts include ensuring and maintaining standardized services requirements at multiple military installations, leveraging the buying power of the purchasing organization, and reducing the number of contracts and contractors managed by the contracting organization. The disadvantages of regionalized contracts include contracts not being responsive to the unique needs of each of the military installations. For example, a regional grounds maintenance contract may not meet the unique mission needs of a military installation with flight operations, if the other military installations under that contract do not have a flight operations mission. Another example would be a regional custodial services contract for a group of military installations, some with 24-hour flight or training operations and other installations with more traditional working hours.

It is important to note that this is an exploratory research in services contracting within the Department of Defense. Consequently, the following research observations and conclusions are somewhat preliminary in nature and should be viewed as such.

1. The Department of Defense's services acquisition volume has continued to increase in scope and dollars in the past decade. GAO found that since FY 1999, DoD's spending on services has increased by 66%, and in FY 2003, DoD spent over $118 billion or approximately 57% of its total procurement dollars on services.[79] DoD procures a variety of services, including both traditional commercial services and services unique to defense. In terms of amount spent, four service categories represent over 50% of total spending on services: (1) professional, administrative, and management support services; (2) construction, repair, and maintenance of structure and facilities; (3) equipment maintenance; and (4) information technology services.

2. Presidio of Monterey (POM) has contracted maintenance of about 155 buildings and structures to Presidio Municipal Services Agency (PMSA), a consortium of the cities of Monterey and Seaside. The PMSA agreement has allowed the two cities to apply their expertise to routine municipal services and the Army to focus on its military mission. Through this partnership and contract with PMSA, the POM has realized a 41% reduction in expenses when compared to previous base operational costs and private contracts. We recommend that DoD explore and evaluate the possibility of establishing such synergistic contractual relations with cities adjacent to other bases in support of their respective operations.

3. Proactive and frequent communications are essential for a successful services contract. Travis AFB is a successful example of this, where 60th CONS uses business requirement advisory groups as the mechanism for conducting such communications. BRAGs are teams made up of cross-functional personnel that

represent the functional organizations involved as customers in the services contracts. These cross-functional teams plan and manage the service contracts throughout the services' life cycle. As the DoD increases the use of centralized contracting organizations and regional contracts, the use of proactive and frequent communications will be even more essential for the successful management and performance of these contracts.

4. Visits and interviews at Travis AFB, Presidio of Monterey (POM), Naval Air Station Whidbey Island (NAS WI), and the Naval Support Detachment Monterey (NSDM) confirmed GAO's finding that "while the Army's and Navy's creation of centralized installation management agencies can potentially create efficiencies and improve the management of the facilities through streamlining and consolidation, implementation of these plans has so far met with mixed results in quality and level of support provided to activities and installations."[80]

5. The centralization of contracting offices and use of regional contracts will result in additional dynamics to DoD's acquisition of services. The use of centralized contracting organizations and regional contracts will require even more proactive and frequent communications between contracting organizations and the customer. Although it is still too early to assess the effectiveness and efficiency of centralized contracting organizations and regional contracts, this study indicates that centralization and regionalization of services contracts are growing trends in the DoD and will significantly change how services contracts are managed.

6. Given the unique characteristics of services, such as intangibility, co-production, diversity, and complexity, establishing service specifications and measuring and monitoring the quality of delivered services are inherently more complex than for manufactured goods. Hence, it is critical to have on board a knowledgeable client and the necessary number of skilled contracting personnel to define the requirements and to supervise outsourced services. DoD has been aggressively complying with OMB's Circular A-76, which directs all federal government agencies "to rely on the private sector for needed commercial activities." This has resulted in dramatic growth in DoD's spending while downsizing its civilian and military acquisition workforce. Although this exploratory study is not yet complete, the two trends contradict the critical need to have a necessary number of skilled contracting personnel.

This could mean that in DoD's outsourced services either the needs are not being fully satisfied or the value for the money spent is not being realized.

7. Although the DoD acquires more services than goods, and the acquisition of services and the use of services contractors are becoming an increasingly critical aspect of its mission, the management infrastructure for the acquisition of services is less developed than for the acquisition of products and systems. There is a less formal program management approach and life-cycle methodology for the acquisition of services, which is confirmed by the lack of standardization in the business practices associated with the services acquisition process. This results from the fact that the functional personnel currently managing the services programs are not considered members of the DoD acquisition workforce and are typically not provided acquisition training under Defense Acquisition Workforce Improvement Act (DAWIA) requirements.

QUESTIONS TO CONSIDER

1. What types of base operations services are typically procured at your military installation?

2. How is the outsourcing decision made in services acquisition?

3. How are these services acquired (what type of acquisition strategy and procurement method is used)?

4. What are the challenges in procuring base operations support services, from both business (acquisition, finance) and operational (military, mission) perspectives?

5. What type of structure is used to manage services programs?

6. What are the emerging trends in the policies and practices used in acquiring base operations services?

ACKNOWLEDGEMENTS

The authors are greatly thankful to RADM Jim Greene, USN (Ret), the NPS Acquisition Research Chair, for securing the sponsor funding for this research. We would also like to acknowledge Keith Snider for his efforts on behalf of the Acquisition Research

Program in the Graduate School of Business and Public Policy at the Naval Postgraduate School.

ENDNOTES

[1] U.S. Government Accountability Office, *Contract Management: Opportunities to Improve Surveillance on Department of Defense Contracts*, GAO-05-274 (2005).

[2] D.G. Levy, et al., *Base Realignment and Closure (BRAC) and Organizational Restructuring in the DoD: Implications for Education and Training and Infrastructure*, RAND, Santa Monica, CA (MG-153, 2004): 36-50.

[3] U.S. Government Accountability Office, *Best Practices: Taking a Strategic Approach Could Improve DoD's Acquisition of Services*, GAO-02-230 (2002).

[4] U.S. Karmarkar and R. Pitbladdo, "Service Markets and Competition," *Journal of Operations Management* 12(3-4) (1995): 397-411.

[5] J.A. Fitzsimmons and M.J. Fitzsimmons, *Service Management: Operations, Strategy, and Information Technology*, 5th ed. (New York: McGraw-Hill, 2006).

[6] R. Chase, "The Customer Contact Approach to Services: Theoretical Bases and Practical Extensions," *Operations Research* 21(4) (1981): 698-705.

[7] W.E. Sasser, R.P. Olsen, and D.D. Wyckoff, *Management of Service Operations: Text, Cases, and Readings* (Boston: Allyn & Bacon, 1978); R.G. Murdick, B. Render, and R.S. Russell, *Service Operations Management* (Needham Heights, MA: Allyn & Bacon, 1990); J.L. Heskett, W.E. Sasser, and C.W.L. Hart, *Service Breakthroughs: Changing the Rules of the Game.* (New York: The Free Press, 1990); C.H. Lovelock, *Managing Services: Marketing, Operations and Human Resources,* 2nd ed. (Englewood Cliffs, NJ: Prentice Hall, 1992); Ibid., note 5.

[8] W.E. Sasser, C.W. L. Hart, and J.L. Heskett, *The Service Management Course* (New York: The Free Press, 1991).

[9] W.E. Sasser, R.P. Olsen, and D.D. Wyckoff, *Management of Service Operations: Text, Cases, and Readings* (Boston: Allyn & Bacon, 1978).

[10] C.H. Lovelock, "Classifying Services to Gain Strategic Marketing Advantage," *Journal of Marketing* 47 (Summer 1983): 9-20.

[11] C.H. Lovelock, "A Basic Toolkit for Service Managers," in C.H. Lovelock, (ed.) *Managing Services: Marketing, Operations and Human Resources,* 2nd Ed. (Englewood Cliffs, NJ: Prentice Hall, 1992) 17-30; R.W. Schmenner, "How can Service Businesses Survive and Prosper?" *Sloan Management Review* (Spring 1986): 21-32; J.B. Quinn, *Intelligent Enterprise: A Knowledge and Service based Paradigm for Industry* (New York: The Free Press, 1992).

[12] R. Chase, "The Customer Contact Approach to Services: Theoretical Bases and Practical Extensions," *Operations Research* 21(4) (1981): 698-705.

[13] U.M. Apte and R.O. Mason, "Global Disaggregation of Information-Intensive Services," *Management Science* 41(7) (1995): 1250-1262.

[14] C.P. McLaughlin and S. Coffey, "Measuring Productivity in Services," *International*

Journal of Service Industries Management 1(1990): 46-64.

15   U.S. Karmarkar and R. Pitbladdo, "Quality, Class and Competition," Simon working paper (1992).

16   R. Buzzell and B.T. Gale, *The PIMS Principle: Linking Strategy to Performance* (New York: The Free Press, 1987).

17   W. Deming, Out of Crisis, MIT (Cambridge, MA: Center for Advanced Engineering Study, 1985).

18   P. B. Crosby, *Quality Is Free* (New York: McGraw-Hill, 1979).

19   C. Gronroos, *Strategic Management and Marketing in the Service Sector* (Helsingfors, Sweden: Swedish School of Economics and Business, 1982).

20   A. Parasuraman, V,A. Zeithaml, and L.L. Berry, "A Conceptual Model of Service Quality and Its Implications for Future Research," *Journal of Marketing* 49 (Fall 1985): 41-50.

21   V. Zeithaml, A. Parasuraman, and L.L. Berry, *Delivering Quality Service* (New York: The Free Press, 1990).

22   D. E. Bowen, R. Chase, and T.G. Cummings, *Service Management Effectiveness* (San Francisco: Jossey-Bass Inc., 1990); S. W. Brown, E. Gummesson, B. Edvardsson, and B.Gustavsson, *Service Quality* (Lexington, MA: Lexington Books, 1991); C. H. Lovelock, *Managing Services: Marketing, Operations and Human Resources*, 2nd ed. (Englewood Cliffs, NJ: Prentice Hall, 1992).

23   R.B. Chase and D.E. Bowen, "Service Quality and the Service Delivery System: A Diagnostic Framework," in S.W. Brown, E. Gummesson, B. Edvardsson, and B. Gustavsson (eds.), *Service Quality* (Lexington, MA: Lexington Books, 1991) 157-176.

24   U.M. Apte, U.S. Karmarkar, and R. Pitbladdo, "Quality Management in Services: Analysis and Applications," in P. Lederer and U. Karmarkar (eds.) *Practice of Quality Management* (Cambridge: Harvard Business School Press, 1996).

25   D.A. Collier, "Measuring and Managing Service Quality," in D. E. Bowen, R. B. Chase, and T. G. Cummings (eds.) *Service Management Effectiveness* (San Francisco: Jossey-Bass Inc., 1990) 234-265.

26   Ibid., note 4.

27   M.A. Abramson and R.S. Harris, III, "The Transformation of Government Procurement," in M.A. Abramson and R.S. Harris, III (eds.) *The Procurement Revolution* (Lanham, MD: Rowman & Littlefield, 2003) 3-11.

28   J.S. Gansler, "A Vision of the Government as a World-Class Buyer: Major Procurement Issues for the Coming Decade," in Mark A. Abramson and Roland S. Harris, III (eds.) *The Procurement Revolution* (Lanham, MD: Rowman & Littlefield Publishers, 2003) 13-57.

29   K.G. Denhardt, "The Procurement Partnership Model: Moving to a Team-Based Approach," in Mark A. Abramson, and Roland S. Harris, III (eds.) *The Procurement Revolution* (Lanham, MD: Rowman & Littlefield Publishers, 2003) 59-86.

30   Ibid.

[31] S.A. Stanberry, *Federal Contracting Made Easy* (Vienna, VA: Management Concepts, 2001).

[32] Federal Procurement Data System-Next Generation (FPDS-NG). *http://www.fpdsng.com/downloads/top_requests/total federal spending_by_dept.pdf.*

[33] G.A. Garrett and R.G. Rendon, *Contract Management: Organizational Assessment Tools* (National Contract Management Association, 2005).

[34] Ibid.

[35] Ibid.

[36] Ibid.

[37] Ibid.

[38] Ibid.

[39] Ibid.

[40] Ibid.

[41] Office of Management and Budget, Executive Office of the President: *Performance of Commercial Activities,* Circular No. A-76 (Rev. 2003).

[42] Air Force Instruction, *Acquisition: Performance Based Services Acquisition (PBSA).* 63-124 (2005); Department of Defense Office of the Inspector General, *Acquisition: Contracts for Professional, Administrative and Management Support Services,* D-2005-015 (2003); Federal Acquisition Council, Federal Acquisition Regulation— Part 37. Services Contracting, March 27, 2006 *http://farsite.hill.af.mil.*

[43] Ibid., note 21.

[44] O.E. Williamson, *Markets and Hierarchies: Analysis and Antitrust Implications* (New York: The Free Press, 1983).

[45] Ibid.

[46] Department of Defense Office of the Inspector General, *Contract Surveillance for Service Contracts,* D-2006-010 (2005).

[47] U.S. Government Accountability Office, *Framework for Assessing the Acquisition Function at Federal Agencies,* GAO-05-218G (2005).

[48] U.S. Government Accountability Office, *Contract Management: Opportunities to Improve Surveillance on Department of Defense Contracts,* GAO-05-274 (2005).

[49] Ibid., note 41

[50] Ibid., note 48.

[51] U.S. Government Accountability Office, *Contract Management: Trends and Challenges in Acquiring Services,* GAO-01-753T (2001).

[52] Air Force Instruction, *Acquisition: Performance-Based Services Acquisition,* PBSA 63-124 (2005).

[53] J. Ausink, F. Camm and C. Cannon, *Performance-Based Contracting in the Air Force: A Report on Experiences in the Field,* RAND, Santa Monica, CA (DB-342-AF).

54   U.S. Government Accountability Office, *Best Practices: Improved Knowledge of DoD Service Contracts Could Reveal Significant Savings,* GAO-03-66 (2003).

55   Ibid, note 47.

56   L.H. Baldwin and S. Hunter, *Defining Needs and Managing Performance of Installation Support Contracts: Perspectives from the Commercial Sector.* RAND, Santa Monica, CA (MR-1812) (2004).

57   Federal Acquisition Council, Federal Acquisition Regulation—Part 37, Services Contracting, March 27, 2006 *http://farsite.hill.af.mil.*

58   Ibid., note 56.

59   U.S. Government Accountability Office, *Framework for Assessing the Acquisition Function at Federal Agencies,* GAO-05-218G (2005).

60   G. Witte, "Suspected Illegal Workers Detained at U.S. Bases: Investigators Question Employees Doing Contract Work at Military Facilities," *The Washington Post,* October 29, 2005: A5.

61   I. Nonaka and H. Takeuchi, *The Knowledge-Creating Company: How Japanese Companies Create the Dynamics of Innovation* (USA: Oxford University Press, 1995) 12.

62   Ibid., note 56; R.G. Rendon, "Commodity Sourcing Strategies: Processes, Best Practices, and Defense Initiatives," *Journal of Contract Management* 3(1) (Summer 2005): 7.

63   C.H. Hanks, et al., *Reexamining Military Acquisition Reform: Are We There Yet?* RAND, Santa Monica, CA (MG-291) (2005).

64   U.S. Government Accountability Office, *Commercial Activities Panel: Improving the Sourcing Decisions of the Government,* GAO-02-866T, (2002).

65   U.S. Government Accountability Office, *High Risk Series: An Update,* GAO-05-207 (2005); U.S. Government Accountability Office, *Human Capital: Agencies Need Leadership and the Supporting Infrastructure to Take Advantage of New Flexibilities,* GAO-05-616T (2005).

66   Ibid., note 53.

67   H, Uslar, The Monterey Model: Monterey's Municipal-Military Partnership with the Department of the Army," PowerPoint Presentation by the Deputy Public Works Director, City of Monterey, 2005 Annual Conference of the Association of Defense Communities, Denver, June 4-7, *http://www.defensecommunities.org* April 3, 2006. (2005)>.

68   Defense Language Institute Foreign Language Center, U.S. Department of the Army. *History of DLI,* March 30, 2006 *http://www.dliflc.edu/about_dliflc;* Department of Defense Office of the Inspector General, *Contract Surveillance for Service Contracts,* D-2006-010) (2005); Presidio of Monterey, Office of the Command Historian, U.S. Department of the Army, *Presidio of Monterey* [history of], March 30, 2006 *http://monterey.army.mil.*

69   J. Cairns, "U.S. Army Garrison—Presidio of Monterey" (IMSW-POM-ZA), PowerPoint Presentation, December 1, 2005; K. Howe, "Money Talks at Language School: $362 Million will help hire teachers, add languages to DLI program," *Monterey County*

Herald, January 22, 2005 (downloaded from LexisNexis, 2006).

[70] S. Government Accountability Office, *Defense Infrastructure: Issues Need to Be Addressed in Managing and Funding Base Operations and Facilities Support,* GAO-05-556 (2005).

[71] Ibid.

[72] Defense Language Institute Foreign Language Center, U.S. Department of the Army, *Partnerships: Base Operations Support,* March 31, 2006 *http://www.dli.army. mil/partnerships/baseops.htm.*

[73] "Presidio of Monterey," U.S. Department of the Army, Information Paper (ATZP-GC): Presidio of Monterey Municipal Services Contract, January 24 (2004).

[74] J. Cairns, "U.S. Army Garrison—Presidio of Monterey" (IMSW-POM-ZA), PowerPoint Presentation, December 1, 2005.

[75] Ibid.

[76] U.S. Air Force, *60th Contracting Squadron Mission Overview,* Travis AFB. (2006).

[77] Ibid., note 33.

[78] R.G. Rendon, *Outsourcing Base Operations Support Functions, Program Manager* (Defense Acquisition University Press, 2001).

[79] Ibid., note 1.

[80] Ibid., note 70.

CHAPTER 10

FEDERAL RESEARCH AND DEVELOPMENT (R&D) SERVICES CONTRACTING

By Steve Stryker

BACKGROUND

The history of federal services contracting is incomplete without a discussion of research and development (R&D). The government has always played a role in funding promising technological advances, whether they be upgraded weapons, new "flying machines" or recent biological treatments. Today, the influence of the federal government is found in all stages of developing solutions to emerging, public concerns. This discussion of the acquisition of R&D spans both the steps for conducting R&D and the supporting elements that services contracting provides.

The primary executive agencies in the federal government that conduct research and development are the National Institute of Standards and Technology (NIST), the National Oceanographic and Atmospheric Administration (NOAA), the Department of Defense (DoD), the Department of Energy (DOE), the National Institutes of Health (NIH), the Department of Homeland Security (DHS), the U.S. Geological Survey (USGS), the Department of Transportation (DOT), the Department of Veterans Affairs (VA), the U.S. Department of Agriculture (USDA), the National Aeronautic and Space Administration (NASA), and the Environmental Protection Agency (EPA). Other agencies have small, limited R&D.

THE ROLE OF R&D IN THE U.S. INNOVATION SYSTEM

Science and technology are recognized as key drivers of economic growth as well as improved health and quality of life in the United States and throughout the world. Economists estimate that up to half of U.S. economic growth over the past five decades is due to advances in technology. A study of recent U.S. patents released several years ago found that nearly two thirds of the papers cited in these patents were published by researchers at organizations supported by federal funds– and these relationships have been growing. Recent advances in genetics and biotechnology, as well as computers and information technology, have raised public awareness of the vital economic role of research-based technology. High-tech industry is sought after by economic development organizations in virtually every state and locality. Policymakers regard universities as catalysts for high-tech economic development both through entrepreneurial activity that spins off from their research and through the concentrations of highly trained human resources they attract and generate. And the federal government plays a central role in supporting research in the nation's universities.

R&D is a substantial and growing enterprise in the United States. The government's investment in R&D has remained stable at about $350 billion. This represents about 2.5% of the nation's Gross Domestic Product (GDP). Two thirds of this money (66.6%) comes from industrial firms. Most of the balance (26.7%) comes from the federal government. Colleges and universities, private foundations, other nonprofit institutions, and state and local governments provide the remainder. Industry's share of national R&D funding has been growing steadily for several decades.

Despite its relatively modest share of total U.S. R&D funding, the federal government's role is critical to the nation's science and technology enterprise. Federal agencies support the majority (59%) of the nation's basic research and nearly two thirds (61.6%) of the R&D performed in U.S. colleges and universities. Basic research is the primary source of the new knowledge that ultimately drives the innovation process. At the same time, federally funded research at colleges and universities plays a key role in educating the next generation of scientists and engineers. Federal applied research and development programs also provide direct support for key government missions, such as improving the nation's health and medical care, exploring space, and facilitating national security.

R&D In The Federal Budget

President Obama's budget invests in four key R&D priorities:

(1) science for a prosperous America,
(2) a clean energy future,
(3) healthy lives for all Americans, and
(4) a safe and secure America.

Federal R&D expenditures have represented about 4% of the overall federal budget. DoD spending accounts for about 60% of the R&D budget, with the non-DoD sector spending the remainder. Of late, non-defense R&D spending is on the rise; whereas defense R&D spending is declining.

It is important to recognize that there is no overall R&D budget and no special treatment for R&D within the federal budget. Expenditures for R&D programs are ordinary budget items. They are contained, along with other types of expenditures, within the budgets of more than 20 federal departments and independent agencies. Some R&D programs are line items in the budget and are relatively easy to identify; others are included within larger line items and are more difficult to recognize. Nearly all federal R&D comes from the discretionary budget, the approximately one third of the budget that is subject to annual appropriations decided by the president and Congress. Less than 1% of the federal R&D portfolio is mandatory spending.

Although the federal government maintains several hundred laboratories around the country, only 22% of federally supported R&D is actually conducted in these labs. Industrial firms under contract perform the most federally funded R&D, at about 40%. Colleges and universities conduct about 20% under federal grants. Other nonprofit institutions perform a small portion, and about 10% of the portfolio is performed by federally funded R&D centers (FFRDCs) operated by contractors. Further, within the R&D portfolio, the work performed by these sectors consists of basic research, applied research, development, R&D facilities construction, and capital equipment for R&D. Recent trends show that in DoD, the largest share of R&D funds is for development; whereas in non-defense agencies, the largest share of R&D funds is used for basic and applied research (see "What Is R&D?" below).

To achieve the four R&D priorities noted above, the following challenges need to be met:

(1) Coordinate better executive and legislative R&D priorities;
(2) Develop data sets to improve tracking of R&D investments and to make the data publicly accessible (see "Federal R&D Opportunities and Awards".
(3) Implement comprehensive surveillance and evaluation tools for research and development projects; and
(4) Take advantage of the open innovation model in submitting agency R&D budgets. (This model is used so that R&D need not occur in one place and the process is open to ideas at different stages of a project.)

Today, there is a stronger push for agencies, wherever possible, to coordinate R&D efforts, both to eliminate duplicative and low-payoff projects and to achieve the goals set by the interagency National Science and Technology Council.

What Is R&D?

Both the Office of Management and Budget Circular A-11[1] and the Federal Acquisition Regulation,[2] Parts 2 and 35, provide the fundamental definitions of research and development:

1. Research and Development (R&D) activities comprise creative work undertaken on a systematic basis in order to increase the stock of knowledge and use this stock of knowledge to devise new applications.
2. Basic research is defined as systematic study directed toward fuller knowledge or understanding of the fundamental aspects of phenomena and of observable facts without specific applications towards processes or products in mind.
3. Applied research is defined as extensions of basic research to do systematic study to gain knowledge or understanding necessary to determine the means by which a recognized and specific need may be met.
4. Development is defined as systematic application of basic and/ or applied research directed toward the production of useful materials, devices, and systems or methods, including design, development, and improvement of prototypes and new processes to meet specific requirements.
5. Construction and rehabilitation of research and development facilities. This includes the acquisition, design, and construction of, or major repairs or alterations to, all physical facilities for use in R&D activities. Facilities include land, buildings, and fixed capital equipment, regardless of whether the facilities are to be used by the Government or by a private organization, and regardless of where title to the property may rest. Facilities also comprise the international space station as well as reactors, wind tunnels, and particle accelerators.

By extension of the definition elements in 2-4, above, in the Department of Defense), the research, development, test, and evaluation (RDT&E) budget activities reflect different types of DoD science and technology activities. The more detailed R&D process steps are as follows:

Budget Activity 1, Basic Research. Basic research is systematic study directed toward greater knowledge or understanding of the fundamental aspects of phenomena and of observable facts without specific applications towards processes or products in mind. It includes all scientific study and experimentation directed toward increasing fundamental knowledge and understanding in those fields of the physical, engineering, environmental, and life sciences related to long-term national security needs. It is farsighted high payoff research that provides the basis for technological progress. Basic research may lead to: (a) subsequent applied research and advanced technology developments in Defense-related technologies, and (b) new and improved military functional capabilities in areas such as communications, detection, tracking, surveillance, propulsion, mobility, guidance and control, navigation, energy conversion, materials and structures, and personnel support...

Budget Activity 2, Applied Research. Applied research is systematic study to understand the means to meet a recognized and specific need. It is a systematic expansion and application of knowledge to develop useful materials, devices, and systems or methods. It may be oriented, ultimately, toward the design, development, and improvement of prototypes and new processes to meet general mission area requirements. Applied research may translate promising basic research into solutions for broadly defined military needs, short of system development. This type of effort may vary from systematic mission-directed research beyond that in Budget Activity 1 to sophisticated breadboard hardware, study, programming and planning efforts that establish the initial feasibility and practicality of proposed solutions to technological challenges. It includes studies, investigations, and non-system specific technology efforts. The dominant characteristic is that applied research is directed toward general military needs with a view toward developing and evaluating the feasibility and practicality of proposed solutions and determining their parameters. Applied Research precedes system specific technology investigations or development...

Budget Activity 3, Advanced Technology Development (ATD). This budget activity includes development of subsystems and components and efforts to integrate subsystems and components into system prototypes for field experiments and/or tests in a simulated environment. ATD includes concept and technology demonstrations of components and subsystems or system models.

The models may be form, fit and function prototypes or scaled models that serve the same demonstration purpose. The results of this type of effort are proof of technological feasibility and assessment of subsystem and component operability and producibility rather than the development of hardware for service use. Projects in this category have a direct relevance to identified military needs. Advanced Technology Development demonstrates the general military utility or cost reduction potential of technology when applied to different types of military equipment or techniques... Projects in this category do not necessarily lead to subsequent development or procurement phases, but should have the goal of moving out of Science and Technology (S&T) and into the acquisition process within the future years defense program (FYDP). Upon successful completion of projects that have military utility, the technology should be available for transition.

Budget Activity 4, Advanced Component Development and Prototypes (ACD&P). Efforts necessary to evaluate integrated technologies, representative modes or prototype systems in a high fidelity and realistic operating environment are funded in this budget activity. The ACD&P phase includes system specific efforts that help expedite technology transition from the laboratory to operational use. Emphasis is on proving component and subsystem maturity prior to integration in major and complex systems and may involve risk reduction initiatives...

Budget Activity 5, System Development and Demonstration (SDD). SDD programs...are conducting engineering and manufacturing development tasks aimed at meeting validated requirements prior to full-rate production... Prototype performance is near or at planned operational system levels. Characteristics of this budget activity involve mature system development, integration and demonstration... and conducting live fire test and evaluation (LFT&E) and initial operational test and evaluation (IOT&E) of production representative articles...

Budget Activity 6, RDT&E Management Support. This budget activity includes research, development, test and evaluation efforts and funds to sustain and/or modernize the installations or operations required for general research, development, test and evaluation. Test ranges, military construction, maintenance support of laboratories, operation and maintenance of test aircraft and ships, and studies and analyses in support of the RDT&E program are funded in this budget activity...

Budget Activity 7, Operational System Development. This budget activity includes development efforts to upgrade systems that have been fielded or have received approval for full rate production and anticipate production funding in the current or subsequent fiscal year.

R&D and Services Contracting

Given this fundamental process for research & development, the question now arises of how s this R&D process relates to services contracting. Table 10-1 shows the connection between services and R&D contracting. Table 10-1 Services are generally shorter-term activities focused on a clear accomplishment. This end state is true whether in a repetitive commercial setting, a process improvement setting, or services purchased as a utility. By contrast, R&D is a series of process steps over a longer term aimed at development and/or implementation of new ideas, processes, or products.

Table 10-1 PBA Context of R&- D Contracting		
The rationale for discussing performance-based acquisition (PBA) in the context of R&D contracting is that performance-based aspects of R&D contracting are a natural extension of service contracting.		
Aspect	**Service Contracting**	**R&D Contracting**
Definition	Effort directed at doing something to something. Major thrust is to provide, maintain, and/or upgrade to objects, people, processes, or information.	Effort directed at developing processes or products. Major thrust is to evolve new ways of doing for processes or services.
Modus Operandi	Based on shorter-term, routine, or state-of-the-art application within a definite time frame.	Based on longer-term, unique use, or breakthrough in a less definite time frame.

Thus, research and development entails effort and output like services. The major distinction between services contracting and R&D is that any R&D uses a common, underlying method and perspective. The matrix in Table 10-2 captures the essence of the R&D process steps.

Table 10-2 Process Steps for Research and Development			
R&D Stage	**Description**	**Results**	**Techniques**
Basic Research	Increase knowledge base to better understand fundamental phenomena	Identify specific idea(s) for further research	• Studies • Literature review • Speak to experts
Applied Research	Develop design for addressing research idea(s)	Proposed solution for problem or opportunity	• Studies • Experiments
Initial Development	Construct process or prototype of item	Operational and cost requirements description	• Experiments • Modeling
Testing	Prove feasibility of prototype	Functional validation	• Testing • Design validation • Focus group
Final Development	Enhance prototype to perform as operational system	Proven operational performance addressing social & environmental concerns	• Design changes • Production method • Focus group
Utilization	Disseminate, sustain, and upgrade item	Need fully met	• Improve design • Marketplace tests • New applications

NOTE: This matrix shows the life cycle events for R&D.

The conventional wisdom is that the R&D process is used to generate new tangible items. In many cases, this is true. Yet, it can also generate new services. For example when the Department of Homeland Security (DHS) was established in 2003, one of its main challenges was to get the message to the country about what the agency is and what it will do. To achieve this objective, an informational program was needed. The six steps of the R&D process were used to ultimately disseminate and upgrade knowledge and understanding about DHS.

R&D ACQUISITION PROCESS

The key events in the source selection process that is being executed for the majority of services purchased are shown in Table 10-3.

Table 10-3 Source Selection Process Events		
Acquisition Phase	**Source Selection Process**	**Source Selection Activities**
Pre-solicitation	Develop Acquisition Plan	• Conduct Effective Market Research • Develop the Acquisition Plan
	Develop Source Selection Plan	Develop the Source Selection Plan with Evaluation Team Members Identified
	Obtain Reviews and Approvals	• Sustain Funding Availability • Request/Receive Agency-Level Reviews/Approval Authorization
Solicitation	Prepare and Issue Solicitation	Write the Requirements
		Develop an Independent Government Cost Estimate
		Obtain Industry Comments on the Draft Solicitation (optional)
		Revise Technical Information
		Finalize the Solicitation
		Issue & Publicize the Solicitation
		Hold Pre-proposal Conference (optional)
		Answer Questions & Amend the Document Solicitation
Evaluation	Evaluate Proposals	Train the Source Selection Team
		Receive Proposals
		Determine Whether Proposals Comply with the Solicitation Instructions
		Scrutinize Proposals Using Evaluation Criteria
		Request Clarification or Correction
		Rate Technical Proposals
		Conduct Initial Cost Evaluation
		Establish Competitive Range
Award	Select Contractor	Conduct Discussions & Orals
		Request Best and Final Offers (BAFOs)
		Re-rate Proposals Based on BAFOs
		Select the Apparent Winner
		Conduct Responsibility Reviews
		Approve the Selection
		Award the Contract & Publicize
		Notify Unsuccessful Offerors
		Debrief Offerors
		Handle Any Protests
Post Award	Contract Administration	• Do Appropriate Monitoring • Accept Deliverables & Final Evaluation

In the performance-based acquisition orientation for R&D, it is important to make the connection between actual performance and the achievement of strategic goals. Figure 10-1 enables this connection for any R&D project.

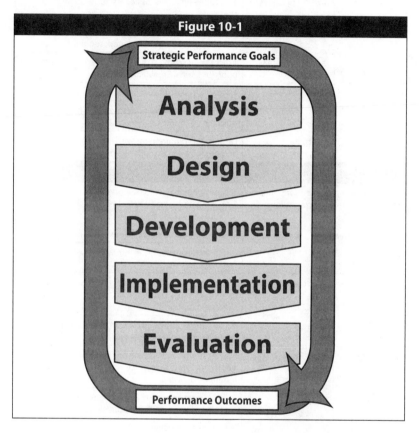

Figure 10-1

Strategic Performance Goals

Analysis

Design

Development

Implementation

Evaluation

Performance Outcomes

Many of the source selection process steps in Table 10-3 are also found in conducting source selection for research and development contracts. Table 10-4 offers insights to improve this process and move toward a stronger performance orientation.

Table 10-4 PBA Context of R&D Contracting		
Aspect	**Challenge**	**Improvement Means**
Definition	Consistent use	Eliminate management & support from R&D categories since it is a service activity.
Scope	Broader perspective	1. Include impact discussion on subsequent R&D stage(s).
		2. Use phased approach to allow for decision points prior to proceeding to next work segment.
	More complete	Articulate description of R&D requirement based upon functional knowledge of similar past experience.
	Output oriented	1. Paradigm shift: Focus on results, not hours used.
		2. For any effort, expect intermediate and final results from the contractor.
Strategic View	Incorporate outcomes	Design R&D requirement with program objectives and organizational mission in mind.
R&D		
Performance Administration	Use performance standards	1. Apply peer review to describe & use incremental & final means to evaluate technical performance, schedule, cost, & quality.
		2. Have common, basic set of standards (see Table 10-5).
		3. Can define multiple performance levels for the same R&D activity.
Incentives	Select meaningful ones	1. Have implicit choices in every contract (e.g., ability to innovate, + performance evaluations and/or exercise of option).
		2. Use explicit choices to obtain greater success (e.g., award term or share-in-savings).
Contract Type	Fixed-Price Application (FPA)	1. Choose among variations: fixed-price, variable [best effort] outcome; fixed-price with re-determination; or indefinite delivery.
		2. Choose among many R&D procurement strategies that using FPA (see "R&D Acquisition Strategies").
		3. Performance defined in incremental, overlapping & consecutive steps.
	Non-FPA	R&D is volatile & changeable and/or has unknown unknowns (e.g., whether to test & if so, what tests to use)

Fixed-price contracting is not anathema in research and development contracting. Why? As shown in Figure 10-2, historically the presumption with carrying out an R&D endeavor was that until all variables are fully controlled the risk cannot be shifted to the performer's shoulders. However, why should the government assume so much of the risk during R&D when other, successful means have demonstrated differently?

For example, what happens in Stage 1, Basic Research? The researcher uses three techniques (as shown in Table 10-2) to discover an idea worthy of further research investigation. Now, has the federal government ever used legal instruments to have basic research done? How about millions of them? So, the government must know what functional activities need to occur, even if the results are not known, because that is what is being purchased.

Thus, again why must the government assume so much risk for an R&D area that is well understood? Again, the government can shift the risk to the R&D performer. An example is the Small Business Innovative Research (SBIR) program (see a more complete description at "R&D Acquisition Strategies," below).

In this endeavor, organizations selected to do research on one or more agency- identified research ideas are given a set amount of money and a time frame to analyze the feasibility of an idea. That is, the initial effort is generally a fixed-price contract.

So, if it can be done for the SBIR program, why not for any basic research?

Figure 10-3 gives a contemporary view of the relationship between government risk and stage of R&D. Here, the risk/R&D connection is a bell-shaped curve. In the first couple of R&D stages, the government can shift the risk to the performer since the functional aspects of the effort are well known. And the last two stages follow suit for the same reason. However, in stages three and four, there may be many more variables. For example, if the prototype is going through testing, the characteristics to test and/or the kinds of tests to use may not be known. And if these unknown, unknowns are present, then having the government take more of the performance risk can be in the best interest of the endeavor. The bottom line is that cost- reimbursement efforts are not bad. They need to be applied where there is not enough information or certainty for the performer to assume the risk. This application needs to occur on an exceptional, not a knee-jerk, basis.

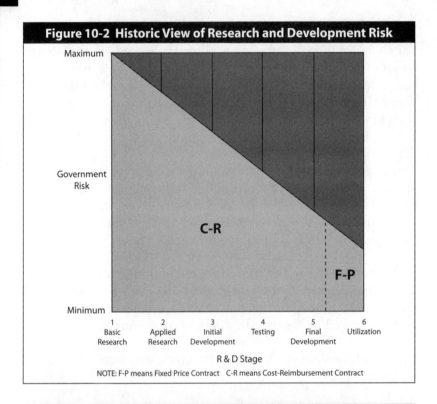

Figure 10-2 Historic View of Research and Development Risk

NOTE: F-P means Fixed Price Contract   C-R means Cost-Reimbursement Contract

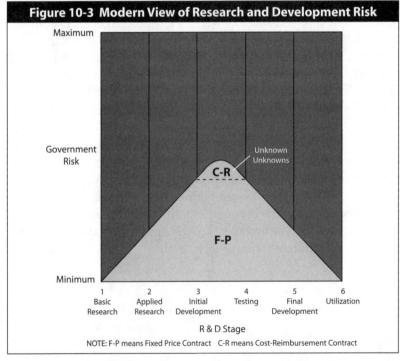

Figure 10-3 Modern View of Research and Development Risk

NOTE: F-P means Fixed Price Contract   C-R means Cost-Reimbursement Contract

Patent Rights and Independent R&D Development Costs

There are two additional contractual aspects common across the R&D contracting spectrum. They are patent rights and independent research and development costs.

Patent Rights

The Bayh-Dole Act of 1980 expressly gave colleges, universities, and other nonprofit entities the right, which had previously been presumptively held by the federal government itself, to patent inventions resulting from federally funded research and development activities they conduct. In the three decades since the Bayh-Dole Act changed the nation's patent laws, some academic institutions have been much more prolific than others at patenting technologies and other inventions discovered in their laboratories. In addition, patient waivers have also been granted to for-profit organizations based on their fulfilling some other economic constraint, such as cost sharing.

Independent Research & Development Costs

(FAR 31-205.18). Independent research and development (IR&D) costs are incurred by a company on its own in conducting projects that fall within the areas of basic research, applied research, development, and systems. In order to be charged to a government contract, IR&D must be of potential interest to the federal government and be related to the R&D areas noted above. IR&D are allowable costs under contracts and subcontracts involving business with the federal government. These costs are treated as overhead. Thus, the government pays its share of the company's IR&D in the price it pays for products and services. This augments the company's expenditures for R&D and allows additional company spending to explore advanced concepts, create new products and processes, improve existing products, and pursue technology advancements in areas where the government's needs are greatest and an organization's capabilities are strongest.

By definition, IR&D costs are independent and cannot be for efforts required in the performance of a contract or grant. A cost incurred to perform a contract is direct and must be charged to the contract. R&D conducted under a contract falls within this category.

R&D Acquisition Strategies

Peer Review Requirements

One of the major distinguishing characteristics of research and development acquisitions is peer review. Administration R&D policy principles issued by the White House's Office of Science and Technology Policy direct federal agencies to use merit review with peer evaluation (peer review) and competitive selection in R&D projects. Chosen activities must be reviewed, in accordance with OMB *Circular A-11*, by appropriately qualified scientists and engineers outside the decision-making or supervisory chain.

Peer review is a means of assessing the potential for R&D efforts as well as the subsequent results of R&D projects. Independent, third-party reviewers carry out competent, qualified, objective, and formal evaluation by using specified criteria. It is a process that can be used at key milestones of the R&D life cycle. Common instances where peer reviews are conducted include:

- Selection of projects from research proposals,
- Prior to competitive award of subcontracts,
- Inclusion of R&D findings in scientific journals and/or conferences, and
- Determination of recognition and awards.

(See Figure 10-4, below, for the Peer Review Process Flow.)

In addition, in response to the Government Performance and Results Act and performance-based contracting, agencies have incorporated peer review into the annual performance of programs and laboratories. The results of these reviews are also used to determine future program direction and to build business cases for subsequent funding of research activities. Success in meeting agency goals for science and technology would be indicated by favorable outside peer reviews and judgments of expert advisory committees.

Three additional challenges to the success of the peer review process are (1) it will provide a complete picture of the project value to the agency, (2) the agency will incorporate the peer review recommendations, and (3) multi-disciplinary teams will be used wherever possible to enable an unbiased and full review.

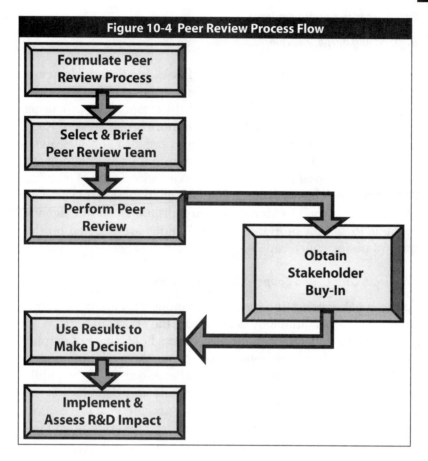

Figure 10-4 Peer Review Process Flow

R&D Acquisition Instruments

Various instruments can be used for procuring research and development services. All of these acquisition instruments follow the source selection process briefly described above whereby the funding entity evaluates proposed effort based on a defined need. The challenge in any acquisition strategy is to ensure that after award, sufficient surveillance is conducted to ascertain that the expected performance and results are indeed occurring. The R&D acquisition strategy definition and use process is shown in Figure 10-5.

For each strategy a Web citation is provided as an example to demonstrate an agency's activities related to the type of procurement instrument used.

Broad Agency Announcements

http://www.darpa.mil/cmo/baa.html

The broad agency announcement (BAA) acquisition device is one of the most commonly used since it can easily reflect the specific R&D activity to be procured. In essence, the procuring office uses peer review to define one or more broad areas of R&D interest to the program office(s). Various organizations are given an opportunity to submit one or more proposals for the research areas. The proposal team can consist of a wide variety of teaming arrangements. Through submitting concept papers, a down selection process is used to identify the organizations that the agency requests to submit proposals. Organizations are selected on the basis of performance capability for a particular research topic.

Contracts, Grants, and Cooperative Agreements

In the R&D context, the distinction among procurement instruments is who will ultimately benefit from the effort put forth. With a contract, the federal program receives the lion's share of outputs and outcomes. In a cooperative agreement, other governmental or organizational entities are the primary beneficiaries (in the public interest). The ultimate recipient of outputs and outcomes is the beneficiary of a grant. However, with any procurement mechanism today, there needs to be a well-defined R&D description and the means to track subsequent performance.

Cooperative Research and Development Agreements

http://www.cuyamaca.edu/cuyamaca/academic/dept/envt/tech_transfer/3e-crada.htm

Cooperative research and development agreements (CRADAs) are developed by federal laboratories to encourage non-federal parties and the government to optimize resources and cost-effectively perform research by sharing the costs of research with a CRADA partner. The collaborating partner agrees to provide resources (such as funding, personnel, services, facilities, or equipment) while the federal laboratory agrees to provide similar resources but no funds directly to the partner. Federal scientists can work closely with their non-federal counterparts to exchange ideas and information while protecting a partner's proprietary information. The CRADA vehicle provides incentives that help speed the commercialization of federally-developed technology. CRADAs also enable the government and a collaborating partner to share patents and patent licenses. Further, a CRADA is not a procurement contract, grant, or cooperative agreement. CRADAs typically consist of two main components: (1) General Provisions (the legal framework) and a (2) Statement of Work or SOW (the objectives, tasks, deliverables and performance criteria) of the CRADA activity.

Other Transactions Agreements

http://www.policyarchive.org/handle/10207/bitstreams/19087.pdf

http://www.ogc.doc.gov/ogc/contracts/cld/hi/otguide.pdf

A class of assistance agreements used by DoD, DHS, DOE, NASA, and DOT to facilitate basic, applied, and advanced research projects when the research is to be performed by a for-profit firm or a consortium that includes for-profit firms is known as Other Transactions. These agreements may be utilized only when a contract, grant, or cooperative agreement is not feasible. In addition, Other Transactions do involve the expenditure of appropriated federal funds and are subject to greater regulation than CRADAs. A company must maintain adequate records to account for its funding contribution, and generally those records must be maintained for three years after the expiration of an agreement. Federal agencies are free to negotiate unique intellectual property coverage for each Other Transaction agreement.

Program Opportunity Notices for Commercial Demonstrations

http://www.management.energy.gov/policy_guidance/615.htm

Program Opportunity Notices are used by the Department of Energy to accelerate the demonstration of the technical feasibility and commercial application of all potentially beneficial non-nuclear energy sources and utilization technologies. Demonstrations can be performed by individuals, educational institutions, commercial or industrial organizations, or other private entities, or public entities, including state and local governments, but not other federal agencies. Commercial demonstration projects include demonstrations of technological advances, field demonstrations of new methods and procedures, and demonstrations of prototype commercial applications for the exploration, development, production, transportation, conversion, and utilization of non-nuclear energy resources.

Program Research and Development Announcements

http://www.management.energy.gov/policy_guidance/615.htm

Program research and development announcements (PRDAs) are used to provide proposers with information concerning the Department of Energy's (DOE's) interest in entering into arrangements for research, development, and related projects in specified areas of the energy field. It is DOE's desire to involve the gamut of small business concerns in research and development undertaken pursuant to a PRDA. The solicitation process is similar to that conducted with a Broad Agency Announcement.

Defense Acquisition Challenge Program

https://cto.acqcenter.com

The Defense Acquisition Challenge (DAC) program is designed to increase the introduction of innovative and cost-saving technologies, products, or processes that demonstrate a near-term potential to improve existing DoD programs. Preference is given to those technologies and products that challenge an incumbent product or process and have the potential to be evaluated within 24 months following project selection for transition to operation/ production at the completion of the evaluation. Proposal review occurs in two phases. In the first phase, any person or activity within or outside the DoD interested in participating must submit a proposal using the DAC website (https://cto.acqcenter.com). All proposals received are subject to peer and scientific review panels. In the second phase, the proposals selected/submitted by DoD program managers compete for DAC funding to test the proposed technology.

Small Business Innovation Research Program

http://www.darpa.mil/sbpo/sbir_program/index.html

This Small Business Innovation Research (SBIR) program was established by Congress to enable small businesses to participate in federal research & development and to increase private sector commercialization of innovations derived from federal R&D. All federal agencies with an annual extramural R&D budget exceeding $100 million participate in the SBIR program. The SBIR program budget is computed as 2.5% of an agency's extramural

R&D budget. The program dynamic has three phases. Phase I is a feasibility study of a selected federal R&D idea. Proposals are competitively selected. Successful Phase I efforts can lead to Phase II work, which is a research and development effort that culminates in a well-defined, deliverable prototype. Phase III requires the small business to seek outside funding to transform the prototype into a commercially saleable item to either the government and/or the private sector. Phase I funding is for a fixed amount over a fixed period of time. Phase II funding can be the same as for Phase I, although in some cases, additional government funds can be provided to match private sector funding.

Small Business Technology Transfer Program

http://www.darpa.mil/sbpo/sttr_program/index.html

The Small Business Technology Transfer (STTR) program is separate from the SBIR program. The purpose of the STTR program is to create partnerships between innovative small business concerns and research institutions to conduct federally funded research or research and development in order to ultimately commercialize innovative technologies. All federal agencies with an annual extramural R&D budget exceeding $1 billion participate in the STTR program. The STTR program budget is computed as 0.3% of an agency's extramural R&D budget. The STTR program process enables R&D to occur through three phases similar to those used in the SBIR program. Further, the appropriate teaming arrangement to execute this program is between a small business and a research institution, i.e., a nonprofit research institution, federally funded research and development center (FFRDC), or university. For STTR program Phase I and II efforts, the principal investigator may be primarily employed with either a small business or a research institution.

Federally Funded Research and Development Centers

FAR Part 35.017 and *http://www.sourcewatch.org/index.php?title=Federally_Funded_Research_and_Development_Center*

An FFRDC meets a special long-term research or development need that cannot be met as effectively using existing in-house or contractor resources. In order to discharge its responsibilities to the sponsoring agency, an FFRDC has access beyond that which is usual for a normal contractual relationship to government and supplier data (including sensitive and proprietary data) and to employees, installation equipment, and real property. However, an FFRDC may perform work for other than the sponsoring agency. FFRDCs are operated, managed, and/or administered by either a university or a consortium of universities, other not-for-profit or nonprofit organizations, or an industrial firm (as an autonomous organization or as an identifiable separate operating unit of a parent organization).

Using GSA Schedules to Purchase R&D

http://www.gsa.gov/Portal/gsa/ep/channelView.do?pageType Id=17112&channelPage=%2Fep%2Fchannel%2Fgsa Overview. jsp&channelId=-24732

It is a myth that the GSA schedules today do not provide the means for the gamut of purchasing that the federal government does. Certainly, supplies, services, information technology, and construction are covered. So why not research and development? The answer is there is no gap in GSA schedules either. Its website conveys that BPAs can be issued from an engineering services schedule that does include specific aspects of the R&D life cycle.

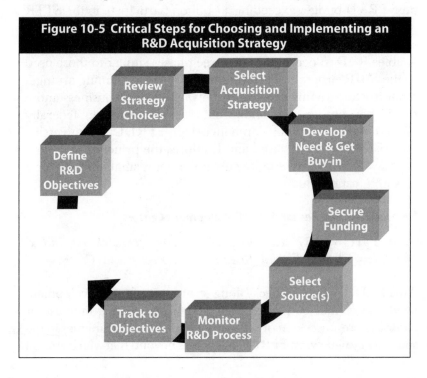

Figure 10-5 Critical Steps for Choosing and Implementing an R&D Acquisition Strategy

MONITORING AND SURVEILLANCE

Fulfilling the requirements of the Government Performance and Results Act of 1993 has presented federal science agencies with the challenge of defining ways to quantify and evaluate research outcomes. Two major facets that come into play here are report tracking and measuring research program performance.

Report Tracking

Report tracking is an action that is taken for granted in the contractual administration of many an R&D project Yet, much on-the-ground experience has shown that to presume an organization will naturally provide the required reports at the right time in the correct format and content does not work. Instead, establishing a means up-front to track the emergence and submittal of these information outputs is key to ensuring that legal commitments are met. A tickler mechanism can be established so that the Contracting Officer representative is always aware of what is due from the R&D contractor, whether it has been received, what the format and content are (relative to what is mandated), and whether the contractor is delinquent. The representative can also take immediate actions to obtain feedback about how and when the R&D organization will deliver the necessary reports. If the delinquency continues, the Contracting Officer can get involved and potentially issue a payment suspension until the required reporting corrections are made. This process can be used for any of the acquisition strategies noted. To enable proper submittals, the postaward conference is an excellent venue to discuss the deliverables sequence and to reiterate the importance of meeting that sequence . Further, it makes sense not to ask for only a draft, final report. Rather, asking for monthly progress reports and/or having periodic review meetings is an opportunity to acknowledge and discuss the progress to date, issues discovered, and ways to handle them. These steps can convey a realistic picture of what an R&D organization is actually performing and how it can do so better.

Performance Measurement

Measuring research program performance is particularly important because of the substantial investments made in research and development activities. Table 10-5 provides a set of standards with examples that have been effectively utilized to demonstrate and sustain effective R&D performance. Together, these standards provide a complete picture of the short- and longer-term impacts of an R&D effort although it should be noted that the standards in Table 10-5 have a longer-term time constant than others, and these standards do not preclude the use of additional standards that focus on the specific R&D activity undertaken.

While these standards are necessary, they may not be sufficient to fully conduct surveillance of an R&D performer's activities. Other means of assessing performance include: (1) timeliness and completeness of reports, (2) regular meetings to discuss progress, and (3) periodic in-process reviews of the overall effort to date and subsequent tasks planned. Any of these actions can help identify what is going well and what concerns need to be addressed sooner to ensure viable R&D results.

Table 10-5 R&D (Basic Performance Standards with Examples)	
Performance Standard	Example
A. Research Quality	1. Percent of deviation in:
	o method(s) given vs. method(s) used
	o timeliness given vs. timeliness used
	o problems found vs. problems resolved
	o results projected vs. actual results
	o test(s) shown vs. test(s) conducted
	o demo(s) shown vs. demo(s) conducted
	2. No. of unexpected or novel results
	3. Percentage match of research method(s) and equivalent research
B. Research Relevance	1. Percent match of:
	o R&D definition to Org.'s mission
	o R&D definition to program objectives
	o R&D priority to actual priority relative to other, equivalent efforts
	o R&D stage to further R&D stage(s)
	2. No. of new R&D generated Strategic or program objectives
	3. No. of new user groups identified
	4. No. of new applications found
C. Research Leadership	Percent match of:
	o R&D impact assertions vs. expert judgment
	o R&D priority vs. international priorities R&D

Best Practices

Building the bridges to effectively conduct an R&D acquisition means using the following Best Practices:

1. Realize the scope of what really needs to occur. Learn to define the requirement and hone it through effective feedback from the R&D peer review group.
2. Understand that the results from an R&D effort will impact the strategic and program goals of an agency. Define performance metrics to ensure these connections are made.
3. Package a solicitation document to resonate well with the key acquisition and program personnel. Doing so eases and accelerates R&D success.
4. Acquisition strategies are a method, not an outcome. Discern the desired outcome of the R&D project and then choose the best strategy to engender that outcome.
5. Generate market research knowledge about the providers of the R&D in advance. Use this information to better reflect the description of what needs to be done.
6. Be clear about the expected outcome to better consider an array of proposed approaches to finding the results.
7. Model performance monitoring that demonstrates the ability to ensure the provision of desired results.
8. A single set of results may not fully meet the need. Sustain the quality of the research by connecting the report information to other existing or emerging findings through peer review.
9. Focus on employing the results generated. Can they be immediately applied? Will they lead to further commercialization activities? How well do the findings demonstrate achievement of program objectives? What additional R&D efforts may be generated from this effort?

IMPLICATIONS FOR FURTHER INNOVATION

The field of research & development in the federal government is in a dynamic mode today. Based on the discussion of ways to procure various R&D projects, several emerging areas of note provide a window to the means of obtaining research and development in the future. They are as follows:

Apps for Army Program

http://www.army.mil/-news/2010/08/05/43293-apps-for-army-to-shape-future-software-acquisition/

The Apps for Army program is the Army's first internal application development challenge and one of the first for the federal government. Its aim was to foster agile development and rapid deployment of software for soldiers in combat. Through May 2010, some 141 participants had registered for Apps for Army as teams or individuals for the application development contest, part of a government-wide effort to engage broader audiences in the contribution of new ideas. Out of 53 submittals, 15 winners were announced at the Army LandWarNet conference in Tampa, Fla., in August 2010. Selected submissions received employee awards from a total cash pool of $30,000. Today, the process to develop applications for Army use is time-consuming and difficult. With the acquisition process that was piloted during the Apps for Army challenge, the Army demonstrated a faster way to get capability to the war fighter – a process the Army can extend now to include industry.

Sustainable Energy

The Department of Energy is amending the Department of Energy Acquisition Regulation (DEAR) to implement Executive Order 13514, Federal Leadership in Environmental, Energy and Economic Performance. The intent of the rule (effective October 22, 2010) is to leverage agency acquisitions to foster markets for sustainable technologies and energy efficient and environmentally sustainable materials, products, and services. This rule was drafted in recognition of changing environmental circumstances and our nation's heightened energy demands. These circumstances demand that the federal government lead by example to create a clean energy economy that will increase prosperity, promote energy security, protect the interests of taxpayers, and safeguard the health of our environment. Executive Order 13514 requires federal agencies to leverage agency acquisitions to foster markets for sustainable technologies and energy-efficient and environmentally sustainable materials, products, and services. Federal agencies are additionally required to design, construct, maintain, and operate high performance sustainable buildings in sustainable locations.

Patent Rights Incentive

The Patent & Trademark office negotiated a contract for an upgraded patent application system with a $1 value contract. However, an incentive in the contract provided that if the contractor were successful in developing and implementing the software, it could market the software without liability to other government or private sector clients.

FEDERAL R&D OPPORTUNITIES AND AWARDS

Following is a useful set of references that provide descriptions of various federal research & development opportunities, awards, in-progress, or/or completed projects.

R&D Opportunities

Research and development opportunities can be found in four places: (1) Fedbizopps.gov, (2) grants.gov, (3) ebuy.gsa.gov, and (4) federal agency websites. In addition, DoD TechMatch (*www.dodtechmatch.dom*) is a government-sponsored (Department of Defense), no-fee, web-based portal that facilitates technology deployment collaboration by providing information and identifying opportunities (FedBizOpps, *Grants.gov*, and SBIR/STTR solicitations), licensable patents, and current technology needs using a unique keyword matching function.

R&D Project Summaries and Awards

R&D project summary information, awards, and current or completed projects follow.

Frequently Asked Questions

http://www.osti.gov/fedrnd/descript

What information is provided by Federal R&D Project Summaries?

Project award information, including agency or organization, project title, project abstract, principal investigator, and project start and end dates, are provided in R&D Project Summaries. Additional information, such as keywords or funding, is sometimes provided as well.

What federal agencies participate in Federal R&D Project Summaries?

Original agency participants are the Department of Agriculture (USDA), the Department of Energy (DOE), the Environmental Protection Agency (EPA), the National Institutes of Health (NIH) and the National Science Foundation (NSF), and the Small Business Administration (SBA). The Department of Defense (DoD), the National Aeronautics and Space Administration (NASA), and the Transportation Research Board (TRB) became participants in 2009.

How many R&D records are searched? How often is information updated?

Over 800,000 records are searched when "All Sources" is used as a search term. Queries are sent in real time, so as soon as an update occurs in a particular database, results are available via Federal R&D Project Summaries.

What are the benefits of the Federal R&D Project Summaries search?

Federal R&D Project Summaries shows how the public's investment in research and development is used. The search is a cross-agency search of R&D and provides an interdisciplinary view of science. A patron may select to search any or all agency databases. The query is sent in real- time to the database(s) selected and full-text records for database matches are returned. You do not need to know which agency or organization performs the R&D when the search is performed, nor do you have to wait for new records to be indexed prior to retrieving them. In addition, the search is full-text so all relevant information is retrieved.

Why do the returned records appear to be different from one another?

Information comes from different sources and is in its original format. OSTI does not duplicate information from the agencies but rather provides the service to make each agency's information searchable via one interface. OSTI hosts the tool that searches and displays the information to a patron so that results can be culled, compiled, and customized into useful sets of information.

Do the results differ from those found at each individual database?

No. The information is not altered in any way. However, only the top results are returned from each participating database, generally the top 100. To view specific details for each search, use the "Summary of All Results" link at the lower right of the results page dashboard. A relevancy filter is also used since results from many sources are compiled. If more database results are needed from a particular source, you can directly access the source you have identified as being most relevant through Federal R&D Project Summaries.

What features are added to this new version of Federal R&D Project Summaries?

Content now includes project summaries from the Department of Defense (DoD), the National Aeronautics and Space Administration (NASA), and the Transportation Research Board (TRB), as well as from original agency participants, the Department of Agriculture (USDA), the Department of Energy (DOE), the Environmental Protection Agency (EPA), the National Institutes of Health (NIH) and the National Science Foundation (NSF), and the Small Business Administration (SBA). An Advanced Search feature has been added to target queries more narrowly, if desired. Enhanced capabilities are also evident on the results page, with clusters of subtopics presented within an area of interest for easier navigation and discovery. Principal investigators are also clustered. Displayed results can be limited to a single agency or organization, and information can be sorted in a variety of ways. In short, the information and capabilities of this new version are greatly enhanced.

Database Descriptions

http://www.osti.gov/fedrnd/descript

DoD R&D Descriptive Summaries (RDDS)

The DoD database includes narrative information on research, development, test and evaluation (RDT&E) programs and program elements (PE Numbers) within the Department of Defense. The collection dates back to FY 1995.

DOE R&D Project Summaries Database

The DOE database contains ongoing or recently completed Department of Energy research projects. Projects pertain to a range of R&D disciplines in basic energy science, physics, biology, fossil energy, environmental management, energy efficiency, renewable energy, and technology.

EPA Science Inventory

The Science Inventory searches EPA science activities and scientific and technical products conducted by EPA and through EPA-funded assistance agreements. Science Inventory records provide descriptions of an activity or product, contact information, and links to available printed material or Web sites.

NASA Research Task Book

This database includes research projects supported by NASA's Advanced Capabilities Division (ACD) and those within the National Space Biomedical Research Institute (NSBRI). Information includes project descriptions, annual research results, research impacts, and a listing of publications resulting from this NASA-funded research from FY2004 to the present.

NIH RePORTER

The NIH RePORTER is a searchable database of federally-funded biomedical research projects conducted at universities, hospitals, and other research institutions funded by the National Institutes of Health (NIH) and other government agencies over the past 25 years. It replaces NIH CRISP, which NIH has retired.

NSF Award Abstracts Database

Information about research projects that NSF has funded since 1989 can be found by searching the Award Abstracts Database. The information includes abstracts that describe the research and names of principal investigators and their institutions. The database includes both completed and in-process research.

SBA Technology Resources Network (Tech-Net)

Tech-Net contains information on Small Business Innovation Research (SBIR) awards and Small Business Technology Transfer (STTR) awards. It facilitates those seeking small business partners, small business contractors and subcontractors, leading-edge technology research, research partners (small businesses, universities, federal labs and non-profit organizations), manufacturing centers, and investment opportunities.

Transportation Research in Progress

Transportation Research in Progress reports include current or recently completed transportation research projects. Most RiP records are projects funded by federal and state departments of transportation. University transportation research is also included. The Transportation Research Board (TRB), administered as part of the National Academies, hosts and maintains the database.

USDA Current Research Information System

The USDA's Current Research Information System (CRIS) is the U.S. Department of Agriculture's (USDA) documentation and reporting system for ongoing and recently completed research projects in agriculture, food and nutrition, and forestry. Projects are conducted or sponsored by USDA research agencies, state agricultural experiment stations, the state land-grant university system, other cooperating state institutions, and participants in a number of CSREES-administered grant programs.

DoD Research and Development Databases

The following are additional databases of the Department of Defense's research and development activities:

- Advanced Concept Technology Demonstration Program *www.acq.osd.mil/actd/*
- Advanced Systems and Concepts Office *www.acq.osd.mil/asc*
- Defense Acquisition Challenge Program *www.acq.osd.mil/cto/*
- Defense Production Act Title III Program *www.acq.osd.mil/ott/dpatitle3/*
- Foreign Comparative Testing Program *www.acq.osd.mil/cto/*
- Independent Research & Development Program *www.dtic.mil/ird/*
- ManTech Program *https://www.dodmantech.com*

National Technical Information Service

http://www.ntis.gov/products/ntisdb.aspx

The National Technical Information Service (NTIS)is the largest central repository for government-funded research in the scientific, technical, engineering, and business-related information areas. For more than 60 years NTIS has assured businesses, universities, and the public timely access to approximately 3 million U.S. federal government technical reports covering over 350 subject areas. NTIS provides a variety of dissemination services for other agencies with the specialized resources, systems, equipment, financial infrastructure, and personnel expertise needed to produce and disseminate the information products on a large scale.

What Is the NTIS Database?

Containing over 2.0 million bibliographic records, the NTIS Database is the preeminent resource for accessing the latest research sponsored by the United States and select foreign governments. The database represents billions of dollars in research. Contents include research reports, computer products, software, video cassettes, audio cassettes and more. The complete electronic file dates back to 1964. On average, NTIS adds over 30,000 new records each year to the database. Most records include abstracts.

Access to the NTIS Database is available through:

- Commercial Services (access media and pricing l vary). Please contact these organizations directly.
- National Technical Reports Library (NTRL) – Subscription access to the NTIS Database metadata with links to over 600,000 digitized full-text reports.
- Direct Lease from NTIS. Contact the NTIS Office of Product Management (703) 605-6515.

Once identified in the NTIS Database, most items are available for purchase directly from NTIS.

National Technical Information Service
Alexandria, Virginia 22312
(703) 605-6000
1-800-553-NTIS (6847)

ENDNOTES

[1] *See* OMB Circular A-11(2010) *http://www.whitehouse.gov/omb/circulars.*

[2] FAR Parts 2 and 25 *http://www.acquistion.gov*

APPENDIX

THE SERVICES ACQUISITION REFORM ACT OF 2003 SECTION-BY- SECTION ANLYSIS

Section 1 – Short Title; Table of Contents

Section 2 – Executive Agency Defined

The section would define the term "executive agency" as that term is defined in section 4(1) of the Office of Federal Procurement Policy Act (41 U.S.C. 403(1)), unless stated otherwise.

TITLE I – ACQUISITION WORKFORCE AND TRAINING

Section 101 – Definition of Acquisition.

The section would amend section 4 of the Office of Federal Procurement Policy Act (41 U.S.C. 403) to provide a comprehensive Government-wide definition of the term "acquisition." The new definition would encompass the entire spectrum of acquisition starting with the development of an agency's requirements through management and measurement of contract performance.

Section 102 – Acquisition Workforce Training Fund.

The section would amend section 37 of the Office of Federal Procurement Policy Act (41 U.S.C. 433) to establish within the General Services Administration an acquisition workforce-training fund to be managed by the Federal Acquisition Institute (FAI). The fund is to be financed by depositing 5% of the fees collected by various executive agencies under their Government-wide contracts. This will provide the stabilized funding needed by FAI to develop training resources needed to enable our acquisition professionals to transition to the new service oriented and technology driven Federal market. The fund can only be used for sorely needed acquisition workforce training across the civilian Government agencies.

Section 103 – Government-Industry Exchange Program.

The section would amend Subpart B of part III of title 5, United States Code by adding a new Chapter 38 establishing an acquisition professional exchange program to permit the temporary exchange of high-performing acquisition professionals between the Federal Government and participating private-sector concerns. Under the program, which is modeled after the Information Technology Exchange Program included in section 209 of the recently passed E-Government Act, Pub. L. 107-347, a participating Federal employee would retain his/her Federal benefits and would be deemed during the period of the assignment (for a period of between 6 months and a year, with possible extensions of up an additional year for both public and private-sector employees) to be detailed to regular work within the agency. Under the section an agency head would take necessary actions to ensure that 20 percent of those Federal employees assigned to private sector firms are assigned to small businesses. Private-sector employees could be assigned to a Federal agency. An assigned employee could still be paid by the private-sector employer and would be deemed a Federal employee for most purposes. The section would amend a number of current government employee ethics provisions to apply to private sector employees assigned to Federal agencies under the program. The Office of Personnel Management would submit semi-annual reports to the Committees on Government Reform and Governmental Affairs summarizing the operation of the program including the number of individuals assigned, the positions involved and the durations of the assignments. No assignments under the section could be made after the end of a 5-year period beginning on the date of enactment. The General Accounting Office would, 4 years after enactment, report on the effectiveness of the program and whether it should be continued. Finally, the section would provide conforming amendments to title 5 and title 18, United States Code and other law in connection with the new professional exchange program.

Section 104 – Acquisition Workforce Recruitment and Retention Program.

The section would permit the head of an agency to determine, for purposes of sections 3304, 5333, and 5753 of title 5, United States Code, that certain Federal acquisition positions are "shortage category" positions in order to recruit and directly hire such employees with high qualifications. The actions under this section would be subject to Office of Personnel Management policies. The Administrator for Federal Procurement Policy would be required to submit a report to Congress prior to the authority's September 2007 expiration date concerning the efficacy of the program and recommending whether the authority should be extended.

Section 105 – Architectural and Engineering Acquisition Workforce.

The section would provide that the Administrator for Federal Procurement Policy in consultation with the Secretary of Defense, the Administrator of General Services and the Director of the

Office of Personnel Management develop and implement a plan to assure that the Federal Government maintains a core in-house architectural and engineering capability to ensure that it has the capability to effectively contract for the performance of architectural and engineering services.

TITLE II – ADAPTATION OF BUSINESS ACQUISITION PRACTICES

Subtitle A – Adaptation of Business Management Practices

Section 201 – Chief Acquisition Officers.

The section would amend section 16 of the Office of Federal Procurement Policy Act (41 U.S.C. 414) to provide for the appointment of a non-career employee as the Chief Acquisition Officer for each executive agency other than the Department of Defense. The Department of Defense currently has a comparable position established pursuant to section 133 of title 10, United States Code. The Chief Acquisition Officer would have acquisition as the official's primary duty and advise and assist the agency head and other senior officials to ensure that the agency mission is achieved through the management of the agency's acquisition activities. The functions of the Chief Acquisition Officer would include monitoring the agency's acquisition activities, evaluating them based on applicable performance measurements, increasing the use of full and open competition in agency acquisitions, making acquisition decisions consistent with applicable laws, and establishing clear lines of authority, accountability, and responsibility for acquisition decisionmaking and developing and maintaining a acquisition career management program. The Chief Acquisition Officer would, as a part of the statutorily required annual strategic planning and performance evaluation process, assess agency requirements for agency personnel knowledge and skills in acquisition resources management and, if necessary, develop strategies and plan for hiring, training and professional development.

Section 202 – Chief Acquisition Officers Council

The section would add a new section 16A to the Office of Federal Procurement Policy (OFPP) Act (41 U.S.C. 403 et seq.) to authorize the establishment of a Chief Acquisition Officers Council to monitor and improve the federal acquisition system. The Council is to be chaired by the Deputy Director for Management (DDM) of the Office of Management and Budget (OMB) and comprised of the

Administrator for Federal Procurement Policy (Administrator), the Chief Acquisition Officers created under section 16 of the OFPP Act, and any other federal officer or employee designated by the chair. The Administrator is to lead the activities of the Council on behalf of the DDM. The General Services Administration is to provide administrative and other support to the Council. The Council will, among other things, develop recommendations for OMB on acquisition policies and requirements, assist the Administrator in the identification, development, and coordination of multiagency and other innovative acquisition initiatives, promote effective business practices to ensure timely delivery of best value products and services to the government, and work with the Office of Personnel Management to assess and address hiring, training, and professional development needs related to acquisition.

Section 203 – Statutory and Regulatory Review.

The section would provide that the Administrator for Federal Procurement Policy establish an advisory panel of at least nine experts in acquisition law and policy who represent diverse public and private sector experiences. The panel would review acquisition laws and regulations with a view toward ensuring the greater use of commercial practices and performance-based contracting and enhancing the performance of acquisition functions across agency lines, and the use of government-wide contracts. The panel would make recommendations for the repeal or amendment of laws or regulations that are unnecessary for the effective, efficient and fair award and administration of Government contracts while retaining the financial and ethical integrity of the acquisition programs and ensuring that the Government's best interest is protected. The report is to be completed within one year after the establishment of the panel and contain the findings and conclusions of the panel.

Subtitle B – Other Acquisition Improvements

Section 211 – Ensuring Efficient Payment.

The section would provide that the Federal Acquisition Regulation be revised to create a streamlined cost-effective, commercial-like payment process for service contracts. The revised process would, to the maximum extent practicable, provide for the submission of biweekly or monthly payment invoices for payments that are not contract financing payments. Biweekly invoices would have to be submitted electronically. All electronic invoices would be accepted or rejected by the agency within 7 working days and all accepted invoices would be paid as soon as possible, but in no case later than 30 days after the invoice date.

Section 212 – Extension of Authority to Carry Out Franchise Fund Programs.

The section would amend section 403 (f) of the Federal Financial Management Act of 1994 (31 U.S.C. 501 note) to reauthorize the Government's franchise funds until October 1, 2006. These six franchise fund programs were authorized in the Departments of the Interior, Commerce, Health and Human Services, Treasury, and Veterans Affairs and the Environmental Protection Agency to provide common administrative support services.

Section 213 – Agency Acquisition Protests.

The section would amend Chapter 137 of title 10, United States Code and the Federal Property and Administrative Services Act of 1949 to provide statutory authority for an agency-level acquisition protest process. It would provide for a "stay" of the award or of contract performance during the 20 working day period an agency is given to decide the protest. The "stay" could be lifted by the head of the agency procuring activity upon a written finding that urgent and compelling circumstances do not permit waiting for the decision. The section would provide that filing an agency-level protest under this section would not affect the right of an interested party to file a protest with the Comptroller General or in the United States Court of Federal Claims. The section would also amend section 3553 (d) (4) of title 31, United States Code to provide that an interested party filing a protest on the same matter with the Comptroller General within 5 days of the issuance of the agency protest decision would qualify for a stay of performance in connection with such protest.

Section 214 – Improvements in Contracting for Architectural and Engineering Services.

The section would amend section 1102 of title 40 of the United States Code to clarify the terms "surveying and mapping" as used in the definition of architectural and engineering services to ensure that the quality-based selection process in chapter 11 of title 40 of the United States Code is used for the full spectrum of surveying and mapping services. The Federal Acquisition

Regulation would also be amended to include the new clarified definition. Further, the section would amend section 2855 (b) of title 10, United States Code to raise from $85,000 to $300,000 the threshold for a participation incentive for small business concerns in acquisitions for architectural and engineering services and to conform section 2855 to the title 40 amendments. Finally, the section would require that architectural and engineering services offered under multiple-award schedule contracts awarded by the General Services Administration or under Government-wide task and delivery order contracts be performed under the supervision of a licensed professional engineer and be awarded pursuant to the quality-based selection procedures in chapter 11 of title 40 of the United States Code.

Section 215– Authorization of Telecommuting for Federal Contractors.

The section would provide for an amendment to the Federal Acquisition Regulation (FAR) providing that solicitations for Federal contracts should not contain any requirement or evaluation criteria that would render an offeror ineligible for award or would reduce the scoring of the offeror's proposal based upon the offeror's inclusion of a plan to allow its employees to telecommute unless the contracting officer first determines in writing that the needs of the agency, including security needs, could not be meet without the requirement. The General Accounting Office would report to Congress on the implementation one year after the FAR amendment is published.

TITLE III – CONTRACT INCENTIVES

Section 301 - Share-in-Savings Initiatives

The section would amend section 2332 title 10, United States Code and section 317 of the Federal Property and Administrative Services Act (Property Act) to authorize government-wide the use of share-in-savings contracts. These contracts represent an innovative approach to encourage industry to share creative solutions with the Government. Through these contracts agencies can lower their costs and improve service delivery without large "up front" investments as the contractor provides the technology and is compensated by receiving a portion of savings achieved. The section would amend and clarify the provisions in title 10 and the Property Act that were added to the United States Code by section 210 of the E-Government Act of 2002, Pub. L. 107-347. The new section would expand the authorization beyond information technology and provide for the use of such contracts whenever the proper approvals are granted.

The section would authorize agencies to enter into share-in-savings contracts for a term of 5 years, and with the appropriate approval, for up to 10 years, to pay contractors from the savings realized, and to retain those savings that exceed the amount paid to the contractor. The section would permit agencies to use various options for funding cancellation or termination costs and would permit the cancellation or termination amount to be negotiated by the parties. The section would require that share-in-savings contracts include a provision containing a quantifiable baseline for savings that is approved by the agency's chief acquisition officer. The section would not permit the award of such contracts where funding for the full cost of cancellation or termination is not available unless the amount of unfunded contingent liability does not exceed the lesser of 50% of the estimated cancellation or termination costs or $10,000,000. Any unfunded contingent liability in excess of $5,000,000 would require approval by the Director of the Office of Management and Budget (OMB). Further, the section would require that the Federal Acquisition Regulation (FAR) be revised to implement this section and to provide for such matters as the use of competitive procedures and innovative provisions for technology refreshment, appropriate regulatory flexibility to facilitate the use of such contracts and assurance that the contractor's share of the savings reflects the risk involved and the market conditions. The Director of OMB is to provide incentives to agencies in identifying additional opportunities for the use of these contracts and guidance for determining baselines and savings share ratios. Finally, the section would require the Director of OMB to report to Congress two years after the FAR revisions are issued describing the number of share-in savings contracts entered into, the total payments made and savings achieved, agency efforts to determine baseline costs and making recommendations for changes in law needed to encourage the effective use of share-in-savings contracts.

Section 302- Incentives for Contract Efficiency

The section would amend the Office of Federal Procurement Policy Act (41 U.S.C. 403 et seq.) to add a new section 41 authorizing agencies to include in service contracts options to extend the contract by one or more performance periods based on exceptional performance as measured by standards set forth in the contract. The contract is, to the maximum extent practicable, to be performance based.

TITLE IV – ACQUISITIONS OF COMMERCIAL ITEMS

Section 401 – Additional Incentive for Use of Performance-Based Contracting for Services.

The section would amend section 41 of the Office of Federal Procurement Policy Act (41 U.S.C. 41), as added by section 302 above, to add a new subsection that would provide that a performance-based service contract or task order may be treated as a contract for a commercial item if it defines tasks to be performed in measurable, mission related terms, identifies specific products or outputs and the source provides similar services to the public under similar terms to those offered the Government. This would authorize the use of special simplified procedures provided in the Federal Acquisition Regulation for commercial items if the performance-based contract or task order is valued at $5,000,000 or less and apply to those contracts the current waivers of requirements and certifications applicable to contracts for commercial items. Finally, the section would require the Administrator for Federal Procurement Policy to establish a center of excellence for service contracting to assist the acquisition community in identifying best practices in service contracting.

Section 402 – Authorization of Additional Commercial Contract Types.

The section would provide that section 8002 (d) of the Federal Acquisition Streamlining Act of 1994 (Public Law 103-355; 41 U.S.C. 264 note) be amended to provide that the Federal Acquisition Regulation (FAR) include a provision that would provide that time and material and labor-hour contracts could be used for commercial services that are commonly sold to the general public through such contracts. Time and material and labor-hour contracts are treated in the current Part 16 of the FAR as a separate contract type, as are fixed-price contracts and cost-reimbursement contracts. While section 8002 (d) provides that the FAR is to prohibit the use of cost-type contracts for commercial items, there is no comparable prohibition applicable to time and material and labor-hour contracts. Section 402 would make clear that, under the appropriate circumstances, time and material and labor-hour contracts should be specifically authorized by the FAR for commercial services.

Section 403 – Clarification of Commercial Services Definition.

The section would amend section 4 of the Office of Federal Procurement Policy Act (41 U.S.C. 403 (12)) to clarify the definition of commercial item to place commercial services on an equal level with supplies in Federal acquisitions.

Section 404 – Designation of Commercial Business Entities.

The section would amend section 4 of the Office of Federal Procurement Policy Act, 41 U.S.C. 403 to add to the definition of commercial item services or items provided or produced by a commercial entity that over the past 3 business years made 90% of its sales to private-sector entities. The section would further provide for a Comptroller General review of the implementation of the new section to determine its effectiveness in increasing the availability of goods and services to the Federal Government at fair and reasonable prices.

TITLE V – OTHER MATTERS

Section 501 –Authority to Enter Into Certain Procurement-Related Transactions and to Carry Out Certain Prototype Projects.

The section would amend title III of the Federal Property and Administrative Services Act of 1949 (Property Act) (41 U.S.C. 251 et seq.) to authorize the head of a civilian executive agency, if authorized by the Director of the Office of Management and Budget (OMB), to enter into transactions (other than contracts, cooperative agreements, and grants) to carry out basic, applied and advanced research, and development projects that are otherwise authorized and necessary to the responsibilities of the agency that may facilitate defense against, or recovery from, terrorism or nuclear, biological, chemical, or radiological, attack. This authority would be similar to that exercised by the Secretary of Defense under section 2317 of title 10, United States Code with certain exceptions.

The section would further amend the Property Act to provide that the head of an executive agency, designated by the Director of OMB to enter into transactions (other than contracts, cooperative agreements, and grants) may, with the approval of the Director of OMB, carryout prototype projects in accordance with the same requirements and conditions for prototype projects as are provided under section 845 of the National Defense Authorization Act for Fiscal Year 1994 (Public Law 103-160; 10 U.S.C. 2371 note).

Section 502 - Amendments Relating to Federal Emergency Procurement Flexibility

The section would amend section 852, and various other sections of subtitle F of The Homeland Security Act of 2002, Pub. L. 107-296 to make permanent and clarify the authorities applicable to agencies other than the Department of Homeland Security for procurements for defense against terror. The procurement flexibilities in subtitle F of the Homeland Security Act, sections 851-858, provide for special streamlined procedures for the procurement of property or services when the head of the agency determines the property or services are to facilitate defense against or recovery from terrorism or nuclear, biological, chemical, or radiological attack.

The section would maintain the current expanded thresholds in subtitle F, but would more closely align the accompanying pro- visions with those in section 833 of the Homeland Security Act that provide special streamlined acquisition authorities for the Department of Homeland Security. Specifically, section 601 would provide for the application of the expanded simplified acquisition threshold to acquisitions other than those in support of humani- tarian or peacekeeping or contingency operations and eliminate notice and reservation restrictions. The section would also provide for the full application of the attributes of a commercial item to an impacted acquisition, as is the case in section 833 of the Homeland Security Act.

Section 503– Authority to Make Inflation Adjustments to Simplified Acquisition Threshold.

The section would provide that the Administrator for Federal Pro- curement Policy may adjust the simplified acquisition threshold as defined in section 4(11) of the Office of Federal Procurement Policy Act (41 U.S.C. 403 (11)) every five years to an amount equal to $100,000 in constant fiscal year 2003 dollars.

Section 504– Technical Corrections Related to Duplicative Amendments.

The section would repeal subchapter II of chapter 35 of title 44 of the United States Code and chapter 115 of title 40 of the United States Code. The section would also conform various amendments made by the Homeland Security Act of 2002, Pub.L. 107-296, with those made by the E-Government Act of 2002, Pub.L. 107-347.

PERFORMANCE-BASED SERVICE ACQUISITION

CONTRACTING FOR THE FUTURE

INTERAGENCY TASK FORCE ON PERFORMANCE-BASED SERVICE ACQUISITION

Foreword

Performance-based service acquisition (PBSA) has been articulated in regulation, guidance, and policy for over two decades. During that time, agencies have made moderate progress in implementing PBSA, also known as performance-based service contracting and performance-based contracting, but have experienced difficulties in applying PBSA effectively.

In April 2002, the Office of Federal Procurement Policy (OFPP) convened an interagency working group to establish a broader understanding of the requirements of PBSA, and to identify ways to increase agency use of PBSA. The attached report includes recommendations for changes to current regulations and guidance that will give agencies more flexibility in applying PBSA effectively, appropriately, and consistently.

The group focused their efforts on three areas of change: 1) modifying the Federal Acquisition Regulation (FAR) to give agencies flexibility in applying PBSA, 2) modifying reporting requirements to ensure that PBSA is applied appropriately, and 3) improving the quality, currency, and availability of guidance. There are six recommendations that support these changes, and the report includes a brief discussion on each of these recommendations. OFPP supports these recommendations and will establish an action plan to ensure they are implemented swiftly.

Members of the interagency working group represented major service contracting agencies such as the Department of Defense (DOD), General Services Administration, the Department of Health and Human Services, Treasury Department, Department of Energy, Department of Veterans Affairs, Department of Commerce, Department of Transportation, National Space and Aeronautics Administration, Environmental Protection Agency, U.S. Nuclear Regulatory Commission, and others.

Special thanks should be given to the following people for their participation in the development of this report: Ronne Rogin, formerly of the Treasury Department, William Timperley, DOD, and Lesley Field, OFPP.

Angela B. Styles
Administrator

I. EXECUTIVE SUMMARY

A. Modifying the FAR.

Recommendation No. 1: Modify the FAR Part 2 to include definitions for: 1) performance work statement, 2) quality assurance surveillance plan, 3) statement of objectives, and 4) statement of work to support changes to Part 37. Modify FAR Parts 11 and 37 to broaden the scope of PBSA and give agencies more flexibility in applying PBSA to contracts and orders of varying complexity.

B. Modifying Reporting Requirements and Procedures.

Recommendation No. 2: Modify the list of eligible service codes for PBSA, as articulated in the Federal Procurement Data System (FPDS) or FPDS B Next Generation (FPDS-NG) manual, to more accurately reflect services to which PBSA can be applied. Agencies are not prohibited from using PBSA on other contracts, but for the purposes of data collection, agencies will not be evaluated on their application of PBSA to efforts that are not considered eligible service contracts.

Recommendation No. 3: Revise FPDS instructions to ensure agencies code contracts and orders as PBSA if more than 50 percent of the requirement is performance based, as opposed to the current 80 percent requirement.

Recommendation No. 4: Allow agencies that do not input data to FPDS to submit supplemental reports in order to accurately reflect their progress toward meeting the goals.

Recommendation No. 5: Consider allowing agencies to establish interim goals, but expect agencies to apply PBSA to 50 percent of their eligible service contracts (see recommendation 2 above) by 2005, in line with DOD policy.

C. Improving Guidance.

Recommendation No. 6: OFPP should rescind its 1998 Best Practices Guide and consider developing web-based guidance to assist agencies in implementing PBSA. This guidance should be kept current and should include practical information, such as samples and templates that agencies would find useful. The website should include "The 7-Steps to Performance-Based Services Acquisition

Guide" and may include elements of existing guidance. The working group will explore the development a web-based PBSA site for guidance, samples, and templates.

Questions and/or comments may be addressed to Lesley Field (Lfield@omb.eop.gov), OFPP, or Bill Timperley (William.Timperley@osd.mil), Office of the Secretary of Defense.

II. RECOMMENDATIONS AND DISCUSSION

A. Modifying the FAR.

Recommendation No. 1: The following revisions to the FAR are proposed:

1. Add the following definitions to section 2.101:

2.101 Definitions.

"Performance Work Statement" (PWS) means a statement in the solicitation that identifies the technical, functional and performance characteristics of the agencies requirements.

"Quality Assurance Surveillance Plan" (QASP) means a plan for assessing contractor performance in order to ensure accomplishment of the government's performance objectives stated in the contract and compliance with the appropriate inspection clauses. The level of surveillance should be commensurate with the dollar amount, risk, and complexity of the requirement.

"Statement of Objectives" (SOO) means an alternative to a performance work statement (PWS); it is a summary of key agency goals, outcomes, or both, that is incorporated into performance-based service acquisitions in order that competitors may propose their solutions, including a technical approach, performance standards, and a quality assurance surveillance plan based upon commercial business practices.

"Statement of Work" (SOW) means a statement that defines the government's requirements in clear, concise language identifying specific work to be accomplished.

2. Revise section 11.101 to clarify the order of precedence for requirements documents by incorporating the use of statements of objectives, as follows:

11.101 Order of precedence for requirements documents.

(a) Agencies may select from existing requirements documents, modify or combine existing requirements documents, or create new requirements documents to meet agency needs, consistent with the following order of precedence:

(1) Documents mandated for use by law.

(2) Performance- or functionally-oriented documents (see 37.602-1).

(3) Detailed design-oriented documents.

(4) Standards, specifications, and related publications issued by the Government outside the Defense or Federal series for the non-repetitive acquisition of items.

3. Revise section 37.102(a) to clarify that PBSA is not generally compatible with procurements using term type contracts (as defined in 16.306(d)), as follows:

37.102 Policy.

(a) Performance-based contracting (see Subpart 37.6) is the preferred method for acquiring services (Public Law 106-398, section 821). When acquiring services, including those acquired under supply contracts, agencies must-

(1) Use performance-based contracting methods to the maximum extent practicable, except for-

(i) Architect-engineer services acquired in accordance with 40 U.S.C. 541-544 (see Part 36);

(ii) Construction (see Part 36);

(iii) Utility services (see Part 41);

(iv) Services that are procured using term type contracts (see 16.306(d)); or

(v) Services that are incidental to supply purchases; and

(2) Use the following orderY

4. Revise Subpart 37.6 to read as follows:

37.600 Scope of subpart. (No change)

37.601 General.

(a) The principal objective of performance-based services acquisition (PBSA) is to express government needs in terms of required performance objectives, rather than the method of performance, to encourage industry-driven, competitive solutions. Either a performance work statement (PWS) or a statement of objectives (SOO) may be used.

(b) PBSA contracts shall include-

(1) Measurable performance standards. These standards may be objective (e.g., response time) or subjective (e.g., customer satisfaction), but shall reflect the level of service required by the government to meet mission objectives. Standards shall enable assessment of contractor performance to determine whether contract results and objectives are being met, and

(2) Quality assurance surveillance plans (QASPs). The level of surveillance described in the plan should reflect the complexity of the acquisition. Plans should enable the contracting officer to fulfill the obligations of the government in accordance with 46.407(f). The contracting officer may rely on the inspection clauses in the contract or order, as appropriate. For example, a contracting officer

may appropriately rely on the inspections clause in a simplified acquisition purchase or order without requiring a detailed QASP.

(c) PBSA contracts may include incentives to promote contractor achievement of the results or objectives articulated in the contract. Incentives may be of any type, including positive, negative, monetary, or non-monetary. (See 37.602-2 (b) and (c).)

37.602 Elements of performance-based services acquisition.

37.602-1 Performance work statements (PWSs) and statements of objectives (SOOs).

(a) Statements of work (SOWs) for PBSA contracts or task orders may be either PWSs or SOOs.

(b) When preparing PWSs, agencies shall, to the maximum extent practicable-

(1) Describe the work in terms of the purpose of the work to be performed rather than either "how" the work is to be accomplished or the number of hours to be provided (see 11.002(a)(2) and 11.101);

(2) Establish performance standards and measures for the program; and

(3) Enable assessment of work performance to determine whether results, objectives, and obligations are being met.

(c) SOOs shall, at a minimum, include the following information with respect to the acquisition:

(1) Purpose.

(2) Scope or mission.

(3) Period and place of performance.

(4) Background.

(5) Performance objectives, goals and outcomes.

(6) Any operating constraints.

37.602-2 Quality assurance.

(a) Agencies shall develop QASPs to ensure the results, objectives, and obligations of the contract are being met. Plans shall recognize the responsibility of the contractor to carry out its quality control obligations (see 46.105) and shall include measurable performance standards corresponding to the desired results or objectives. QASPs shall focus on achievement of desired results or objectives and not on the methodology used by the contractor to achieve them. Agencies are encouraged to take advantage of best commercial practices in the development of plans.

(b) In accordance with 46.407(f), invoice payment amounts may be adjusted via an equitable price reduction to reflect the actual level of services received. Deductions shall not be arbitrary or punitive.

(c) Incentives, if used, shall correspond to the performance standards set forth in the contract or order, either in a QASP or in a clause incorporated in accordance with Part 46. (See 37.601(b)(4).)

37.602-3 Selection procedures. (No change)

37.602-4 Contract type.

Agencies shall follow the order of precedence set forth in 37.102(a)(2) for selecting contract and order types. In applying the order of precedence, the agency shall use the contract type most likely to motivate contractors to perform at optimal levels (see Subpart 16.1).

37.602-5 Follow-on and repetitive requirements. (No change)

Discussion of Proposed FAR Changes: *The interagency working group discussed the general description of PBSA and the required elements. Use of the term APBSA@ is proposed to provide common terminology throughout the government. FAR section 37.601 currently reads as follows:*

> *Performance-based contracting methods are intended to ensure that required performance quality levels are achieved and that total payment is related to the degree that services performed meet contract standards. Performance-based contractsC*
>
> *(a) Describe the requirements in terms of results required rather than the methods of performance of the work;*
>
> *(b) Use measurable performance standards (i.e., terms of quality, timeliness, quantity, etc.) and quality assurance surveillance plans......;*
>
> *(c) Specify procedures for reductions of fee or for reductions to the price of a fixed-price contract when services are not performed or do not meet contract requirements......; and*
>
> *(d) Include performance incentives where appropriate.*

This description is restrictive and does not allow an agency to apply performance-based principles (or receive credit for goaling purposes) if the work is described in terms of outcomes, but one of the other elements (e.g., a price decrement formula) is not present. After considerable discussion, the working group is recommending changes to FAR Subpart 37.6. The proposed changes will allow more agency discretion while still adhering to the basic concept of PBSA.

Additionally, the complexity of QASPs should reflect the complexity of the acquisition. If appropriate, the contracting officer may rely on the 'Inspection of Services' clauses, as prescribed in FAR Part 46.

Discussion on excluding term contracts from the requirement to use performance based requirements: *Term type contracts should be excluded from the requirement to use PBSA because, under these contracts, the contractor only guarantees to provide its best efforts. Payment is predicated on effort and not necessarily on outcome. This is generally* *in conflict with PBSA, which requires an outcome and where payment is contingent upon achieving that outcome in accordance with prescribed performance standards.*

Discussion on adding new definitions: *One of the perceived obstacles to PBSA is the difficulty associated with converting statements of work from the traditional, familiar style to one that uses a performance-based approach. Utilization of a SOO allows program personnel to summarize their requirements, identify constraints, and request that offerors submit not only a performance-based solution, but also a set of metrics and a QASP. (See "The 7 Steps Guide to Performance-Based Service Acquisition," Step 4, at http://www.acqnet.gov.) These documents require government review and approval, but using a SOO can assist agencies in applying PBSA more easily. Several different agencies have used this approach successfully, and many more are beginning to adopt the practice.*

PWS is often referenced in the FAR, but the group found that the definition is not included in Part 2. The proposed definition comes from the revised OMB Circular A-76. SOW is often referenced in the FAR, but the definition was not included in Part 2.

Discussion on Order of Precedence: *This change makes it clear that it is appropriate to use either performance or functional specifications. Section 2711(a)(2) of the Competition in Contracting Act of 1984 (41, U.S.C 253(a)(3)), states in pertinent part that, ". . . the type of specification included in a solicitation shall depend on the nature of the needs of the executive agency and the market available to satisfy such needs. Subject to such needs, specifications may be stated in terms of -*

> *(A) function, so that a variety of products or services may qualify;*

> *(B) performance, including specifications of the range of acceptable characteristics or of the minimum acceptable standards..."*

B. Modifying Reporting Requirements and Procedures.

Recommendation No. 2: The FPDS service codes listed below are recommended for removal from the "eligible services" categories listed in the FPDS manual (http://www.fpdc.gov/fpdc/rm2002. pdf). If this recommendation is adopted, agencies can implement this change immediately as it does not require a coding change to FPDS, but only a change to the FPDS manual.

- General Science and Technology R&D - AJ1_ through AJ9_
- Medical R&D - AN11 through AN14 (this leaves in AN15-16; there are different stages of research)
  - AN21 through AN24
    (Retain final two stages of R&D as eligible)
  - AN31 through AN34
    (Retain final two stages of R&D as eligible)
  - AN41 through AN44
    (Retain final two stages of R&D as eligible)
  - AN51 through AN54
    (Retain final two stages of R&D as eligible)
  - AN61 through AN64
    (Retain final two stages of R&D as eligible)
  - AN71 through AN74
    (Retain final two stages of R&D as eligible)
  - AN81 through AN84
    (Retain final two stages of R&D as eligible)
  - AN91 through AN94
    (Retain final two stages of R&D as eligible)
- Social Services R&D - AQ11 through AQ14 (Retain final two stages of R&D as eligible)
- AQ91 through AQ94 (Retain final two stages of R&D as eligible)
- Purchase of Structures and Facilities B E***
- Hazardous Substance Cleanup - F108
- Oil Spill Response - F112
- Non-nuclear Ship Repair, East and West - J998 and J999
- Medical Services (not facility-related) - Q501-Q527
- Education and Training Services B U001-U099
- Lease or Rental of Equipment B W0**
- Lease or Rental of Facilities B X***

Add a new service code for design/build projects for FY 04. If this recommendation is adopted, FPDS (or the successor to FPDS, FPDS-NG) will have to be modified; therefore this change would not go into effect until October 1, 2003.

Discussion on AEligible Services. *"The proposed changes to FAR section 37.601 in recommendation #1 naturally led* *to a discussion of other changes. One area is the definition of Aeligible services." Currently, the FAR only exempts construction, architect and engineering services, and utilities from PBSA requirements. The working group believed that the large universe of potential performance-based service acquisitions could result in "force-fitting" some requirements when doing so might not be in the government's best interest. For example, pure medical research, where the outcome is truly unknown and the contractor's success or failure may be a poor indicator of results achieved, is not a good fit. The working group queried a number of different agencies and departments, and this report recommends additional exclusions from the universe of eligible service contracts that are currently contained in the FPDS manual. Further, the working group recommends that a new service code be developed for "design-build" projects, which the group thinks are appropriate for a performance-based management approach.*

The working group believes that reducing the universe of eligible (i.e., appropriate) services will increase use of PBSA. Relieving agencies of the requirement to force-fit nearly all service acquisitions to be PBSA, when this may not be appropriate or desirable, will improve agency application of PBSA. The group thinks that for those services where a performance-based approach is used, there should be a high return on the investment of time and resources. A PBSA approach can be used for many types of services, but only those eligible services will be reported.

Recommendation No. 3: Revise the FPDS/FPDS-NG instructions (Amendment 4, block 20) as follows: "If more than 50 percent of the requirement is performance-based, then the contract or order may be coded as a performance-based acquisition."

Discussion on Reporting. *All federal agency contract specialists must complete a data entry form for every procurement action, for transmission to FPDS. Current coding instructions for SF-279, block 20, dictating an 80 percent standard (i.e., 80 percent of the dollars) to determine whether an action is performance-based. This language has been carried over to the proposed FPDS replacement system,*

FPDS-NG. With the increase in multi-purpose contracts (e.g., supplies and services), the working group thinks that agencies should apply PBSA to more contracts, some of which might not lend themselves to the 80 percent rule. The group recommends making a change in the instructions as follows: "If more than 50 percent of the requirement is performance-based, then the contract or order may be coded as a performance-based acquisition."

Recommendation No. 4: Allow agencies that do not input data to FPDS to submit supplemental reports in order to accurately reflect their progress toward meeting the goals.

> **Discussion on non-FPDS actions:** *Some agencies do not feed data to FPDS, and others have contracts that are not covered by the FAR and, therefore, are not recorded in FPDS. However, PBSA principles can be applied to many of these contracts, and these agencies should be able to count these actions toward their goals. Further, agencies that transfer funding to another agency for a contract or task order action should receive PBSA credit, not the contracting agency. Clarification of this point should reduce instances of dual reporting.*

Recommendation No. 5: Consider allowing agencies to establish interim goals, but expect agencies to apply PBSA to 50 percent of their eligible service contracts (see recommendation 2, above) by 2005, in line with DOD policy.

> **Discussion on Meeting the Performance Goals.** *Because there is so much momentum for PBSA now, the group supports the idea of goals. The group recommends that OFPP consider following DOD's lead by setting a goal that PBSA be applied to 50 percent of eligible service contracts by 2005. Based upon the actual percentages attained by the various agencies for FY02 and the pace of implementation of these recommendations, OFPP should consider allowing agencies to establish interim goals for future years.*

C. Improving Guidance.

Recommendation No. 6: OFPP should rescind its 1998 Best Practices Guide and consider developing web-based guidance to assist agencies in implementing PBSA. This guidance should be kept current and should include practical information, such as samples and templates that agencies would find useful. The website should include "The 7-Steps to Performance-Based Services Acquisition Guide" and may include elements of existing guidance. The working group will explore the development a web-based PBSA site for guidance, samples, and templates.

> **Discussion on Government-Wide Guidance.** *Since OMB first mandated the use of PBSA, no new government-wide guidance has been issued for agencies to follow. The group thinks that the current OFPP guide is outdated and should be rescinded. In the absence of current government-wide guidance, there has been a proliferation of department- and agency-wide guides. As a result of a Procurement Executive Council's initiative to improve guidance, the Department of Commerce gathered a team of experts from six different agencies to develop more current guidance; contractor support was also used. The result was the release of "The 7 Steps to Performance-Based Services Acquisition Guide," which provides basic information to assist agencies in using PBSA. However, more guidance is needed to accommodate the needs of the acquisition community. If this recommendation is accepted, the next phase of effort for the working group is to establish a credible, current, on-line presence for PBSA guidance.*

III. ADDITIONAL DISCUSSION ON PBSA

Although the working group does not offer specific recommendations regarding cost savings and incentives, it believes a discussion on these topics is appropriate.

Cost Savings: The working group thinks that the acquisition community should work together to re-shape the expectation that PBSA will save money. While it may be possible to save money on non-professional types of services, or by the use of share-in-savings techniques, the government spends most of its service contracting dollars where contractors are chosen by "best value" techniques, not low price. There is little current data to support monetary savings, and if such data did exist, it would be extremely difficult to isolate the exact reasons the savings occurred. The working group does agree that we are seeing improved quality of performance and improved customer satisfaction.

Incentives: Just as contractors deserve incentives for outstanding performance, federal employees deserve recognition for their efforts in changing the way they work with contractors. In discussing various methods of incentivizing contractor performance, the group considered both the government view and the industry view of incentives. Contractor feedback indicates that while the contractor may have monetary or non-monetary incentives in the contract, the government personnel managing the contract appear to have no stake in how well the contractor performs. The lack of incentives on the government side might result in a failure to excel on the contractor side. The working group recommends that government managers consider including successful program management in individuals' performance standards. The intended result would be to provide an incentive for government program managers to team with contractors for mutually beneficial results. Consideration should also be given to creating an award for outstanding achievement in this area.

Documents Reviewed for This Effort: In addition to reviewing individual agency guidance, OFPP's "Guide to Best Practices for Performance-Based Service Contracts" (1998), and the old OFPP Pamphlet No. 4, "A Guide to Writing and Administering Performance Statements of Work for Service Contracts" (1980), the Task Force also reviewed a report prepared by Dr. Lawrence Martin, PricewaterhouseCoopers Endowment for the Business of Government. That report, "Making Performance-Based Contracting Perform: What the Federal Government Can Learn from State and Local Governments," provides a number of innovative approaches that have been successful at the state and local level. The working group met with Dr. Martin; the exchange of ideas and viewpoints was thought provoking, and the ideas presented were considered in preparation of this report. The group also reviewed OFPP's "Solicitation/Contract/Task Order Review Checklist," dated August 1997, as well as "The 7 Steps to Performance-Based Services Acquisition Guide."

GLOSSARY

acceptance

(1) The taking and receiving of anything in good part, and as if it were a tacit agreement to a preceding act, which might have been defeated or avoided if such acceptance had not been made. (2) Agreement to the terms offered in a contract. An acceptance must be communicated, and (in common law) it must be the mirror image of the offer.

acquisition cost

The money invested up front to bring in new customers.

acquisition plan

A plan for an acquisition that serves as the basis for initiating the individual contracting actions necessary to acquire a system or support a program.

acquisition strategy

The conceptual framework for conducting systems acquisition. It encompasses the broad concepts and objectives that direct and control the overall development, production, and deployment of a system.

act of God

An inevitable, accidental, or extraordinary event that cannot be foreseen and guarded against, such as lightning, tornadoes, or earthquakes.

actual authority
The power that the principal intentionally confers on the agent or allows the agent to believe he or she possesses.

actual damages
See *compensatory damages*.

affidavit
A written and signed statement sworn to under oath.

agency
A relationship that exists when there is a delegation of authority to perform all acts connected within a particular trade, business, or company. It gives authority to the agent to act in all matters relating to the business of the principal.

agent
An employee (usually a contract manager) empowered to bind his or her organization legally in contract negotiations.

allowable cost
A cost that is reasonable, allocable, and within accepted standards, or otherwise conforms to generally accepted accounting principles, specific limitations or exclusions, or agreed-on terms between contractual parties.

alternative dispute resolution
Any procedure that is used, in lieu of litigation, to resolve issues in controversy, including but not limited to, settlement negotiations, conciliation, facilitation, mediation, fact finding, mini-trials and arbitration.

amortization
Process of spreading the cost of an intangible asset over the expected useful life of the asset.

apparent authority
The power that the principal permits the perceived agent to exercise, although not actually granted.

as is

A contract phrase referring to the condition of property to be sold or leased; generally pertains to a disclaimer of liability; property sold in as-is condition is generally not guaranteed.

assign

To convey or transfer to another, as to assign property, rights, or interests to another.

assignment

The transfer of property by an assignor to an assignee.

audits

The systematic examination of records and documents and/or the securing of other evidence by confirmation, physical inspection, or otherwise, for one or more of the following purposes: determining the propriety or legality of proposed or completed transactions; ascertaining whether all transactions have been recorded and are reflected accurately in accounts; determining the existence of recorded assets and inclusiveness of recorded liabilities; determining the accuracy of financial or statistical statements or reports and the fairness of the facts they represent; determining the degree of compliance with established policies and procedures in terms of financial transactions and business management; and appraising an account system and making recommendations concerning it.

base profit

The money a company is paid by a customer, which exceeds the company's cost.

best value

The best trade-off between competing factors for a particular purchase requirement. The key to successful best-value contracting is consideration of life-cycle costs, including the use of quantitative as well as qualitative techniques to measure price and technical performance trade-offs between various proposals. The best-value concept applies to acquisitions in which price or price-related factors are *not* the primary determinant of who receives the contract award.

bid

> An offer in response to an invitation for bids (IFB).

bid development

> All of the work activities required to design and price the product and service solution and accurately articulate this in a proposal for a customer.

bid phase

> The period of time a seller of goods and/or services uses to develop a bid/proposal, conduct internal bid reviews, and obtain stakeholder approval to submit a bid/proposal.

bilateral contract

> A contract formed if an offer states that acceptance requires only for the accepting party to promise to perform. In contrast, a *unilateral contract* is formed if an offer requires actual performance for acceptance.

bond

> A written instrument executed by a seller and a second party (the surety or sureties) to ensure fulfillment of the principal's obligations to a third party (the obligee or buyer), identified in the bond. If the principal's obligations are not met, the bond ensures payment, to the extent stipulated, of any loss sustained by the obligee.

breach of contract

> (1) The failure, without legal excuse, to perform any promise that forms the whole or part of a contract. (2) The ending of a contract that occurs when one or both of the parties fail to keep their promises; this could lead to arbitration or litigation.

buyer

> The party contracting for goods and/or services with one or more sellers.

cancellation

> The withdrawal of the requirement to purchase goods and/or services by the buyer.

capture management

The art and science of winning more business.

capture management life cycle

The art and science of winning more business throughout the entire business cycle.

capture project plan

A document or game plan of who needs to do what, when, where, how often and how much to win business.

change in scope

An amendment to approved program requirements or specifications after negotiation of a basic contract. It may result in an increase or decrease.

change order/purchase order amendment

A written order directing the seller to make changes according to the provisions of the contract documents.

claim

A demand by one party to contract for something from another party, usually but not necessarily for more money or more time. Claims are usually based on an argument that the party making the demand is entitled to an adjustment by virtue of the contract terms or some violation of those terms by the other party. The word does not imply any disagreement between the parties, although claims often lead to disagreements. This book uses the term *dispute* to refer to disagreements that have become intractable.

clause

A statement of one of the rights and/or obligations of the parties to a contract. A contract consists of a series of clauses.

collaboration software

Automated tools that allow for the real-time exchange of visual information using personal computers.

collateral benefit

The degree to which pursuit of an opportunity will improve the existing skill level or develop new skills which will positively affect other or future business opportunities.

compensable delay

A delay for which the buyer is contractually responsible that excuses the seller's failure to perform and is compensable.

compensatory damages

Damages that will compensate the injured party for the loss sustained and nothing more. They are awarded by the court as the measure of actual loss, and not as punishment for outrageous conduct or to deter future transgressions. Compensatory damages are often referred to as "actual damages." See also *incidental* and *punitive damages*.

competitive intelligence

Information on competitors or competitive teams which is specific to an opportunity.

competitive negotiation

A method of contracting involving a request for proposals that states the buyer's requirements and criteria for evaluation; submission of timely proposals by a maximum number of offerors; discussions with those offerors found to be within the competitive range; and award of a contract to the one offeror whose offer, price, and other consideration factors are most advantageous to the buyer.

condition precedent

A condition that activates a term in a contract.

condition subsequent

A condition that suspends a term in a contract.

conflict of interest

Term used in connection with public officials and fiduciaries and their relationships to matters of private interest or gain to them. Ethical problems connected therewith are covered by statutes in most jurisdictions and by federal statutes on the federal level. A conflict of interest arises when an employee's personal or financial interest conflicts or appears to conflict with his or her official responsibility.

consideration

(1) The thing of value (amount of money or acts to be done or not done) that must change hands between the parties to a contract. (2) The inducement to a contract – the cause, motive, price, or impelling influence that induces a contracting party to enter into a contract.

contract negotiation

Is the process of unifying different positions into a unanimous joint decision, regarding the buying and selling of products and/or services.

contract negotiation process

A three phased approach composed of planning, negotiating, and documenting a contractual agreement between two or more parties to buy or sell products and/or services.

constructive change

An oral or written act or omission by an authorized or unauthorized agent that is of such a nature that it is construed to have the same effect as a written change order.

contingency

The quality of being contingent or casual; an event that may but does not have to occur; a possibility.

contingent contract

A contract that provides for the possibility of its termination when a specified occurrence takes place or does not take place.

contra proferentem

A legal phrase used in connection with the construction of written documents to the effect that an ambiguous provision is construed most strongly against the person who selected the language.

contract

(1) A relationship between two parties, such as a buyer and seller, that is defined by an agreement about their respective rights and responsibilities. (2) A document that describes such an agreement.

contract administration

The process of ensuring compliance with contractual terms and conditions during contract performance up to contract closeout or termination.

contract closeout

The process of verifying that all administrative matters are concluded on a contract that is otherwise physically complete – in other words, the seller has delivered the required supplies or performed the required services, and the buyer has inspected and accepted the supplies or services.

contract fulfillment

The joint Buyer/Seller actions taken to successfully perform and administer a contractual agreement and met or exceed all contract obligations, including effective changes management and timely contract closeout.

contract interpretation

The entire process of determining what the parties agreed to in their bargain. The basic objective of contract interpretation is to determine the intent of the parties. Rules calling for interpretation of the documents against the drafter, and imposing a duty to seek clarification on the drafter, allocate risks of contractual ambiguities by resolving disputes in favor of the party least responsible for the ambiguity.

contract management

The art and science of managing a contractual agreement(s) throughout the contracting process.

contract type
A specific pricing arrangement used for the performance of work under the contract.

contractor
The seller or provider of goods and/or services.

controversy
A litigated question. A civil action or suit may not be instigated unless it is based on a "justifiable" dispute. This term is important in that judicial power of the courts extends only to cases and "controversies."

copyright
A royalty-free, nonexclusive, and irrevocable license to reproduce, translate, publish, use, and dispose of written or recorded material, and to authorize others to do so.

cost
The amount of money expended in acquiring a product or obtaining a service, or the total of acquisition costs plus all expenses related to operating and maintaining an item once acquired.

cost of good sold (COGS)
Direct costs of producing finished goods for sale.

cost accounting standards
Federal standards designed to provide consistency and coherency in defense and other government contract accounting.

cost-plus-award fee (CPAF) contract
A type of cost-reimbursement contract with special incentive fee provisions used to motivate excellent contract performance in such areas as quality, timeliness, ingenuity, and cost-effectiveness.

cost-plus-fixed fee (CPFF) contract
A type of cost-reimbursement contract that provides for the payment of a fixed fee to the contractor. It does not vary with actual costs, but may be adjusted if there are any changes in the work or services to be performed under the contract.

cost-plus-incentive fee (CPIF) contract

A type of cost-reimbursement contract with provision for a fee that is adjusted by a formula in accordance with the relationship between total allowable costs and target costs.

cost-plus-a-percentage-of-cost (CPPC) contract

A type of cost-reimbursement contract that provides for a reimbursement of the allowable cost of services performed plus an agreed-on percentage of the estimated cost as profit.

cost-reimbursement (CR) contract

A type of contract that usually includes an estimate of project cost, a provision for reimbursing the seller's expenses, and a provision for paying a fee as profit. CR contracts are often used when there is high uncertainty about costs. They normally also include a limitation on the buyer's cost liability.

cost-sharing contract

A cost-reimbursement contract in which the seller receives no fee and is reimbursed only for an agreed-on portion of its allowable costs.

cost contract

The simplest type of cost-reimbursement contract. Governments commonly use this type when contracting with universities and nonprofit organizations for research projects. The contract provides for reimbursing contractually allowable costs, with no allowance given for profit.

cost proposal

The instrument required of an offeror for the submission or identification of cost or pricing data by which an offeror submits to the buyer a summary of estimated (or incurred) costs, suitable for detailed review and analysis.

counteroffer

An offer made in response to an original offer that changes the terms of the original.

customer revenue growth

The increased revenues achieved by keeping a customer for an extended period of time.

customer support costs

Costs expended by a company to provide information and advice concerning purchases.

default termination

The termination of a contract, under the standard default clause, because of a buyer's or seller's failure to perform any of the terms of the contract.

defect

The absence of something necessary for completeness or perfection. A deficiency in something essential to the proper use of a thing. Some structural weakness in a part or component that is responsible for damage.

defect, latent

A defect that existed at the time of acceptance but would not have been discovered by a reasonable inspection.

defect, patent

A defect that can be discovered without undue effort. If the defect was actually known to the buyer at the time of acceptance, it is patent, even though it otherwise might not have been discoverable by a reasonable inspection.

definite-quantity contract

A contractual instrument that provides for a definite quantity of supplies or services to be delivered at some later, unspecified date.

delay, excusable

A contractual provision designed to protect the seller from sanctions for late performance. To the extent that it has been excusably delayed, the seller is protected from default termination or liquidated damages. Examples of excusable delay are acts of God, acts of the government, fire, flood, quarantines, strikes, epidemics, unusually severe weather, and embargoes. See also *forbearance* and *force majeure clause*.

depreciation
Amount of expense charged against earnings by a company to write off the cost of a plant or machine over its useful live, giving consideration to wear and tear, obsolescence, and salvage value.

design specification
(1) A document (including drawings) setting forth the required characteristics of a particular component, part, subsystem, system, or construction item. (2) A purchase description that establishes precise measurements, tolerances, materials, in-process and finished product tests, quality control, inspection requirements, and other specific details of the deliverable.

direct cost
The costs specifically identifiable with a contract requirement, including but not restricted to costs of material and/or labor directly incorporated into an end item.

direct labor
All work that is obviously related and specifically and conveniently traceable to specific products.

direct material
Items, including raw material, purchased parts, and subcontracted items, directly incorporated into an end item, which are identifiable to a contract requirement.

discount rate
Interest rate used in calculating present value.

discounted cash flow (DCF)
Combined present value of cash flow and tangible assets minus present value of liabilities.

discounts, allowances and returns
Price discounts, returned merchandise.

dispute
A disagreement not settled by mutual consent that could be decided by litigation or arbitration. Also see *claim*.

e-business

Technology-enabled business that focuses on seamless integration between each business, the company, and its supply partners.

EBITDA

Earnings Before Interest, Taxes, Depreciation and Amortization, but after all product/service, sales and overhead (SG&A) costs are accounted for. Sometimes referred to as Operating Profit.

EBITDARM

Acronym for Earnings Before Interest, Taxes, Depreciation, Amortization. Rent and Management fees.

e-commerce

A subset of e-business, Internet-based electronic transactions.

electronic data interchange (EDI)

Private networks used for simple data transactions, which are typically batch-processed.

elements of a contract

The items that must be present in a contract if the contract is to be binding, including an offer, acceptance (agreement), consideration, execution by competent parties, and legality of purpose.

enterprise resource planning (ERP)

An electronic framework for integrating all organizational functions, evolved from Manufacturing Resource Planning (MRP).

entire contract

A contract that is considered entire on both sides and cannot be made severable.

e-procurement

Technology-enabled buying and selling of goods and services.

estimate at completion (EAC)

The actual direct costs, plus indirect costs allocable to the contract, plus the estimate of costs (direct or indirect) for authorized work remaining.

estoppel

A rule of law that bars, prevents, and precludes a party from alleging or denying certain facts because of a previous allegation or denial or because of its previous conduct or admission.

ethics

Of or relating to moral action, conduct, motive, or character (such as ethical emotion). Also, treating of moral feelings, duties, or conduct; containing precepts of morality; moral. Professionally right or befitting; conforming to professional standards of conduct.

e-tool

An electronic device, program, system, or software application used to facilitate business.

exculpatory clause

The contract language designed to shift responsibility to the other party. A "no damages for delay" clause would be an example of one used by buyers.

excusable delay

See *delay, excusable*.

executed contract

A contract that is formed and performed at the same time. If performed in part, it is partially executed and partially executory.

executed contract (document)

A written document, signed by both parties and mailed or otherwise furnished to each party, that expresses the requirements, terms, and conditions to be met by both parties in the performance of the contract.

executory contract

A contract that has not yet been fully performed.

express

Something put in writing, for example, "express authority."

fair and reasonable

A subjective evaluation of what each party deems as equitable consideration in areas such as terms and conditions, cost or price, assured quality, timeliness of contract performance, and/or any other areas subject to negotiation.

Federal Acquisition Regulation (FAR)

The government-wide procurement regulation mandated by Congress and issued by the Department of Defense, the General Services Administration, and the National Aeronautics and Space Administration. Effective April 1, 1984, the FAR supersedes both the Defense Acquisition Regulation (DAR) and the Federal Procurement Regulation (FPR). All federal agencies are authorized to issue regulations implementing the FAR.

fee

An agreed-to amount of reimbursement beyond the initial estimate of costs. The term "fee" is used when discussing cost-reimbursement contracts, whereas the term "profit" is used in relation to fixed-price contracts.

firm-fixed-price (FFP) contract

The simplest and most common business pricing arrangement. The seller agrees to supply a quantity of goods or to provide a service for a specified price.

fixed cost

Operating expenses that are incurred to provide facilities and organization that are kept in readiness to do business without regard to actual volumes of production and sales. Examples of fixed costs consist of rent, property tax, and interest expense.

fixed price

A form of pricing that includes a ceiling beyond which the buyer bears no responsibility for payment.

fixed-price incentive (FPI) contract

A type of contract that provides for adjusting profit and establishing the final contract price using a formula based on the relationship of total final negotiated cost to total target cost. The final price is subject to a price ceiling, negotiated at the outset.

fixed-price redeterminable (FPR) contract

A type of fixed-price contract that contains provisions for subsequently negotiated adjustment, in whole or in part, of the initially negotiated base price.

fixed-price with economic price adjustment

A fixed-price contract that permits an element of cost to fluctuate to reflect current market prices.

forbearance

An intentional failure of a party to enforce a contract requirement, usually done for an act of immediate or future consideration from the other party. Sometimes forbearance is referred to as a nonwaiver or as a onetime waiver, but not as a relinquishment of rights.

force majeure clause

Major or irresistible force. Such a contract clause protects the parties in the event that a part of the contract cannot be performed due to causes outside the control of the parties and could not be avoided by exercise of due care. Excusable conditions for nonperformance, such as strikes and acts of God (e.g., typhoons) are contained in this clause.

fraud

An intentional perversion of truth to induce another in reliance upon it to part with something of value belonging to him or her or to surrender a legal right. A false representation of a matter of fact, whether by words or conduct, by false or misleading allegations, or by concealment of that which should have been disclosed, that deceives and is intended to deceive another so that he or she shall act upon it to his or her legal injury. Anything calculated to deceive.

free on board (FOB)

A term used in conjunction with a physical point to determine (a) the responsibility and basis for payment of freight charges and (b) unless otherwise agreed, the point at which title for goods passes to the buyer or consignee. *FOB origin* – The seller places the goods on the conveyance by which they are to be transported. Cost of shipping and risk of loss are borne by the buyer. *FOB destination* – The seller delivers the goods on the seller's conveyance at destination. Cost of shipping and risk of loss are borne by the seller.

functional specification

A purchase description that describes the deliverable in terms of performance characteristics and intended use, including those characteristics that at minimum are necessary to satisfy the intended use.

general and administrative (G&A)

(1) The indirect expenses related to the overall business. Expenses for a company's general and executive offices, executive compensation, staff services, and other miscellaneous support purposes. (2) Any indirect management, financial, or other expense that (a) is not assignable to a program's direct overhead charges for engineering, manufacturing, material, and so on, but (b) is routinely incurred by or allotted to a business unit, and (c) is for the general management and administration of the business as a whole.

general accepted accounting principles (GAAP)

A term encompassing conventions, rules, and procedures of accounting that are "generally accepted" and have "substantial authoritative support." The GAAP have been developed by agreement on the basis of experience, reason, custom, usage, and to a certain extent, practical necessity, rather than being derived from a formal set of theories.

General Agreement on Tariffs and Trade (GATT)

A multi-national trade agreement, signed in 1947 by 23 nations.

gross profit margin

Net Sales minus Cost of Goods Sold. Also called Gross Margin, Gross Profit or Gross Loss.

gross profit margin % or ratio
Gross Profit Margin $ divided by Net Sales.

gross sales
Total revenues at invoice value before any discounts or allowances.

horizontal exchange
A marketplace that deals with goods and services that are not specific to one industry.

imply
To indirectly convey meaning or intent; to leave the determination of meaning up to the receiver of the communication based on circumstances, general language used, or conduct of those involved.

incidental damages
Any commercially reasonable charges, expenses, or commissions incurred in stopping delivery; in the transportation, care and custody of goods after the buyer's breach; or in connection with the return or resale of the goods or otherwise resulting from the breach.

indefinite-delivery/indefinite-quantity (IDIQ) contract
A type of contract in which the exact date of delivery or the exact quantity, or a combination of both, is not specified at the time the contract is executed; provisions are placed in the contract to later stipulate these elements of the contract.

indemnification clause
A contract clause by which one party engages to secure another against an anticipated loss resulting from an act or forbearance on the part of one of the parties or of some third person.

indemnify
To make good; to compensate; to reimburse a person in case of an anticipated loss.

indirect cost
Any cost not directly identifiable with a specific cost objective but subject to two or more cost objectives.

indirect labor
All work that is not specifically associated with or cannot be practically traced to specific units of output.

intellectual property
The kind of property that results from the fruits of mental labor.

internet
The World Wide Web.

interactive chat
A feature provided by automated tools that allow for users to establish a voice connection between one or more parties and exchange text or graphics via a virtual bulletin board.

intranet
An organization specific internal secure network.

joint contract
A contract in which the parties bind themselves both individually and as a unit.

liquidated damages
A contract provision providing for the assessment of damages on the seller for its failure to comply with certain performance or delivery requirements of the contract; used when the time of delivery or performance is of such importance that the buyer may reasonably expect to suffer damages if the delivery or performance is delinquent.

mailbox rule
The idea that the acceptance of an offer is effective when deposited in the mail if the envelope is properly addressed.

marketing
Activities that direct the flow of goods and services from the producer to the consumers.

market intelligence
Information on your competitors or competitive teams operating in the marketplace or industry.

market research

The process used to collect and analyze information about an entire market to help determine the most suitable approach to acquiring, distributing, and supporting supplies and services.

memorandum of agreement (MOA)/ memorandum of understanding (MOU)

The documentation of a mutually agreed-to statement of facts, intentions, procedures, and parameters for future actions and matters of coordination. A "memorandum of understanding" may express mutual understanding of an issue without implying commitments by parties to the understanding.

method of procurement

The process used for soliciting offers, evaluating offers, and awarding a contract.

modifications

Any written alterations in the specification, delivery point, rate of delivery, contract period, price, quantity, or other provision of an existing contract, accomplished in accordance with a contract clause; may be unilateral or bilateral.

monopoly

A market structure in which the entire market for a good or service is supplied by a single seller or firm.

monopsony

A market structure in which a single buyer purchases a good or service.

NCMA CMBOK

Definitive descriptions of the elements making up the body of professional knowledge that applies to contract management.

negotiation

A process between buyers and sellers seeking to reach mutual agreement on a matter of common concern through fact-finding, bargaining, and persuasion.

net marketplace

Two-sided exchange where buyers and sellers negotiate prices, usually with a bid-and-ask system, and where prices move both up and down.

net present value (NPV)

The lifetime customer revenue stream discounted by the investment costs and operations costs.

net sales

Gross sales minus discounts, allowances and returns.

North America Free Trade Agreement (NAFTA)

A trilateral trade and investment agreement, between Canada, Mexico, and the United States ratified on January 1, 1994.

novation agreement

A legal instrument executed by (a) the contractor (transferor), (b) the successor in interest (transferee), and (c) the buyer by which, among other things, the transferor guarantees performance of the contract, the transferee assumes all obligations under the contract, and the buyer recognizes the transfer of the contract and related assets.

offer

(1) The manifestation of willingness to enter into a bargain, so made as to justify another person in understanding that his or her assent to that bargain is invited and will conclude it. (2) An unequivocal and intentionally communicated statement of proposed terms made to another party. An offer is presumed revocable unless it specifically states that it is irrevocable. An offer once made will be open for a reasonable period of time and is binding on the offeror unless revoked by the offeror before the other party's acceptance.

oligopoly

A market dominated by a few sellers.

operating expenses

SG&A plus depreciation and amortization.

opportunity

A potential or actual favorable event

opportunity engagement

The degree to which your company or your competitors were involved in establishing the customer's requirements.

opportunity profile

A stage of the Capture Management Life Cycle, during which a seller evaluates and describes the opportunity in terms of what it means to your customer, what it means to your company, and what will be required to succeed.

option

A unilateral right in a contract by which, for a specified time, the buyer may elect to purchase additional quantities of the supplies or services called for in the contract, or may elect to extend the period of performance of the contract.

order of precedence

A solicitation provision that establishes priorities so that contradictions within the solicitation can be resolved.

Organizational Breakdown Structure (OBS)

A organized structure which represents how individual team members are grouped to complete assigned work tasks.

outsourcing

A contractual process of obtaining another party to provide goods and/or services that were previously done internal to an organization.

overhead

An accounting cost category that typically includes general indirect expenses that are necessary to operate a business but are not directly assignable to a specific good or service produced. Examples include building rent, utilities, salaries of corporate officers, janitorial services, office supplies, and furniture.

overtime

The time worked by a seller's employee in excess of the employee's normal workweek.

parol evidence

Oral or verbal evidence; in contract law, the evidence drawn from sources exterior to the written instrument.

parol evidence rule

A rule that seeks to preserve the integrity of written agreements by refusing to permit contracting parties to attempt to alter a written contract with evidence of any contradictory prior or contemporaneous oral agreement (*parol* to the contract).

payments

The amount payable under the contract supporting data required to be submitted with invoices, and other payment terms such as time for payment and retention.

payment bond

A bond that secures the appropriate payment of subcontracts for their completed and acceptable goods and/or services.

Performance-based contract (PBC)

A documented business arrangement, in which the buyer and seller agree to use: a performance work statement, performance-based metrics, and a quality assurance plan to ensure contract requirements are met or exceeded.

performance bond

A bond that secures the performance and fulfillment of all the undertakings, covenants, terms, conditions, and agreements contained in the contract.

performance specification

A purchase description that describes the deliverable in terms of desired operational characteristics. Performance specifications tend to be more restrictive than functional specifications, in that they limit alternatives that the buyer will consider and define separate performance standards for each such alternative.

Performance Work Statement (PWS)
> A statement of work expressed in terms of desired performance results, often including specific measurable objectives.

post-bid phase
> The period of time after a seller submits a bid/proposal to a buyer through source selection, negotiations, contract formation, contract fulfillment, contract closeout, and follow-on opportunity management.

pre-bid phase
> The period of time a seller of goods and/or services uses to identify business opportunities prior to the release of a customer solicitation.

pricing arrangement
> An agreed-to basis between contractual parties for the payment of amounts for specified performance; usually expressed in terms of a specific cost-reimbursement or fixed-price arrangement.

prime/prime contractor
> The principal seller performing under the contract.

private exchange
> A marketplace hosted by a single company inside a company's firewall and used for procurement from among a group of preauthorized sellers.

privity of contract
> The legal relationship that exists between the parties to a contract that allows either party to (a) enforce contractual rights against the other party and (b) seek remedy directly from the other party.

procurement
> The complete action or process of acquiring or obtaining goods or services using any of several authorized means.

procurement planning
> The process of identifying which business needs can be best met by procuring products or services outside the organization.

profit

The net proceeds from selling a product or service when costs are subtracted from revenues. May be positive (profit) or negative (loss).

program management

Planning and execution of multiple projects that are related to one another.

progress payments

An interim payment for delivered work in accordance with contract terms; generally tied to meeting specified performance milestones.

project management

Planning and ensuring the quality, on-time delivery, and cost of a specific set of related activities with a definite beginning and end.

promotion

Publicizing the attributes of the product/service through media and personal contacts and presentations, e.g., technical articles/ presentations, new releases, advertising, and sales calls.

proposal

Normally, a written offer by a seller describing its offering terms. Proposals may be issued in response to a specific request or may be made unilaterally when a seller feels there may be an interest in its offer (which is also known as an unsolicited proposal).

proposal evaluation

An assessment of both the proposal and the offeror's ability (as conveyed by the proposal) to successfully accomplish the prospective contract. An agency shall evaluate competitive proposals solely on the factors specified in the solicitation.

protest

A written objection by an interested party to (a) a solicitation or other request by an agency for offers for a contract for the procurement of property or services, (b) the cancellation of the solicitation or other request, (c) an award or proposed award of the contract, or (d) a termination or cancellation of an award of the contract, if the written objection contains an allegation that the termination or cancellation is based in whole or in part on improprieties concerning the award of the contract.

punitive damages

Those damages awarded to the plaintiff over and above what will barely compensate for his or her loss. Unlike compensatory damages, punitive damages are based on actively different public policy consideration, that of punishing the defendant or of setting an example for similar wrongdoers.

purchasing

The outright acquisition of items, mostly off-the-shelf or catalog, manufactured outside the buyer's premises.

quality assurance

The planned and systematic actions necessary to provide adequate confidence that the performed service or supplied goods will serve satisfactorily for the intended and specified purpose.

quotation

A statement of price, either written or oral, which may include, among other things, a description of the product or service; the terms of sale, delivery, or period of performance; and payment. Such statements are usually issued by sellers at the request of potential buyers.

reasonable cost

A cost is reasonable if, in its nature and amount, it does not exceed that which would be incurred by a prudent person in the conduct of competitive business.

request for information (RFI)

A formal invitation to submit general and/or specific information concerning the potential future purchase of goods and/or services.

request for proposals (RFP)

A formal invitation that contains a scope of work and seeks a formal response (proposal), describing both methodology and compensation, to form the basis of a contract.

request for quotations (RFQ)

A formal invitation to submit a price for goods and/or services as specified.

request for technical proposals (RFTP)

Solicitation document used in two-step sealed bidding. Normally in letter form, it asks only for technical information; price and cost breakdowns are forbidden.

revenue value

The monetary value of an opportunity.

risk

Exposure or potential of an injury or loss

sealed-bid procedure

A method of procurement involving the unrestricted solicitation of bids, an opening, and award of a contract to the lowest responsible bidder.

selling, general & administrative (SG&A) expenses

Administrative costs of running business.

severable contract

A contract divisible into separate parts. A default of one section does not invalidate the whole contract.

several

A circumstance when more than two parties are involved with the contract.

single source

One source among others in a competitive marketplace that, for justifiable reason, is found to be most worthy to receive a contract award.

small business concerns
A small business is one that is independently owned and operated, and is not dominant in its field; a business concern that meets government size standards for its particular industry type.

socioeconomic programs
Programs designed to benefit particular groups. They represent a multitude of program interests and objectives unrelated to procurement objectives. Some examples of these are preferences for small business and for American products, required sources for specific items, and minimum labor pay levels mandated for contractors.

solicitation
A process through which a buyer requests, bids, quotes, tenders, or proposes orally, in writing, or electronically. Solicitations can take the following forms: request for proposals (RFP), request for quotations (RFQ), request for tenders, invitation to bid (ITB), invitation for bids, and invitation for negotiation.

solicitation planning
The preparation of the documents needed to support a solicitation.

source selection
The process by which the buyer evaluates offers, selects a seller, negotiates terms and conditions, and awards the contract.

Source Selection Advisory Council
A group of people who are appointed by the Source Selection Authority (SSA). The Council is responsible for reviewing and approving the source selection plan (SSP) and the solicitation of competitive awards for major and certain less-than-major procurements. The Council also determines what proposals are in the competitive range and provides recommendations to the SSA for final selection.

source selection plan (SSP)
The document that describes the selection criteria, the process, and the organization to be used in evaluating proposals for competitively awarded contracts.

specification

A description of the technical requirements for a material, product, or service that includes the criteria for determining that the requirements have been met. There are generally three types of specifications used in contracting: performance, functional, and design.

stakeholders

Individuals who control the resources in a company needed to pursue opportunities or deliver solutions to customers.

standard

A document that establishes engineering and technical limitations and applications of items, materials, processes, methods, designs, and engineering practices. It includes any related criteria deemed essential to achieve the highest practical degree of uniformity in materials or products, or interchangeability of parts used in those products.

standards of conduct

The ethical conduct of personnel involved in the acquisition of goods and services. Within the federal government, business shall be conducted in a manner above reproach and, except as authorized by law or regulation, with complete impartiality and without preferential treatment.

statement of work (SOW)

That portion of a contract describing the actual work to be done by means of specifications or other minimum requirements, quantities, performance date, and a statement of the requisite quality.

statute of limitations

The legislative enactment prescribing the periods within which legal actions may be brought upon certain claims or within which certain rights may be enforced.

stop work order

A request for interim stoppage of work due to nonconformance, funding, or technical considerations.

subcontract
> A contract between a buyer and a seller in which a significant part of the supplies or services being obtained is for eventual use in a prime contract.

subcontractor
> A seller who enters into a contract with a prime contractor or a subcontractor of the prime contractor.

supplementary agreement
> A contract modification that is accomplished by the mutual action of parties.

technical factor
> A factor other than price used in evaluating offers for award. Examples include technical excellence, management capability, personnel qualifications, prior experience, past performance, and schedule compliance.

technical leveling
> The process of helping a seller bring its proposal up to the level of other proposals through successive rounds of discussion, such as by pointing out weaknesses resulting from the seller's lack of diligence, competence, or inventiveness in preparing the proposal.

technical/management proposal
> That part of the offer that describes the seller's approach to meeting the buyer's requirement.

technical transfusion
> The disclosure of technical information pertaining to a proposal that re-suits in improvement of a competing proposal. This practice is not allowed in federal government contracting.

term
> A part of a contract that addresses a specific subject.

termination
> An action taken pursuant to a contract clause in which the buyer unilaterally ends all or part of the work.

terms and conditions (Ts and Cs)

All clauses in a contract, including time of delivery, packing and shipping, applicable standard clauses, and special provisions.

unallowable cost

Any cost that, under the provisions of any pertinent law, regulation, or contract, cannot be included in prices, cost-reimbursements, or settlements under a government contract to which it is allocable.

uncompensated overtime

The work that exempt employees perform above and beyond 40 hours per week. Also known as competitive time, deflated hourly rates, direct allocation of salary costs, discounted hourly rates, extended work week, full-time accounting, and green time.

Uniform Commercial Code (UCC)

A U.S. model law developed to standardize commercial contracting law among the states. It has been adopted by 49 states (and in significant portions by Louisiana). The UCC comprises articles that deal with specific commercial subject matters, including sales and letters of credit.

unilateral

See *bilateral contract.*

unsolicited proposal

A research or development proposal that is made by a prospective contractor without prior formal or informal solicitation from a purchasing activity.

variable costs

Costs associated with production that change directly with the amount of production, e.g., the direct material or labor required to complete the build or manufacturing of a product.

variance

The difference between projected and actual performance, especially relating to costs.

vertical exchange

A marketplace that is specific to a single industry.

waiver

The voluntary and unilateral relinquishment a person of a right that he or she has. See also *forbearance*.

warranty

A promise or affirmation given by a seller to a buyer regarding the nature, usefulness, or condition of the goods or services furnished under a contract. Generally, a warranty's purpose is to delineate the rights and obligations for defective goods and services and to foster quality performance.

warranty, express

A written statement arising out of a sale to the consumer of a consumer good, pursuant to which the manufacturer, distributor, or retailer undertakes to preserve or maintain the utility or performance of the consumer good or provide compensation if there is a failure in utility or performance. It is not necessary to the creation of an express warranty that formal words such as "warrant" or "guarantee" be used, or that a specific intention to make a warranty be present.

warranty, implied

A promise arising by operation of law that something that is sold shall be fit for the purpose for which the seller has reason to know that it is required. Types of implied warranties include implied warranty of merchantability, of title, and of wholesomeness.

warranty of fitness

A warranty by the seller that goods sold are suitable for the special purpose of the buyer.

warranty of merchantability

A warranty that goods are fit for the ordinary purposes for which such goods are used and conform to the promises or affirmations of fact made on the container or label.

warranty of title

An express or implied (arising by operation of law) promise that the seller owns the item offered for sale and, therefore, is able to transfer a good title and that the goods, as delivered, are free from any security interest of which the buyer at the time of contracting has no knowledge.

web portals

A public exchange in which a company or group of companies list products or services for sale or provide other transmission of business information.

win strategy

A collection of messages or points designed to guide the customer's perception of you, your solution, and your competitors.

Work Breakdown Structure (WBS)

A logical, organized, decomposition of the work tasks within a given project, typically uses a hierarchical numeric coding scheme.

World Trade Organization (WTO)

A multi-national legal entity which serves as the champion of fair trade globally, established April 15, 1995.

REFERENCES

Agrawal, Raj., *Overcoming Software Estimation Challenges*, McLean VA, MITRE, May 22, 2007.

Albert, Neil F., *Cost Estimating: The Starting Point of Earned Value Management*, McLean VA, MCR LLC, June 2005.

Albert, Neil F., *Developing a Work Breakdown Structure*, McLean VA, MCR LLC, June 16, 2005.

Anderson, Mark, and David Nelson, *Developing an Averaged Estimate at Completion Utilizing Program Performance Factors and Maturity*, Arlington VA, Tecolote Research Inc., June 14-17, 2005.

Atkinson, William, *Beyond the Basics*, PM Network Magazine, May 2003 (Project Management Institute).

Badgerow, Dana B., Gregory A. Garrett, Dominic F. DiClementi, and Barbara M. Weaver, *Managing Contracts for Peak Performance*, Vienna VA, National Contract Management Association, 1990.

Black, Hollis M., *Impact of Cost Risk Analysis on Business Decisions*, Huntsville AL, Boeing, June 14-17, 2005.

Bonaldo, Guy, *Interview with Business 2.0 Magazine*, Business Intelligence, February 2003.

Bossidy, Larry, and Ram Charan, *Confronting Realty: Doing What Matters to Get Things Right,* New York NY, Crown Business, 2004.

Bruce, David L., Norby, Marlys, and Ramos, Victor, *Guide to the Contract Management Body of Knowledge, 1st Ed.,* Vienna VA, National Contract Management Association, 2002.

Christensen, David S., and Carl Templin, *An Analysis of Management Reserve Budget on Defense Acquisition Contracts,* Cedar City UT, Southern Utah University, 2000.

Coleman, Richard L., Shishu S. Gupta, and Jessica R. Summerville, *Two Timely Short Topics: Independence and Cost Realism,* Chantilly VA, Northrop Grumman, The Analytical Sciences Corporation and Intelligence Community Cost Analysis Improvement Group, June 16, 2005.

Coleman, Richard L., and Jessica R. Summerville, *Advanced Cost Risk,* Chantilly VA, Northrop Grumman, The Analytical Sciences Corporation, June 16, 2005.

Coleman, Richard L., and Jessica R. Summerville, *Basic Cost Risk,* Chantilly VA, Northrop Grumman, The Analytical Sciences Corporation, June 15, 2005.

Collins, Jim, *Good to Great: Why Some Companies Make the Leap... and Others Don't,* New York NY, Harper Collins, 2001.

Defense Acquisition University, *Cost Estimating Methodologies,* Fort Belvoir VA: April, 2005.

Fleming, Quentin W., *Earned Value Management Light...But Adequate for All Projects,* Tustin CA: Primavera Systems, Inc., November 2006.

Fleming, Quentin W., and Joel M. Koppelman, *The Earned Value Body of Knowledge,* Presented at the 30th Annual Project Management Institute Symposium, Philadelphia PA, October 10-16, 1999.

Flett, Frank, *Organizing and Planning the Estimate,* McLean VA: MCR LLC, June 12-14-2005.

Galorath, Daniel D., *Software Estimation Handbook*, El Segundo CA: Galorath Inc., n.d..

Government Accountability Office, *Cost Assessment Guide, GAO-07-11345P*, Washington DC: July 2007.

Garrett, Gregory A., *Achieving Customer Loyalty*, National Contract Management Association, Vienna VA: August 2002.

Garrett, Gregory A., *Contract Negotiations: Skills, Tools, & Best Practices*, Chicago IL, CCH, 2005.

Garrett, Gregory A., *Cost Estimating and Contract Pricing*, Chicago IL, CCH, 2008.

Garrett, Gregory A., *Government Contract Cost Accounting*, Chicago IL, CCH, 2010.

Garrett, Gregory A., *Managing Complex Outsourced Projects*, Chicago IL, 2004.

Garrett, Gregory A., *Performance-Based Acquisition: Pathways to Excellence*, McLean VA, National Contract Management Association, 2005.

Garrett, Gregory A., *Risk Management for Complex U.S. Government Contracts and Projects*, Ashburn VA, National Contract Management Association, 2009.

Garrett, Gregory A., *World-Class Contracting, 5th ed.*, Chicago IL, CCH, 2010.

Garrett, Gregory A., and Ed Bunnik, *Creating a World-Class PM Organization*, PM Network Magazine, September 2000.

Garrett, Gregory A., and Reginald J. Kipke, *The Capture Management Life-Cycle: Winning More Business*, Chicago IL, CCH, 2003.

Garrett, Gregory A., and Rene G. Rendon, *Contract Management Organizational Assessment Tools*, McLean VA, National Contract Management Association, 2005.

Garrett, Gregory A. and Rene G. Rendon, *U.S. Military Program Management: Lessons Learned and Best Practices,* McLean VA, Management Concepts, 2007.

Johnson, Jim, et. al., *Collaboration: Development and Management – Collaborating on Project Success,* Software Magazine, Sponsored Supplement, February-March 2001.

Kirk, Dorthy, *Managing Expectations,* PM Network Magazine, August 2000.

Kratzert, Keith, *Earned Value Management (EVM): The Federal Aviation Administration Program Manager's Flight Plan,* Washington DC, Federal Aviation Administration, January 2006.

Kumley, Alissa, et al., *Integrating Risk Management and Earned Value Management: A Statistical Analysis of Survey Results,* June 14-17, 2005.

Lewis, James P., *Mastering Project Management: Applying Advanced Concepts of Systems Thinking, Control and Evaluation, Resource Allocation,* New York NY, McGraw-Hill, 1998.

Liker, Jeffrey K., and Thomas Y. Choi, *Building Deep Supplier Relationships,* Harvard Business Review, December 2004.

McFarlane, Eileen Luhta, *Developing International Proposals in a Virtual Environment,* Journal of the Association of Proposal Management, Spring 2000.

Monroe, Kent B., *Pricing: Making Profitable Decisions, 2nd ed.,* New York NY, McGraw-Hill, 1990.

The National Contract Management Association, *The Desktop Guide to Basic Contracting Terms, 4th ed.,* Vienna VA, 1994.

O'Connell, Brian, *B2B.com: Cashing-in on the Business-to-Business E-commerce Bonanza,* Holbrook MA, Adams Media Corp., 2000.

Ohmae, Kenichi, *The Borderless World: Power and Strategy in the Interlinked Economy,* New York NY, Harper Collins, 1991.

Patterson, Shirley, *Supply Base Optimization and Integrated Supply Chain Management,* Contract Management Magazine, McLean VA, January 2005.

RAND Corporation, *Impossible Certainty: Cost Risk Analysis for Air Force Systems,* Arlington VA, 2006.

Society of Cost Estimating and Analysis, *Cost Programmed Review of Fundamentals: Basic Data Analysis Principles – What to Do Once You Get the Data,* Vienna VA, 2003.

Tichy, Noel, *The Leadership Engine,* New York NY, Harper Business Press, 1997.

Webster' Dictionary, The New Lexicon of the English Language, New York NY, Lexicon Publications, 1989.

Zubrow, Dave, *Earned Value Management: Basic Concepts,* Pittsburgh PA, Carnegie Mellon Software Engineering Institute, 2002.

Zubrow, Dave, *Implementing Earned Value Management to Manage Program Risk,* Pittsburg, PA, Carnegie Mellon Software Engineering Institute, 2002.

INDEX